Microsoft Dynamics CRM 2011 Applications (MB2-868) Certification Guide

A practical guide on how to use and manage Microsoft Dynamics CRM 2011 that focuses on helping you to pass the Microsoft certification exam

Danny Varghese

[PACKT] PUBLISHING enterprise
professional expertise distilled

BIRMINGHAM - MUMBAI

Microsoft Dynamics CRM 2011 Applications (MB2-868) Certification Guide

First published: April 2013

Production Reference: 1100413

Published by Packt Publishing Ltd.
Livery Place
35 Livery Street
Birmingham B3 2PB, UK.

ISBN 978-1-84968-650-1

www.packtpub.com

Cover Image by Artie Ng (artherng@yahoo.com.au)

Credits

Author
Danny Varghese

Reviewers
Neil Benson
Guillermo Barker Cruz
Ian Grieve

Acquisition Editor
Edward Bowkett

Lead Technical Editor
Sweny M. Sukumaran

Technical Editors
Vrinda Nitesh Bhosale
Manmeet Singh Vasir

Project Coordinator
Anurag Banerjee

Proofreader
Dirk Manuel

Indexer
Rekha Nair

Graphics
Ronak Dhruv
Aditi Gajjar

Production Coordinator
Nilesh R. Mohite

Cover Work
Nilesh R. Mohite

About the Author

Danny Varghese is a business applied technology consultant committed to providing clients with highly valued business solutions. His mission is to offer a unique blend of industry, project-management, technical, and customer-support skills to ensure his work supports the strategic objectives of his clients.

His colleagues would describe him as an energetic leader and effective communicator who works productively with clients and all levels of management. It is clear to everyone who works with him, that he is passionate about what he does, and adept in integrating technological advancement with the correct amount of improvement to the business process.

It is this same passion and aptitude that inspired him to take on the challenge of writing this book. He believes in the exponential potential of business and in sharing the knowledge required to attain that potential with others in the community. It is his hope that this book serves as a resource to solving business problems with the highest possible valued solutions.

He has been a consultant at Slalom Consulting for two years. Slalom Consulting has won numerous Microsoft Country Partner of the Year awards, and consistently ranks in the top 10 best places to work by Consulting Magazine and `glassdoor.com`.

Acknowledgement

1 Corinthians 10:31

To my Lord and Savior Jesus Christ, thank you for loving me. Everything I do and all that I am is because of you. The skills and opportunity to write this book have been a blessing and I owe everything to you.

To my wife Sharon, thank you for being the model of love, patience, and understanding. You've supported me in everything I've ever done and for that I can never repay you.

To my daughter Ariana, you are the absolute joy of my life. I didn't believe in love at first sight until you were born. "For you see, each day I love you more, today more than yesterday and less than tomorrow." - Rosemonde Gérard.

Mom, Dad, Denny, and Daley thank you for your continued support, teaching me to love God, work hard, and seize every opportunity.

Mom and Dad, thank you for raising such a strong Christian woman, making me feel like your son, and taking care of us with unconditional love. Shawn, thank you for being another great brother and supporting me in writing this book.

My friends, whom I consider family, you've helped mold me into the man I am today, keeping me honest and always being there when I've needed anything. Words cannot express what you've meant to me in my life.

My colleagues and friends, including Jeff Shaffer, Bryan Van Antwerp, Darren Liu, Luke Simpson, and Shelley Schmelter, you've helped me to grow professionally and to become a well-rounded technology consultant.

My colleagues and friends at Slalom Consulting including Jason Davis and Giovanni Spiteri, you are two in a long list of excellent managers giving me the support, tools, time, and latitude to pursue any career goal I've had. Jamie Burton, thank you for being the first face of the organization and always being there as a friend whenever I needed one. Charles Fabiano, Sheila Hernandez, Nirnay Patel, Jenny Meilander, Yolande Du Preez, and Stan Ray, you are one of the best and brightest teams I've ever worked with.

Last but not least, a very big thanks to everyone at Packt Publishing for giving me this opportunity. Thank you for your encouragement, guidance, and support throughout this process.

About the Reviewers

Neil Benson has been a CRM addict since 1999 and is an experienced CRM solution architect. He is a certified Microsoft Dynamics CRM consultant, and has been a Microsoft CRM MVP since 2010. An active member of the Microsoft CRM community, he runs the LinkedIn Microsoft Dynamics CRM group on behalf of Microsoft, and has spoken at numerous Microsoft conferences and CRM User Group meetings.

Neil is the author of *Microsoft Dynamics CRM 2011 Customization & Configuration (MB2-866) Certification Guide, Packt Publishing*, and a contributing author to *The CRM Field Guide, We Speak You Learn, LLC*. He lives in Manhattan Beach, California with his wife and son.

Guillermo Barker Cruz is a professional in the service industry with experience in personnel management and in working with multidisciplinary working groups. His areas of expertise are to implement creative solutions to complex problems and create a suitable work culture to ensure customer satisfaction. He has wide experience in negotiating agreements with companies, analytical skills, creativity, goal-orientation, and ability and willingness to work as a team. His experiences include working as a CRM division manager at UruIT DynamiX and Axxon Consulting, and as a service and support director at Epson.

He is an Electrical Engineer from the Universidad de Chile, a Microsoft Certified Professional, and a Microsoft Certified Trainer. He is a Microsoft Dynamics CRM trainer at Golden Training. His LinkedIn profile is `http://www.linkedin.com/profile/view?id=32635763&trk=tab_pro`.

Ian Grieve is a Microsoft Dynamics GP and CRM certified consultant specializing in the delivery of Microsoft Dynamics GP and CRM projects. He is a senior consultant at Perfect Image Ltd., a Microsoft Partner and VAR in the North East of England.

Ian has worked with Microsoft Dynamics GP since 2003 and, over the nine years since, has dealt with all aspects of the product life cycle, from presales, to implementation, to technical and functional training, to post go-live support, and subsequent upgrades and process reviews. Alongside his work with Microsoft Dynamics GP, he has fulfilled a similar role dealing with Microsoft Dynamics CRM, with special emphasis on project delivery and the training of end users on the management of sales, marketing, and service.

In his spare time, Ian runs the *azurecurve | Ramblings of a Dynamics GP Consultant* blog dedicated to Microsoft Dynamics GP and related products and tries, often unsuccessfully, to squeeze in extra time for the Dynamics CRM-related blog *coralcurve | A Consultant's Dabblings In Dynamics CRM.*

www.packtpub.com

Support files, e-books, discount offers, and more

You might want to visit www.packtpub.com for support files and downloads related to your book.

Did you know that Packt offers e-book versions of every book published, with PDF and ePub files available? You can upgrade to the eBook version at www.packtpub.com and as a print book customer, you are entitled to a discount on the e-book copy. Get in touch with us at service@packtpub.com for more details.

At www.packtpub.com, you can also read a collection of free technical articles, sign up for a range of free newsletters, and receive exclusive discounts and offers on Packt books and e-books.

PACKTLIB

http://packtlib.packtpub.com

Do you need instant solutions to your IT questions? PacktLib is Packt's online digital book library. Here, you can access, read and search across Packt's entire library of books.

Why subscribe?

- Fully searchable across every book published by Packt
- Copy and paste, print and bookmark content
- On demand and accessible via web browser

Free access for Packt account holders

If you have an account with Packt at www.packtpub.com, you can use this to access PacktLib today and view nine entirely free books. Simply use your login credentials for immediate access.

Instant updates on new Packt books

Get notified! Find out when new books are published by following @PacktEnterprise on Twitter, or the *Packt Enterprise* Facebook page.

Table of Contents

Preface

This book will teach readers how to manage the Microsoft Dynamics CRM 2011 application, including marketing automation, sales, service management, and services scheduling.

This book will also assist individuals in passing the Microsoft Dynamics CRM 2011 Applications (MB2-868) Certification Exam by reviewing in depth each topic covered by the exam, providing questions to test your knowledge at the end of each chapter, and finally by providing a 75-question practice exam including answers.

What this book covers

Chapter 1, Microsoft Dynamics CRM 2011 Overview, teaches you about the applications available and how they can address your organization's requirements. You will also learn about the value of the Microsoft Dynamics CRM 2011 Applications Certification Exam (MB2-868) and the role of this exam in certification for Microsoft IT professionals and developers.

Chapter 2, Activities and Notes, introduces you to the sales process and activities.

Chapter 3, Managing Marketing Automation Applications – Marketing Lists and Campaigns, teaches you how to create and manage marketing lists, campaigns, and campaign responses. You will also learn how to analyze marketing data to provide your organization with effective reporting.

Chapter 4, Managing Sales Applications, teaches you how to create and maintain lead, customer, opportunity, and competitor records. You'll also learn how go through an entire sales process, starting with leads, converting a lead to an account, contact and/or opportunity.

Chapter 5, Managing the Product Catalog and Order Processing, walks you through working the opportunity to close, creating a quote, and then converting the quote to an order and finally to an invoice. You will then analyze sales metrics and use goals, dashboards, personal views, and reports.

Chapter 6, Managing CRM 2011 Outlook Client, teaches you about the Outlook client and how it integrates with CRM. You'll be able to track e-mails, convert e-mails to leads or opportunities, and learn how to configure the views in the Dynamics CRM Outlook client.

Chapter 7, Managing Service Management Applications, teaches you how to create and manage cases, subject trees, knowledge base articles, queues, and contracts. You will then learn how to analyze cases by using service metrics, goals, and dashboards.

Chapter 8, Managing Service Scheduling Applications, teaches you about service scheduling scenarios, users, facilities/equipment, and service activities. You'll also learn how to report and analyze service activities.

Appendix A, Sample Certification Exam Questions, assesses your understanding of applications within Microsoft Dynamics CRM 2011 and your readiness for the certification exam by providing 75 questions similar to those found in the MB2-868 exam.

Appendix B, Answers to Sample Certification Exam Questions, contains answers and explanations to the sample certification exam questions found in *Appendix A, Sample Certification Exam Questions*.

Appendix C, Answers to Self-test Questions, contains answers to the self-test questions found in chapters 2 to 8.

What you need for this book

For this book, it's recommended that you have a grasp of the overall customer relationship management concept, and understand how to solve business problems through the use of technology.

You can use a Microsoft Dynamics CRM Online 30-day trial to follow along with this book. The trial can be obtained from `http://crm.dynamics.com`.

Another option is to set up a Microsoft Dynamics CRM on-premise deployment. For this, the following software is required:

- 64-bit Microsoft Windows Server 2008 or higher version
- 64-bit Microsoft SQL Server 2008 or higher version
- Microsoft Dynamics CRM 2011 Server
- Microsoft Office Outlook 2003 or higher version
- Microsoft Dynamics CRM 2011 Outlook client
- Microsoft Internet Explorer 7.0 or higher version

In addition to software, it's a good idea to have working knowledge of the Microsoft Windows operating system, Microsoft Internet Explorer, and Microsoft Office.

Who this book is for

Microsoft Dynamics CRM 2011 Applications (MB2-868) Certification Guide is for individuals who will implement and support Microsoft Dynamics CRM 2011. These individuals can include, but are not limited to, IT consultants, professionals, business users, and even key business stakeholders.

Conventions

In this book, you will find a number of styles of text that distinguish between different kinds of information. Here are some examples of these styles, and an explanation of their meaning.

Code words in text, database table names, folder names, filenames, file extensions, pathnames, dummy URLs, user input, and Twitter handles are shown as follows: "This is a free text field where you can enter text such as `PTO` or `Sick`."

New terms and **important words** are shown in bold. Words that you see on the screen, in menus or dialog boxes for example, appear in the text like this: "Start CRM, click on the **Workplace** module, and then click on **Activities**."

> Warnings or important notes appear in a box like this.

> Tips and tricks appear like this.

Reader feedback

Feedback from our readers is always welcome. Let us know what you think about this book—what you liked or may have disliked. Reader feedback is important for us to develop titles that you really get the most out of.

To send us general feedback, simply send an e-mail to `feedback@packtpub.com`, and mention the book title via the subject of your message.

If there is a topic that you have expertise in and you are interested in either writing or contributing to a book, see our author guide on `www.packtpub.com/authors`.

Customer support

Now that you are the proud owner of a Packt book, we have a number of things to help you to get the most from your purchase.

Errata

Although we have taken every care to ensure the accuracy of our content, mistakes do happen. If you find a mistake in one of our books—maybe a mistake in the text or the code—we would be grateful if you would report this to us. By doing so, you can save other readers from frustration and help us improve subsequent versions of this book. If you find any errata, please report them by visiting `http://www.packtpub.com/submit-errata`, selecting your book, clicking on the **errata submission form** link, and entering the details of your errata. Once your errata are verified, your submission will be accepted and the errata will be uploaded on our website, or added to any list of existing errata, under the Errata section of that title. Any existing errata can be viewed by selecting your title from `http://www.packtpub.com/support`.

Piracy

Piracy of copyright material on the Internet is an ongoing problem across all media. At Packt, we take the protection of our copyright and licenses very seriously. If you come across any illegal copies of our works, in any form, on the Internet, please provide us with the location address or website name immediately so that we can pursue a remedy.

Please contact us at `copyright@packtpub.com` with a link to the suspected pirated material.

We appreciate your help in protecting our authors, and our ability to bring you valuable content.

Questions

You can contact us at `questions@packtpub.com` if you are having a problem with any aspect of the book, and we will do our best to address it.

1
Microsoft Dynamics CRM 2011 Overview

In this chapter you will learn about:

- CRM 2011
- Training and certifications

Introduction to CRM 2011

Every organization is dependent on customers, and every organization is challenged to manage these customers. Businesses need a way to attract, sell to, service, and track every interaction these customers have with their organization. To do so, they often implement a **Customer Relationship Management** (**CRM**) system.

Microsoft offers a CRM solution as part of their Dynamics suite, which allows companies to implement a system that manages more than just their customers. Microsoft Dynamics CRM is a web-based application that can be accessed online through an Internet browser or through Microsoft Office Outlook.

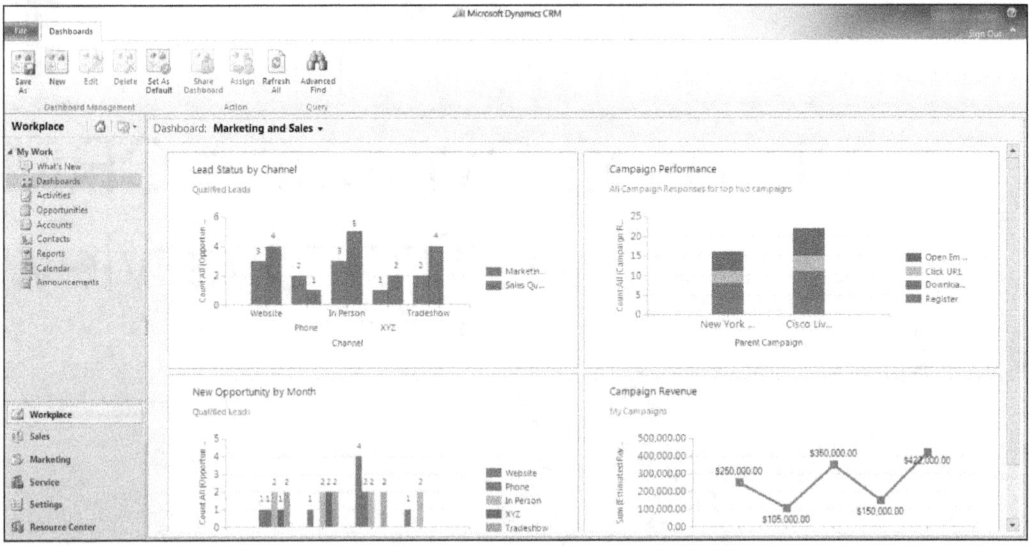

Microsoft Dynamics CRM 2011 Web client

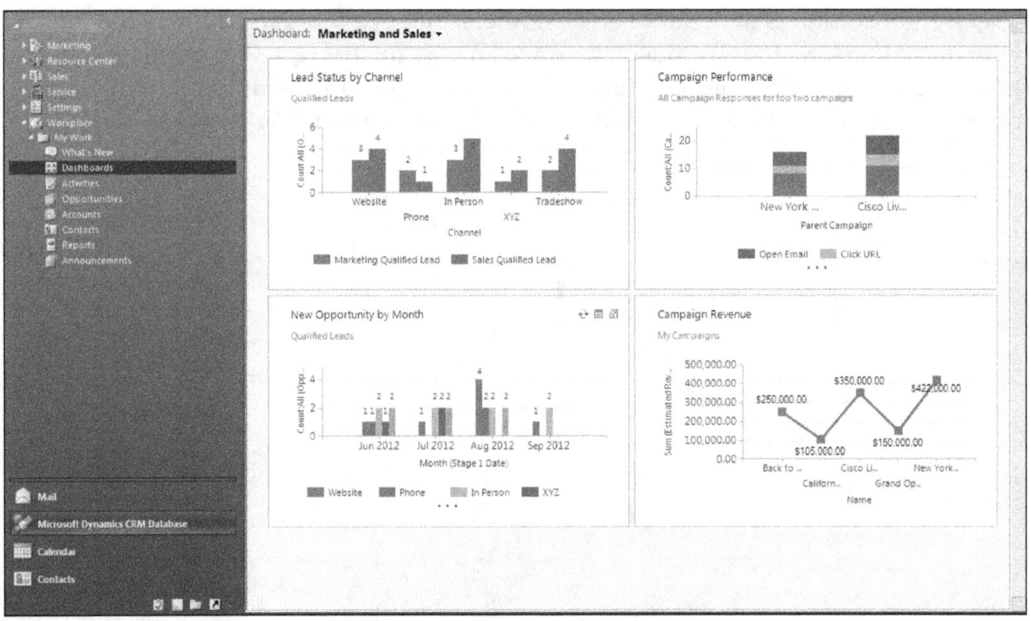

Microsoft Dynamics CRM 2011 Outlook client

Microsoft Dynamics CRM includes three main modules:

- Sales
- Marketing
- Customer service

Each module contains **entities**, which are objects in CRM, and are used to help model data.

Throughout this book, business examples will be used to explain various concepts. A fictitious company called Race2Win Insurance Company will be used to further illustrate these concepts.

Sales module

Microsoft Dynamics CRM allows businesses to optimize their sales processes and customer tracking efforts. With CRM, an organization can increase interactions with current customers, shorten sales cycles, and increase opportunity close rates to gain new customers.

The sales module within CRM consists of the following entities:

- Leads
- Accounts
- Contacts
- Opportunities
- Marketing lists
- Products
- Sales literature
- Quotes
- Orders
- Invoices
- Competitors
- Quick campaigns
- Goals
- Goal metrics
- Rollup queries

Each of these entities are explained in more detail in the upcoming chapters of this book, but let's give a high-level overview of how users could potentially use these out of the box capabilities.

Business scenarios

The business scenarios that we'll cover in a moment outlines the use of the sales module for our fictitious insurance company. Although entities such as marketing lists, quick campaigns, and sales literature are found in the sales module, these will be discussed in the marketing business scenarios. For our scenarios, we'll illustrate examples from the viewpoint of various individual roles within the organization.

Leads

Race2Win Insurance Company needs a way to track leads they've acquired as a result of efforts by their marketing team. Microsoft Dynamics CRM allows the company to track and qualify leads. For example, let's say Race2Win is capturing information on the lead record related to a potential insurance customer. Based on information entered, business rules can be applied to categorize the lead as hot, warm, or cold. CRM has out of the box functionality to apply these business rules automatically.

Once a lead is qualified, Dynamics CRM provides the ability to convert the lead into an opportunity, account, contact, or a combination of the three.

Accounts

The organizations or companies that Race2Win Insurance views as customers can be tracked as accounts in CRM. These accounts may be managed by one or more salespeople. A salesperson may receive commission on sales made to their managed accounts, thus making accounts critical. Accounts contain the address, industry, and various other demographic data about the customer.

Contacts

As part of the sales process, Race2Win Insurance Company's sales force may reach out to individuals or employees at a company. Individuals, either on their own or tied to a company, can be tracked as contacts in Microsoft Dynamics CRM. Like the account, contact records can store addresses and industry/professional information, but can also store more personal data, such as birthdays, anniversaries, and information about various family members. A salesperson may find personal information critical to start and maintain a personal relationship with people at a company.

Opportunities

Opportunities can allow the Race2Win sales force to track potential sales opportunities with their customers. The opportunities can go through various sales cycles, and can track the estimated versus actual revenue of a particular sale. Opportunities can have products from the product catalog associated to them in order to help estimate the revenue more accurately. The Race2Win Insurance salespeople receive their commission when an opportunity is won, and the commission amount is based on the estimated revenue.

Products

Race2Win Insurance Company has various insurance products and services it may sell. Products can be sold to different customers at different prices, and some products may be eligible for discounts based on the quantity ordered. Dynamics CRM allows all of the above functionality through the use of the product catalog.

Quotes

Let's say that during the course of a sales cycle, the customer wishes to receive more detailed pricing information such as an estimate from the Race2Win salesperson. Dynamics CRM allows a quote to be generated ad hoc or from an opportunity. In either case, products from the product catalog can be added, prices from the price list can be used, and discounts can be applied—all to create an accurate quote.

Orders

If a customer wishes to proceed with purchasing products or services, the opportunity can be closed as won. The salesperson will receive commission, and the process is now handed off to someone in order entry to create an order. Orders can be created ad hoc, from an opportunity, or quote. If an opportunity or quote has products, prices, and/or discounts, these can be inherited, making the generation of the order timely and accurate.

Invoices

An invoice can be generated for a customer in place of an order if needed. Many other organizations like Race2Win have their billing department typically create an invoice once the order is ready to be billed. An invoice can be created ad hoc or from an opportunity, quote, or order. Like an order, invoices can inherit the products, prices, and/or discounts from an opportunity, quote, or order.

> While quotes, orders, and invoices can be created in Microsoft Dynamics CRM, sometimes they are created in an ERP system and then imported into Dynamics CRM for reference or reporting.

Competitors

Race2Win Insurance Company has now been using the leads generated to attain new customers, increase sales, and generate quotes, orders, and invoices for customers quickly and efficiently. Like any successful organization, Race2Win has to deal with competition. Dynamics CRM gives the organization's sales force and management the ability to track competitors, analyze their sales strategies, products, and the business they win.

Goals

Throughout a period of time, say fiscal year, an organization like Race2Win can set up goals to track various metrics such as sales performance. These goals can be tracked for each individual, and managers have the ability to see each of their team member's goals. The entire business scenario we just outlined can be achieved by using the Microsoft Dynamics CRM sales module.

Marketing module

Microsoft Dynamics CRM allows an organization to launch and maintain marketing campaigns. The responses to a campaign can be tracked to gauge the effectiveness of a campaign. These responses can also be converted into accounts, contacts, leads, quotes, orders, or opportunities.

The Dynamics CRM marketing module consists of the following entities:

- Leads
- Accounts
- Contacts
- Marketing lists
- Campaigns
- Quick campaigns
- Sales literature
- Products

Each of these entities are explained in more detail in the upcoming chapters of this book, but let's again look at a high-level overview.

Business scenarios

The business scenarios that we'll cover in a moment outlines the use of the marketing module using our fictitious company, Race2Win Insurance Company. Race2Win's marketing team has analyzed its existing customer base and found areas to expand the company's business. They can market new products and services to their existing customer base, and try and turn potential customers into new ones.

Marketing lists

Race2Win has realized that it needs to market new insurance products to an existing list of accounts, and market existing products to potential customers in China. Microsoft Dynamics CRM allows Race2Win to set up a marketing list containing a static list of accounts. They can also use CRM to set up a dynamic marketing list of all leads where the address has the country set to China.

Campaigns

Using marketing lists, an organization can kick off, run, and evaluate marketing campaigns. Race2Win can kick off a campaign very quickly for the existing accounts and it can also execute a more lengthy campaign, containing multiple communication channels, for the leads in China. Depending on the campaign type, the marketing team can create planning activities, track the cost of the campaign, and target certain products.

Sales literature

At times, customers or even internal business users may want to know more about a product that an organization is selling or marketing. Race2Win is no different, dealing with multiple inquiries about products from customers on a weekly basis. The sales literature in CRM can offer collateral for marketing or sales teams to share. An example can be a brochure of their latest insurance products.

The scenarios we just described illustrates how the Microsoft Dynamics CRM marketing module can be used to achieve any marketing goal.

Customer service module

Obtaining new customers is an important goal of any organization, but servicing existing customers is just as important. Microsoft Dynamics CRM offers a solution to service an organization's customers, manage service resources, and maintain a knowledge base repository that can be used to efficiently resolve future service incidents.

The Dynamics CRM service module consists of the following entities:

- Cases
- Service calendar
- Accounts
- Contacts
- Knowledge base articles
- Contracts
- Products
- Goals
- Goal metrics
- Rollup queries

Each of these entities are explained in more detail in the upcoming chapters of this book, but let's look at a high-level overview of how an organization could potentially use these out of the box capabilities.

Business scenarios

Thanks to CRM, Race2Win Insurance Company has been able to effectively market and sell its products to companies in a wide range of industries all over the world. Now it's time for Race2Win to start servicing their clients, and it's Dynamics CRM to the rescue once again.

Cases

Let us say a customer didn't receive their invoice for insurance products that they purchased. This customer e-mails this issue to a client service representative at Race2Win. With Dynamics CRM, this e-mail can be converted to a case. During that process of conversion, an account or contact can be linked (the case can reference a product if needed). Once converted, the original e-mail will be tied to the newly opened case. After the case is created, it can be assigned to a user, or routed to a queue. Throughout its lifecycle, activities such as e-mails, phone calls, and/or tasks can be tracked as a part of the case.

Knowledge base articles

In trying to resolve the case, users can access a repository of knowledge base articles to reference past issues and resolutions.

Contracts

Race2Win can use CRM to create service contracts to define the type and level of support required. These contracts can then be referenced when new cases are opened.

Service calendar

If the servicing of customers requires the allocation of resources, whether that is an individual employee, a contractor, a facility or equipment, Dynamics CRM's scheduling features can assist. The service calendar can show users how each resource is being allocated for a given time period. With this knowledge, you can schedule resources more efficiently in order to deliver a prompt resolution to a case.

As you can see, CRM has a rich feature set that can be used to service any type of client. We just went through a high-level introduction of the three main modules in Microsoft Dynamics CRM. This book is a guide to help pass the CRM 2011 Applications exam (MB2-868) and we will delve deeper into each of the modules to help you better understand the application. The next section gives you an introduction to Microsoft Dynamics CRM 2011 training and certifications.

Microsoft Dynamics CRM 2011 training and certifications

The majority of the content for this section was created by my colleague, Neil Benson, who is also writing a Dynamics CRM certification guide. He was gracious enough to offer this material as a resource for folks preparing for the MB2-868 (Dynamics CRM 2011 Applications) certification exam.

Training courses and examination

On the *Microsoft Learning* website (`http://learning.microsoft.com`), you can find more information about the courses and exams. Here, you can also find a local training course provider or buy an online training course collection.

For users

Microsoft Dynamics CRM 2011 users will find the following two courses very useful:

- **What's New in Microsoft Dynamics CRM 2011 (Course 80289A)**: This one-day course provides an introduction to the new features of CRM 2011 for users who already have experience with Microsoft Dynamics CRM 4.0 or higher

- **Introduction to Microsoft Dynamics CRM 2011** (**Course 80442A**): This one-day course provides an overview of CRM 2011 to users with no previous experience with Microsoft Dynamics CRM

There are no exams or certifications associated with these courses.

For implementers and administrators

If you are an implementation team member or a system administrator, there are eight training courses and four exams available.

Applications

There are four courses available for learning about the major application areas of Microsoft Dynamics CRM 2011:

- **Marketing Automation in Microsoft Dynamics CRM 2011** (**Course 80290A**): This one-day course covers the marketing features of CRM 2011. These marketing features include campaigns and quick campaigns, lists, templates, campaign activities, and campaign responses.
- **Sales Management in Microsoft Dynamics CRM 2011** (**Course 80291A**): This one-day course covers the sales features of CRM 2011. These sales features include leads, opportunities, quotes, orders, invoices, and the product catalog.
- **Service Management in Microsoft Dynamics CRM 2011** (**Course 80292A**): This one-day course covers the service management features of CRM 2011. These features include cases, queues, teams, and the knowledge base.
- **Service Scheduling in Microsoft Dynamics CRM 2011** (**Course 80293A**): This one-day course covers the service scheduling features of CRM 2011. These features include services, service activities, and the service calendar.

There is one exam covering all four of these application areas. This exam is **Microsoft Dynamics CRM 2011 Applications** (**Exam MB2-868**). After passing this exam, you will earn a **Microsoft Certified Technology Specialist** (**MCTS**) certification.

There are two other useful courses available for implementers and administrators. These courses are as follows:

- **Reporting in Microsoft Dynamics CRM 2011** (**Course 80445A**): This one-day course covers the advanced reporting features of CRM 2011
- **Workflow and Dialog Processes in Microsoft Dynamics CRM 2011** (**Course 80444A**): This one-day course covers the configuration and use of the workflows and dialogs processes in CRM 2011

There are no exams or certifications associated with these courses.

Installation

There is one training course and an exam that covers the installation and deployment of Microsoft Dynamics CRM 2011:

- **Microsoft Dynamics CRM 2011 Installation and Deployment (Course 80296A)**: This two-day course covers the deployment options, prerequisites, and installation procedures for Microsoft Dynamics CRM 2011
- **Microsoft Dynamics CRM 2011 Installation and Deployment (Exam MB2-867)**: After passing this exam, you will earn an MCTS certification

Customization and configuration

There is one training course and an exam that covers the customization of Microsoft Dynamics CRM 2011:

- **Microsoft Dynamics CRM 2011 Customization and Configuration (Course 80294B)**: This three-day course covers the customization features of CRM 2011. These features include configuring the organization structure, customizing entities, forms, views, and charts.
- **Microsoft Dynamics CRM 2011 Customization and Configuration (Exam MB2-866)**: After passing this exam, you will earn an MCTS certification.

For developers

For developers, there is one CRM 2011 training course and an exam available.

Extending

There is one training course and an exam that covers extending Microsoft Dynamics CRM 2011:

- **Extending Microsoft Dynamics CRM 2011 (Course 80295A)**: This three-day course covers CRM 2011's extensibility options described in the Microsoft Dynamics CRM 2011 SDK
- **Extending Microsoft Dynamics CRM 2011 (Exam MB2-876)**: After passing this exam, you will earn an MCTS certification

> In addition to the Extending Microsoft Dynamics CRM 2011 training course and exam, developers should also consider the Microsoft Dynamics CRM 2011 Customization and Configuration training course and exam listed earlier in this chapter.

Certifications

This section describes the two levels of certification available for Microsoft Dynamics CRM 2011, and the benefits of becoming certified.

Microsoft Certified Technology Specialist (MCTS)

MCTS certifications demonstrate your proficiency in a feature area of a Microsoft product. Passing any one of the four CRM 2011 exams described earlier in this chapter will earn you an MCTS certification.

Microsoft Certified IT Professional (MCITP)

MCITP certifications demonstrate your in-depth expertise across a number of Microsoft products. There are three MCITP certifications available:

Benefits of certification

Whether you work as an independent consultant, work for a Microsoft customer, or work for a Microsoft partner, earning a Microsoft Dynamics CRM certification leads the way to better career opportunities.

Microsoft partners value certified individuals because employing **Microsoft Certified Professionals** (**MCPs**) enables them to achieve silver and gold competencies that demonstrate their commitment to, and expertise in, Microsoft Dynamics CRM.

Microsoft customers value certified individuals because Microsoft Dynamics CRM solutions implemented, managed, and supported by MCPs have a lower total cost of ownership and a higher return on investment.

Achieving certification demonstrates the technical proficiency that validates your knowledge, adds credibility to your resume, and will help you advance in your career. When combined with real-world experience, certification will mean that you are more highly regarded than other individuals with similar experience who haven't taken training or shown sufficient initiative to achieve certification.

Exam MB2-868

The focus of this certification guide is exam MB2-868: Microsoft Dynamics CRM 2011 Applications. In this section we'll learn:

- How to study for the exam
- How to register for your exam
- What to expect at the test center
- How to make the best use of your time
- How to answer the different types of questions

How to study for the exam

There are several ways to study for the MB2-868 exam:

- **Take an official instructor-led training course**: For the applications exam, there are four courses you can take:
    - **Course 80290A**: **Marketing Automation in Microsoft Dynamics CRM 2011** is a one-day, instructor-led classroom training course available for a fee from Microsoft Learning Partners worldwide, in a number of languages
    - **Course 80291A**: **Sales Management in Microsoft Dynamics CRM 2011** is a one-day, instructor-led classroom training course available for a fee from Microsoft Learning Partners worldwide, in a number of languages
    - **Course 80292A**: **Service Management in Microsoft Dynamics CRM 2011** is a one-day, instructor-led classroom training course available for a fee from Microsoft Learning Partners worldwide, in a number of languages
    - **Course 80293A**: **Service Scheduling in Microsoft Dynamics CRM 2011** is a one-day, instructor-led classroom training course available for a fee from Microsoft Learning Partners worldwide, in a number of languages
- **Take an official e-learning course**: A subscription to e-learning collection 80290A, 80291A, 80292A, and 80293A is available for a fee from Microsoft Learning, in a number of languages

- **Study the official courseware**: If your organization has purchased a Microsoft Dynamics service plan, you can download the official courseware for courses 80290A, 80291A, 80292A, and 80293A from PartnerSource or CustomerSource
- **Use this certification guide**: This certification guide follows the syllabus examined in the MB2-868 Microsoft Dynamics CRM 2011 Applications exam

The best study method will depend upon your training budget, learning style, and the available time. Note, however, that certification guide is the only option available that includes practice exam questions.

Hands-on experience

Hands-on experience with Microsoft Dynamics CRM 2011 is essential, regardless of your preferred study method. Follow all of the procedures covered in this guide several times in a CRM test environment. Use a 30-day trial subscription to Microsoft Dynamics CRM Online if you don't have a training deployment available. You don't need to have completed a full implementation project, but some hands-on experience will greatly improve your chances of success.

How to register for your exam

Regardless of which study method you choose, the only way to register for your MB2-868 exam is with Prometric: Microsoft's official certification exam provider.

Visit the Prometric website to register for your exam (`http://www.prometric.com/Microsoft/Dynamics.htm`).

You must take your exam in person at one of the Prometric's worldwide test centers. Candidates can use any test center, except in India, China, or Pakistan where you must provide proof that you are a legitimate resident of that country.

If you are taking an official training course with a Microsoft Learning Partner, check whether or not the course includes an exam before you book directly with Prometric.

Exam languages

MB2-868 is available in the following languages:

- English
- French
- German
- Italian

- Japanese
- Russian
- Spanish
- Portuguese (Brazil)
- Chinese (Simplified)

Exam fees

The exam fee for MB2-868 is USD 150 (at the time of writing). The exam fees in your country may vary.

Your organization may be entitled to, or have purchased, exam credits. Check with your manager before booking your exam.

Retaking the exam

If you need to retake your exam, you will need to rebook with Prometric and pay for your retake exam. If you need to retake the exam for a third time, you will need to wait for 14 days after the date of your second exam.

What to expect at the test center

Prometric test centers are located in a wide variety of IT training and test centers worldwide. Microsoft Learning Partners often have a test center so that you can take the exam directly after completing an instructor-led training course.

You should arrive at the test center about 30 minutes before you are scheduled to take your exam. You will be asked to present a photographic identification to the test center administrator and to sign in to a log book.

You cannot take anything into the exam room with you. This certification guide is so exciting that it can be hard to put down, but you'll have to do so while taking your exam!

The exam room usually has a number of workstations screened off from each other, and you may be taking your MB2-868 exam along with candidates taking the same or different exams. Communicating with other candidates is not allowed.

An exam supervisor will set up the exam on your computer and may or may not remain in the exam room during your exam. Video surveillance might be installed in the exam room to ensure all that candidates comply with the exam rules.

A wipe-clean notepad will be provided, but any notes that you take during the exam cannot be retained after the exam.

How to make the best use of your time

Once the test center administrator has set up the exam on your computer, you will be able to start the exam. You have 3 hours to complete 75 exam questions, although some of this time will be spent reading the legal preamble regarding copyright and personal data protection.

Almost all candidates will comfortably complete the exam within the time limit. The questions in your test are taken at random from a large pool of possible questions, so no two exams will ever be exactly the same.

The passing mark is 700 points, but Prometric does not reveal the points awarded for each question.

The following are some tips to help you make the best use of your time:

- Spend lots of time reading the terms and conditions, privacy statements, and other legal preamble only if you've missed your calling to the legal profession. Otherwise, accept the statements and move on to the exam as quickly as possible.
- Read each question carefully. In particular, pay attention to phrases that indicate how many answers are required—for example, select one, choose three, or select all that apply—and whether you are expected to select true or false statements.
- Answer each question as best as you can in sequence. Do not skip questions by leaving them unanswered. Instead, if you are not confident in your answer, mark the question for review at the end.
- After you have answered all questions, reassess all of the questions that you have marked for review.
- Before finishing the exam, quickly review all of your answers to ensure that you have left no questions unanswered, and, where appropriate, that you have provided the required number of answers.
- Your intuition is often right. Change an answer only if you have an overwhelming feeling that your first answer was wrong.

How to answer the questions

There are two types of multiple choice questions in the exam:

- Multiple choice with one correct answer (radio buttons)
- Multiple choice with multiple possible answers (checkboxes)

Read the question carefully to see how many answers are required. Consider the following example question:

Q.1. The required fields when creating a marketing list are:
(Choose all that apply.)

1. Member Type.
2. Campaign Type.
3. List Name.
4. Type.
5. Owner.

The answer to this question is 1, 3, 4, and 5.

This question is a good example of an off-syllabus question that sometimes appears in Microsoft certification exams. The Microsoft training course syllabuses and exams are written by different groups of people and do not always cover exactly the same material. So, it is possible to encounter an exam question that wasn't included in the syllabus. This guide covers the course syllabus, and a deep understanding of all of the material covered here will be sufficient to achieve a passing score, but broader hands-on experience and additional reading is recommended if you want to achieve a perfect score.

Summary

In this chapter, a brief introduction to Microsoft Dynamics CRM 2011 was presented. Each of the three main modules—sales, marketing, and service—were covered at a high level, along with business scenarios centered around a fictitious organization called Race2Win Insurance Company. Race2Win Insurance Company's inside sales team uses CRM to track the leads they've generated. They use business rules to qualify the leads and hand them off to other sales representatives who manage accounts. The leads, if needed, can be converted to an account, contact, opportunity, or a combination of the three. Accounts allow Race2Win to manage organizations they do business with; contacts are individuals that may or may not be tied to an account; and opportunities enable the tracking of potential sales to their customers. Opportunities can also track estimated and actual revenue. To get a more accurate measure of revenue, opportunities can reference Race2Win's products, prices, and discounts. Quotes can be used to give a customer an estimate of costs. Once a customer agrees to make a purchase, Race2Win's order entry team can generate an order and/or an invoice. As Race2Win continues to grow its business, the competition will grow stiffer. Dynamics CRM allows Race2Win to analyze a competitor's sales strategies, products, and the business they win. Lastly, the sales module can help Race2Win to set up goals for their employees, such as sales goals. These goals can also be rolled up to a larger goal.

To grow their customer base even more, Race2Win's marketing team can use the Dynamics CRM marketing module to create marketing lists. These lists group accounts, contacts, or leads into a list for use in marketing campaigns. The campaigns can be very simple with one communication channel and an abbreviated timeline. They can also be more complex, tracking planning activities, campaign costs, and even targeted products. If a potential or existing customer would like to learn more about a specific product, Race2Win can send them sales literature, including marketing collateral around products or services.

Every organization, including Race2Win, must keep their customers happy. Race2Win must ensure that any issues with the quality of their products, the level of customer service, and billing get resolved efficiently. CRM's service module allows Race2Win to open up cases any time an issue arises. Knowledge base articles can be created or referenced throughout the life cycle of a case, allowing cases to be resolved more efficiently. If Race2Win has set up any service contracts (for example, a contract limiting the number of cases that can be opened for a customer), these can be referenced as well.

The second half of the chapter revolved around Microsoft Dynamics CRM 2011 training and certification. There are several Microsoft courses you can take, from learning about the application itself, to installing, configuring, and extending it. These courses are not mandatory, but can help, along with books like this, to pass the related certification exams.

Dynamics CRM 2011 has four certification exams:

- Exam MB2-866: Microsoft Dynamics CRM 2011 Customization and Configuration
- Exam MB2-867: Microsoft Dynamics CRM 2011 Installation and Deployment
- Exam MB2-868: Microsoft Dynamics CRM 2011 Applications
- Exam MB2-876: Extending Microsoft Dynamics CRM 2011

If you pass any one of the four exams, you will be a Microsoft Certified Technology Specialist (MCTS). Certifications can help to validate the knowledge you've gained in your training, as well as bolster your resume.

Specifically about the Dynamics CRM application's certification (MB2-868), there are different ways to pass the exam. You can take any of the instructor-led or e-learning courses mentioned earlier in this chapter. You can also download the official courseware from Microsoft CustomerSource or PartnerSource if you have access to either. In conjunction with this, or alternatively, you can use this book! With that said, one of the most important tools to supplement your learning is *hands-on experience* to help reinforce the knowledge you've attained.

Once you feel confident and are ready to take the exam, you can book it online at Prometric (`http://www.prometric.com/Microsoft/Dynamics.htm`). The exam is written in different languages, such as Spanish, French, and German, and usually costs USD 150.

Once you are at the test taking center, some helpful exam taking tips are: quickly accept the legal statements at the beginning of the exam and move on to the questions as quickly as possible; read each question carefully, paying attention to phrases that indicate how many answers are required; answer each question as best as you can in sequence; and if you are not confident in your answer, mark the question for review at the end.

This chapter has provided you with an introduction to the Dynamics CRM application, and the MB2-868 certification exam. In the next chapter, you'll learn how to track interactions between other users and customers by using activities and notes.

2
Activities and Notes

In this chapter you will learn about:

- Activities
- Notes

Activities

Activities are a way for an organization to track interactions both with users in their own company and with their customers. An example of a type of activity is a manager creating a **task** for someone on their team to set up an **appointment** for the rest of the team. The appointment itself can also be an activity that is tracked in CRM. Another example is when a salesperson makes a **phone call** to a customer: they can track the content of the conversation and duration in CRM.

Business scenarios

Race2Win Insurance Company sells insurance products all over the world. They recently launched a campaign around new products they'll be offering in the upcoming year. One of their best customers responded to the campaign, expressing interest. The marketing team creates a **campaign response** activity to record the interest expressed. They then pass on this information to the salesperson managing this account.

The salesperson assigned to the account starts the selling process and can use CRM **activities** to track all interactions they have with the customer. To track this interaction, each activity created can be associated to a record in the system (see the *Activity attributes* section and the *Common attributes* sub-section for more information on the field used to associate a record to an activity).

The salesperson begins by making a **phone call** to one of their contacts at the company, in order to understand the selling environment, and to figure out the best date and time for a meeting. They can create a phone call activity in CRM to enter some notes about the conversation. The salesperson can associate the activity to both the account on which they are working and the contact they are calling. Doing this allows the salesperson to track the interaction they have had with this contact about the account.

After the salesperson gets some background information, they set up a **task** to create an agenda for the meeting. While they are working on the agenda, they set up an **appointment** with the expected attendees. After the agenda is completed, the salesperson sends an **e-mail** to the group with the agenda attached.

One day before the meeting the sales representative's contact e-mails them to fax more information about the product they will be selling. The e-mail sent by the contact can also be tracked in Dynamics CRM. The sales representative finds sales literature tied to the product and prints it out. They then fax over a copy of the document to their contact. The salesperson creates a **fax** activity record to track the fact that they sent a fax to her contact.

The salesperson gives their sales pitch, and hours later the company decides to purchase the insurance product. The salesperson is elated and sends a letter to the individuals at the meeting thanking them for the business. The salesperson can create a **letter** activity record recording this interaction as well.

Fast forward a few months, and it's time for another sales opportunity with the same customer. The salesperson assigned to the account is out on vacation, so another sales representative steps in. That salesperson can look at the account and see the history of communication the previous salesperson had.

Tracking communications within Dynamics CRM can play a vital role in understanding a customer, and their history. The different types of activities in CRM are:

- **Task**: Records a to-do or a follow-up item
- **E-mail**: Records a sent or received e-mail message
- **Phone call**: Records a phone call started or received
- **Letter**: Records the mailing of a letter
- **Fax**: Records a sent or received fax
- **Appointment**: Records a meeting
- **Recurring appointment**: Records a recurring meeting.
- **Service activity**: Records service performed for a customer
- **Campaign response**: Records a response to a campaign
- **Custom activity**: Records a custom activity

Custom activities

Microsoft Dynamics CRM 2011 includes new functionality that allows an organization to create custom activity types. With ever-changing communication channels, and activities being crucial in tracking those communications, it's imperative that there are other activity types. An example is a custom activity for a text message. Text messages sent or received could potentially be recorded in CRM.

Activity attributes

Most activity types have a set of common **attributes**. Attributes are essentially fields in Dynamics CRM.

Common attributes

A list of common attributes available for nearly all activity types, is shown in the following table:

Attribute	Description
Subject	A clear, concise description of the activity.
Description	Description of the activity.
Regarding	The record related to the activity. This field is used to link the activity record to a record in the CRM system.
Owner	The user in CRM that owns the record.
Duration	The estimated time it would take the activity to be completed.
Priority	Level of importance of getting the activity completed.
Due Date	Date on which the activity is estimated to be completed.
Status	The status of the activity.
Actual Duration	The actual time it took to complete the activity.
Scheduled Start	The estimated start date of the activity.
Actual Start	The date the activity actually started.
Actual End	The date the activity actually ended.
Category	A way to categorize an activity at a high level.
Sub-Category	A more finite categorization than the one defined in the Category attribute.

Certain activity types have their own specific attributes, in addition to the common attributes listed above. These activity-specific attributes are listed below.

E-mail specific attributes

The following screenshot shows an e-mail activity record in CRM, highlighting attributes that are specific to this particular type of activity.

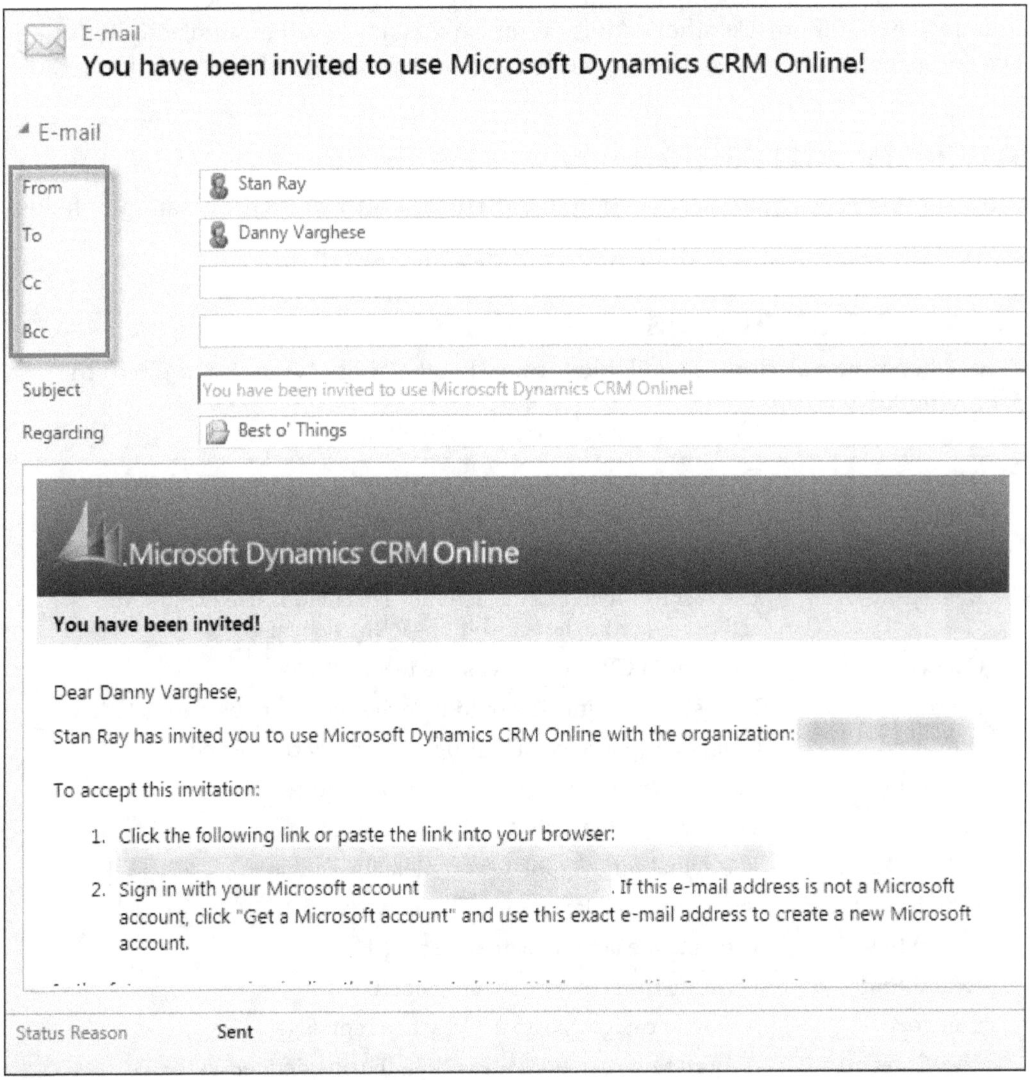

The following table lists the attributes that are specific to an e-mail activity, along with a description of the data that each field stores:

Attribute	Description
From	The CRM user that sent the e-mail.
To	Any record type that has an e-mail address field can be included in this field. There can be multiple records of different types in this field. For example, an account, contact, and lead can all be a value in this field.
Cc	Recipients carbon copied on the e-mail. The record types allowed as values for this field are the same as the **To** field.
Bcc	Recipients blind carbon copied on the e-mail. The record types allowed as values for this field are the same as the **To** field.

Phone call specific attributes

The following screenshot is of a phone call activity record in CRM, highlighting attributes that are specific to this particular type of activity:

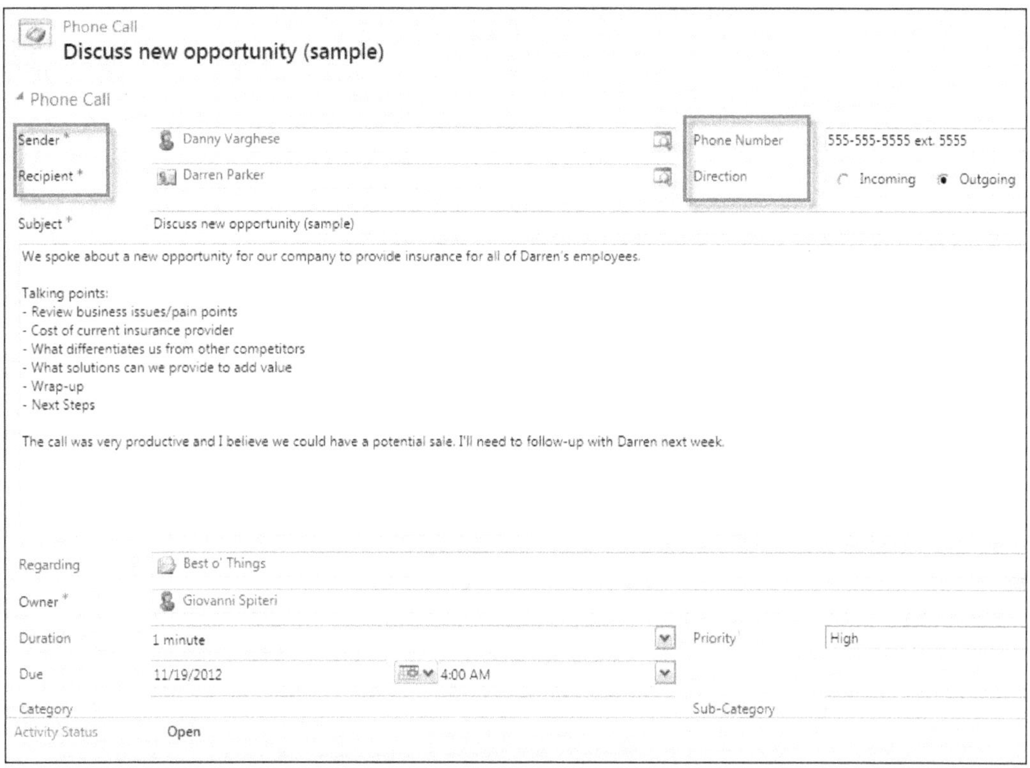

The following table lists all of the attributes that are specific to a phone call activity, along with a description of the data that each field stores:

Attribute	Description
Sender	Defaults to the currently logged in user, but it can be an account, contact, lead, or user.
Recipient	Can be an account, contact, lead, or user record.
Phone Number	Phone number dialed or received.
Direction	Possible values are outgoing (phone call was made) or incoming (phone call was received).

Letter specific attributes

The following screenshot is of a letter activity in CRM, highlighting attributes that are specific to this particular type of activity:

The following table lists all of the attributes that are specific to a letter activity, along with a description of the data that each field stores:

Attribute	Description
Sender	Defaults to the currently logged in user, but it can be an account, contact, lead, or user.
Recipient	Can be an account, contact, lead, or user record.
Direction	Possible values are outgoing (letter was sent) or incoming (letter was received).
Address	Address of sender (if letter was received) or recipient (if letter was sent).

Fax specific attributes

The following screenshot is of a fax activity in CRM, highlighting attributes that are specific to this particular type of activity:

The following table lists all the attributes that are specific to a fax activity, along with a description of the data that each field stores:

Attribute	Description
Sender	Defaults to the currently logged in user, but it can be an account, contact, lead, or user.
Recipient	Can be an account, contact, lead, or user record.
Fax Number	Fax number of sender (if fax was received) or recipient (if fax was sent).
Direction	Possible values are outgoing (fax was sent) or incoming (fax was received).
Cover Page	Description of cover page or even some verbiage included on the cover page.

Appointment specific attributes

The following screenshot is of an appointment activity in CRM, highlighting attributes that are specific to this particular type of activity.

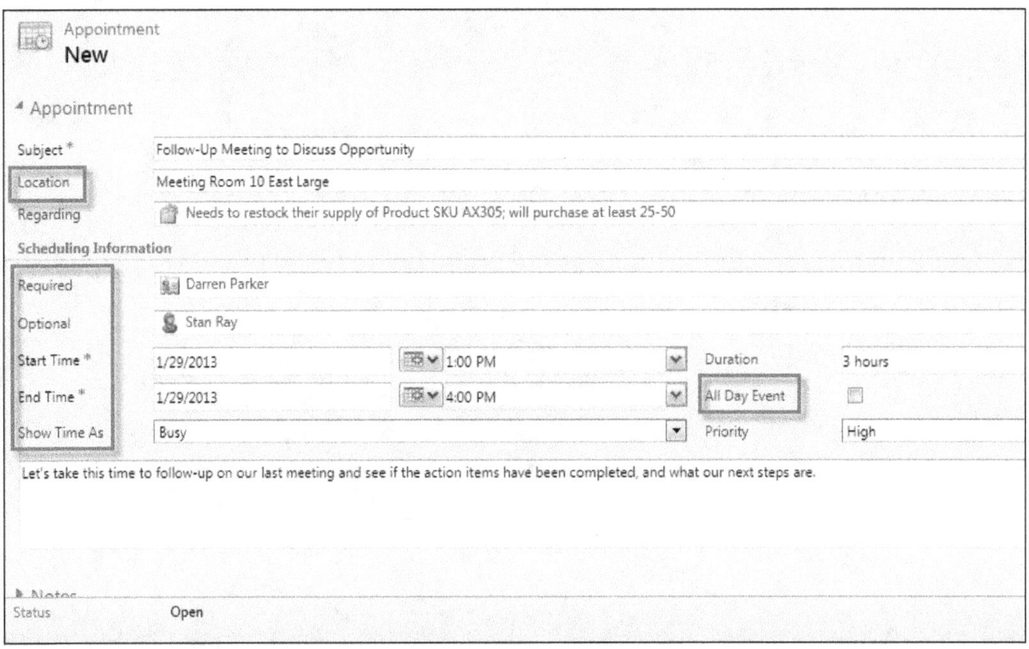

The following screenshot is a continuation of the appointment activity record form:

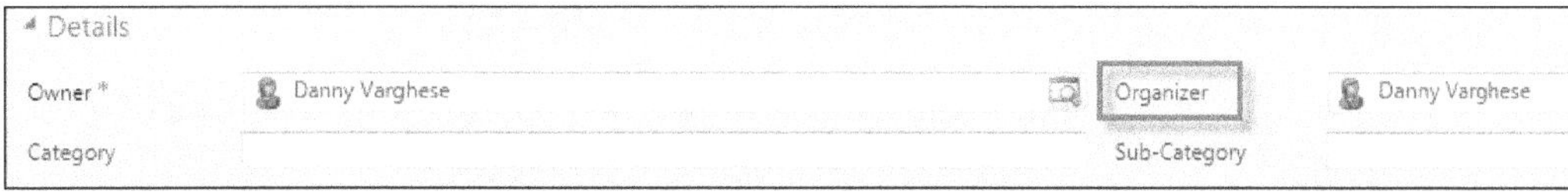

The following table lists all of the attributes that are specific to an appointment activity, along with a description of the data that each field stores:

Attribute	Description
Location	Location of appointment; can be a room, building, or even a conference call number.
Required	Attendees required for the meeting. The values can be account, contact, facility/equipment, lead and/or user record. There can be multiple records of different types in this field. For example, an account, contact, and lead can all be a value in this field.
Optional	Attendees that are optional for the meeting. The values can be account, contact, facility/equipment, lead, and/or user record. There can be multiple records of different types in this field. For example, an account, contact, and lead can all be a value in this field.
Start Time	Start date and time of the appointment.
End Time	End date and time of appointment.
Show Time As	Status of the appointment, indicating if during this time-block the creator of the appointment is free, tentative, busy, or out of office.
All Day Event	Indicating if the appointment is an all-day event.
Organizer	User in CRM that is the organizer of the appointment.

The campaign response activity is explained in *Chapter 3, Managing Marketing Automation Applications – Marketing Lists and Campaigns*. The service activity is explained in *Chapter 8, Managing Service Scheduling Applications*, where we go into the service scheduling aspect of Dynamics CRM. For now let's take a look how to create an activity record in CRM.

Creating activities

For this example, let's create a task activity record. Follow these steps :

1. Start CRM, click on the **Workplace** module, and then click on **Activities**.

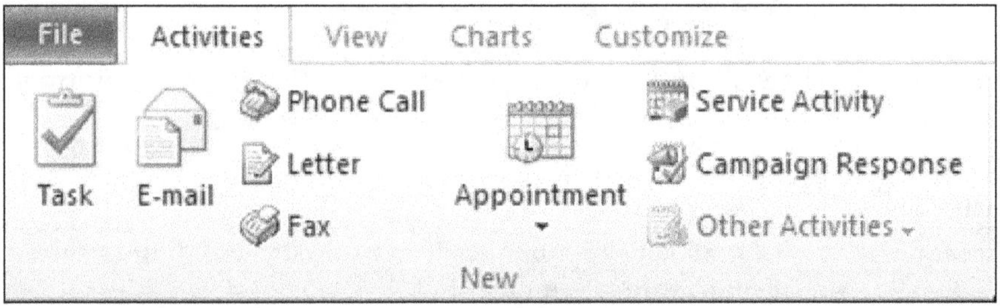

2. Click on the **Task** button.

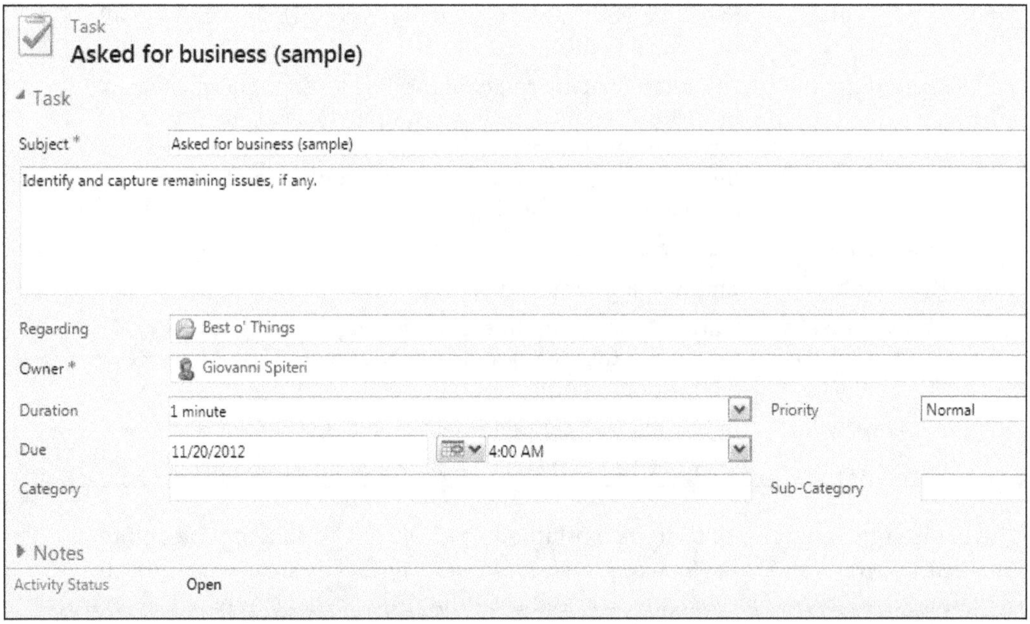

3. Enter the following required fields:
   i. **Subject**: Enter a clear, concise description of the task.
   ii. **Owner**: This defaults to the currently logged in user, but can be changed.

Although the **Regarding** field not a required, it is highly recommended to populate this field. This field helps link the activity to a particular record. Click on the lookup and find a record to associate the task to.

> If you are on a record, say an account, and then create a task from the context of the account, the **Regarding** field will be auto-populated with the account that you were on.

4. Click on **Save**.

Once an activity is created, the activity can be re-assigned to a user or team. In this way, multiple users can perform the various interactions both internally and with customers. The next step in the activity lifecycle is to complete the activity.

For different activities the concept of completing an activity varies. All out of the box activities other than **E-mail** and **Campaign Response** have a button, **Mark Complete**, to complete the activity. For an e-mail, when the e-mail is sent, the activity is essentially complete. For a campaign response, the activity is closed (not completed) when the campaign is either converted or marked closed. More about campaign responses is covered in *Chapter 3, Managing Marketing Automation Applications – Marketing Lists and Campaigns*.

Completing activities

For this example, let us complete a task activity. To do so, follow these steps:

1. Start CRM, click on the **Workplace** module, and then click on **Activities**.
2. Find the task that you wish to complete and open the record.

3. Click the **Mark Complete** button.

Once an activity is completed, the certain parts of the activity form become read only, but **notes** can be added, files can be attached, and the activity can be shared with other users or teams. Notes are discussed later in this chapter.

Viewing activities

Activities can be seen by using Dynamics CRM views or on the entity that the **Regarding** field was set to. For example, if on a task activity record, the **Regarding** field was set to an account with the name of ABC Company, then you can view the task in the list of activities associated to ABC Company.

Viewing activities on a record

By default, every activity record has the following statuses:

- **Open**
- **Completed**
- **Canceled**
- **Scheduled**

In the left-hand navigation of records that have activities associated to them, activities are broken out into **Activities** and **Closed Activities**:

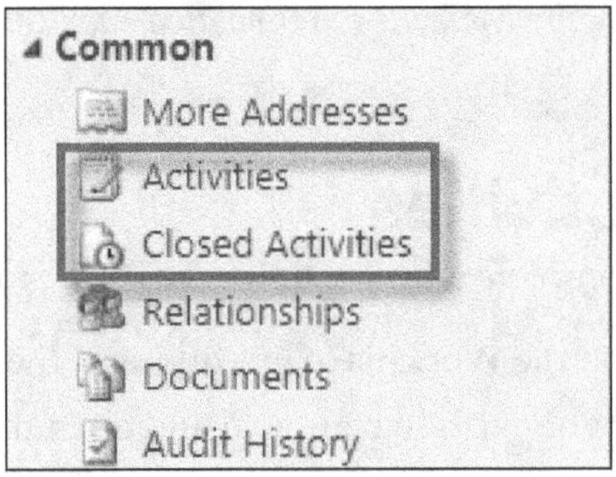

Activities with a status of open or scheduled are found when clicking on **Activities**. Activities with a status of completed or canceled can be found when click on **Closed Activities**. Not only are activities related to records via the **Regarding** field, but some activities are rolled up to other records.

When a user navigates to the list of activities or closed activities, they will be directed to an **associated view**. A view is an area that displays data, and an associated view displays data about an associated or related record. Most views in CRM can be configured to display filtered data, and give users the ability to sort certain columns.

The associated view for open activities has two filters, as shown in the preceding screenshot. The first filter displays activities that are overdue or are due within the time period specified. For example, if the filter of **Next 30 days** is selected, then it will display all activities that are overdue and with a due date within the next 30 days.

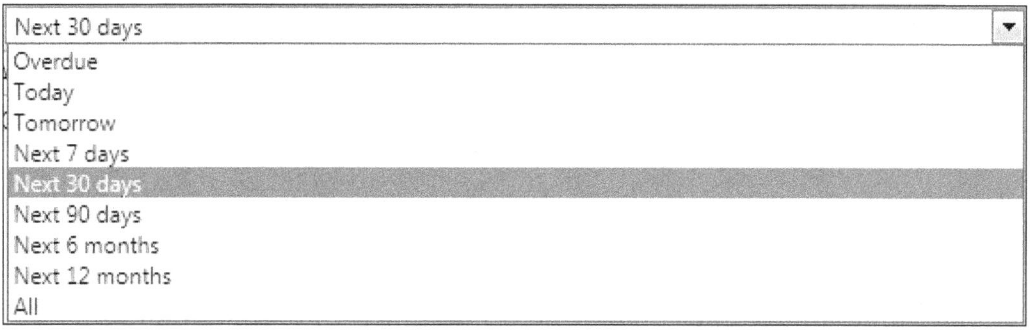

The second filter has two options—**This Record Only** and **Related "Regarding" Records**. The first option displays all activities where the **Regarding** field is set to the record you're viewing. It also displays activities where other system relationship fields are set to the record, for example, on an e-mail, if the **To** field is set to the record, or on a phone call if the **Recipient** field is set to the record.

The second option shows all activities with the **Regarding** field set to the record itself or any related record using the activity roll-up functionality.

Activity roll-up

Dynamics CRM boasts the ability to give users a 360 degree view of their customers. One of the features that helps to give users a big-picture view when it comes to activities is the activity roll-up. The activity roll-up allows users to see activities of certain **child records** on the **parent record**.

Dynamics CRM allows a hierarchal relationship between entities, allowing an organization to model its data around real-world situations. For example, a company can have one or more people that can serve as contacts associated to it. Another example is that a company can have a parent company. For example, Race2Win Insurance Company may have a parent company called Race2Win LLC. To allow for this, an account can have a relationship to another account, and one or more contacts. In the aforementioned example, the account is a parent record to another account (child record), and a parent to one or more contacts (child record(s)).

When it comes to the activity roll-up, if you were to open an account record, and click on the left-hand side navigation on either **Activities** or **Closed Activities**, you'll be able to see a list of activities associated to the record. If the view filter was set to include **Related "Regarding" Records**, then you will see activities where the **Regarding** field or another system field on the activity (to, from, recipient and so on), was set to that account. You will also see all activities where the **Regarding** field is set to related records to that account, such as contacts or opportunities.

An illustration of this can be found on Jukka Niiranen's blog (`http://niiranen.eu/crm`), and is replicated below:

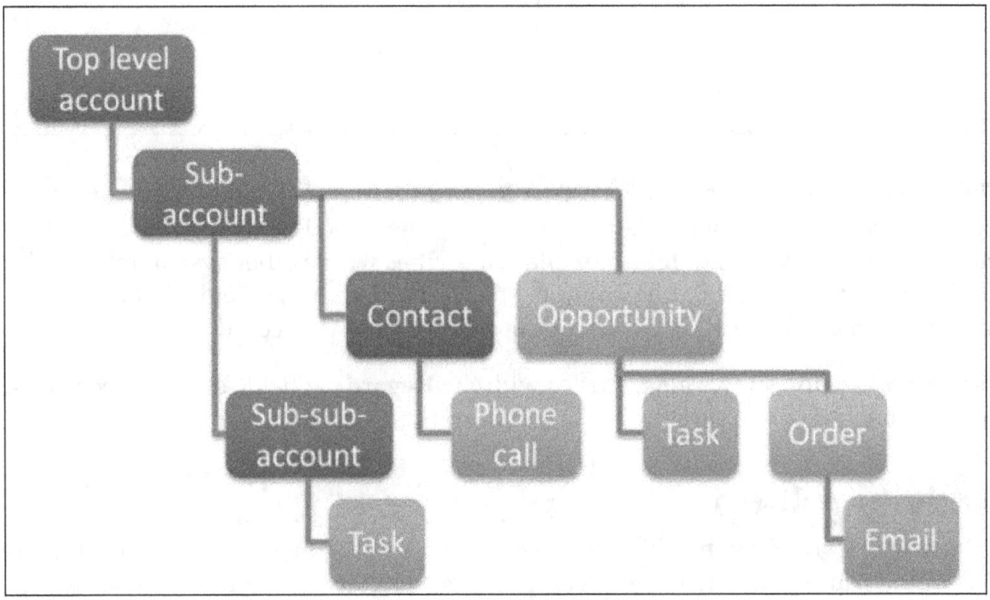

In the illustration above, you can see a relationship between two accounts, one contact, one opportunity, one order, and some activities. The way activity roll-up works is that from the sub-account's activity associated view, you can see activities tied to the sub-sub-account, contact, opportunity and order. However, from the top-level account, you can only see the task on the sub-sub-account. Jukka says the reason for this is that none of the activities in the sub-account's activity view were set as regarding that particular account record. Essentially CRM, behind the scenes, looks at the child record's view to determine which activities to roll-up.

Activity views

Activities can also be viewed by going to the **Workplace** area and clicking on **Activities**. In the view list you'll see the following:

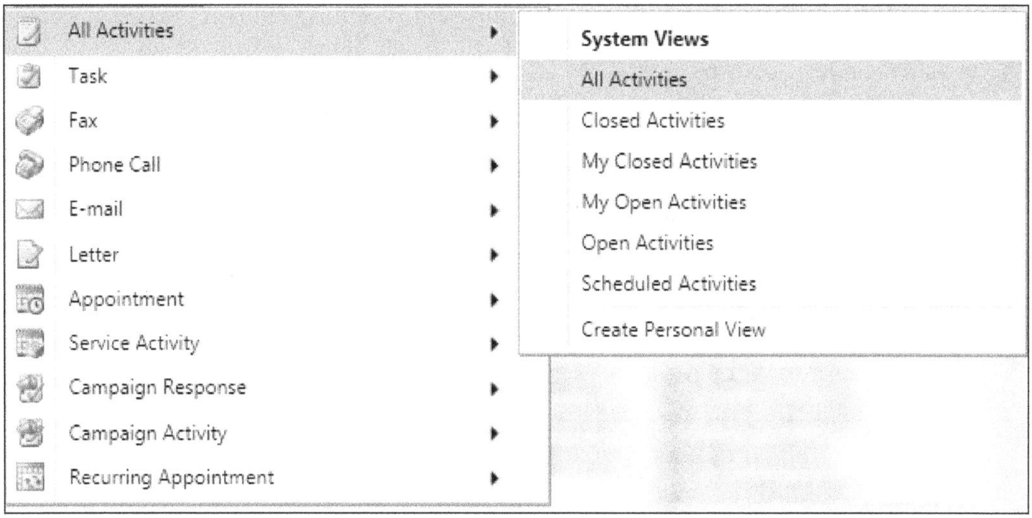

The **All Activities** view can be further broken down into the following basic views:

- **All Activities**: This is a list of all activities regardless of status.
- **Closed Activities**: This is a list of all activities with a status of completed or canceled.
- **My Closed Activities**: This is a list of all activities with a status of completed or canceled and where the owner is the currently logged in user.
- **My Open Activities**: This is a list of all activities with a status of open or scheduled and where the owner is the currently logged in user.
- **Open Activities**: This is a list of all activities with a status of open or scheduled.
- **Scheduled Activities**: This is a list of all activities with a status of scheduled.

Each of the other activity types shown in the preceding screenshot have their own views as well. For example, the task entity has the following views:

- **All Tasks**
- **My Tasks**
- **Tasks Being Followed**
- **Tasks I Follow**

Delving into each view for each activity entity is not necessary for the certification exam and we will not cover these any further.

E-mail templates

We've just seen how an e-mail in CRM is a type of activity. CRM uses an e-mail template to help users send the same e-mail to multiple recipients such as accounts and/or contacts.

Creating e-mail templates

To create an e-mail template, follow these steps :

1. Start CRM, click on the **Settings** module, and then click on **Templates**.
2. Click on **E-mail Templates**.

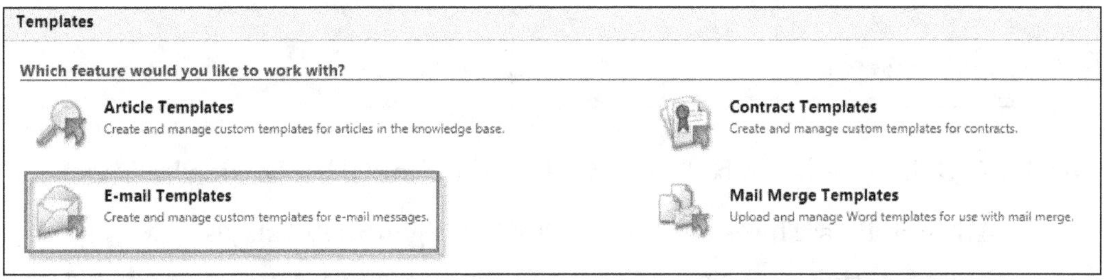

3. Click on **New**.

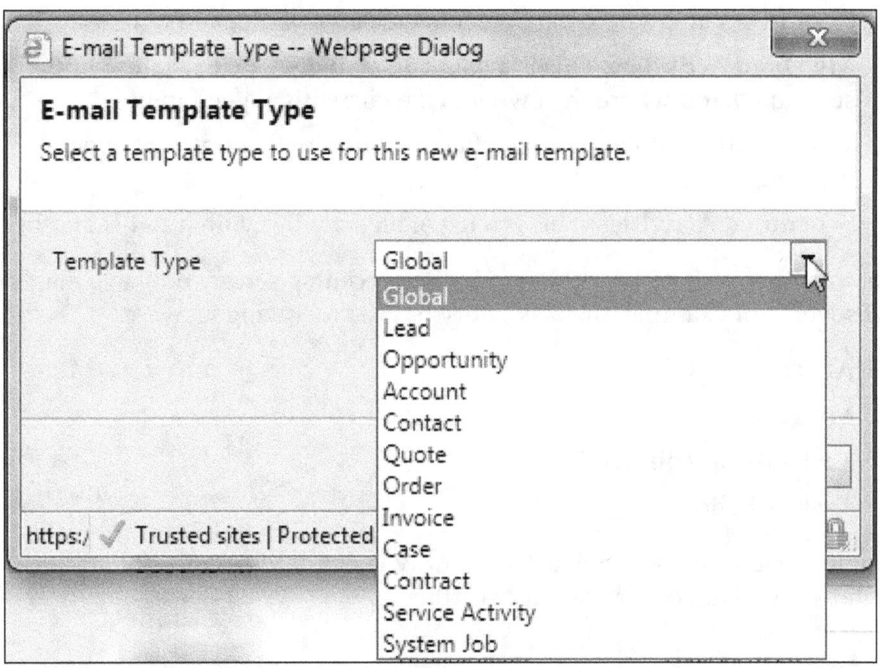

4. In the **E-mail Template Type** dialog, select the type of template that you want to create. The template type defines which entity the e-mail will apply to. The **Global** template type means the e-mail can be applied to any entity.
5. Click on **OK**.

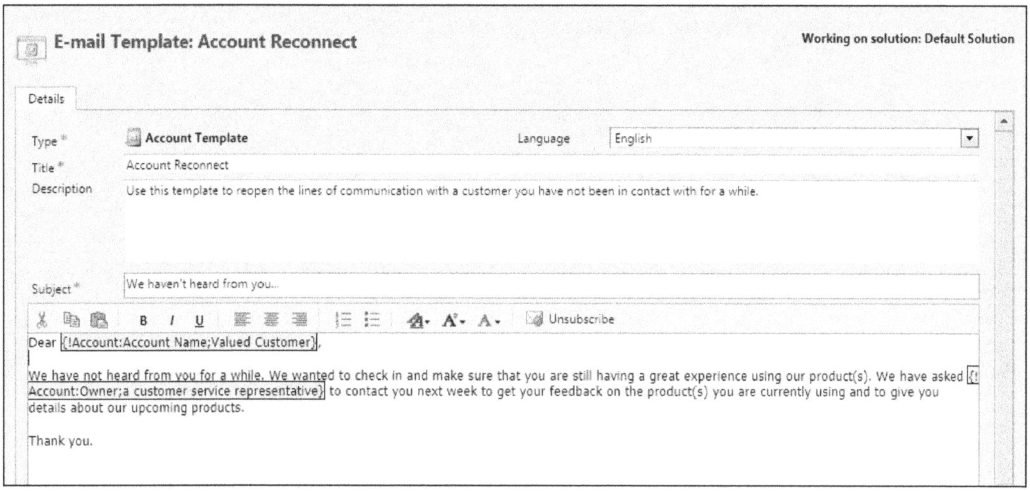

6. Enter the following required fields:
   i. **Title**: Enter a clear concise title for the e-mail template
   ii. **Subject**: Enter a subject for the e-mail

7. While entering values for either the **Subject** or **Body**, you can enter placeholders for fields from an entity or related record. To do this, click on the **Insert/Update** button.

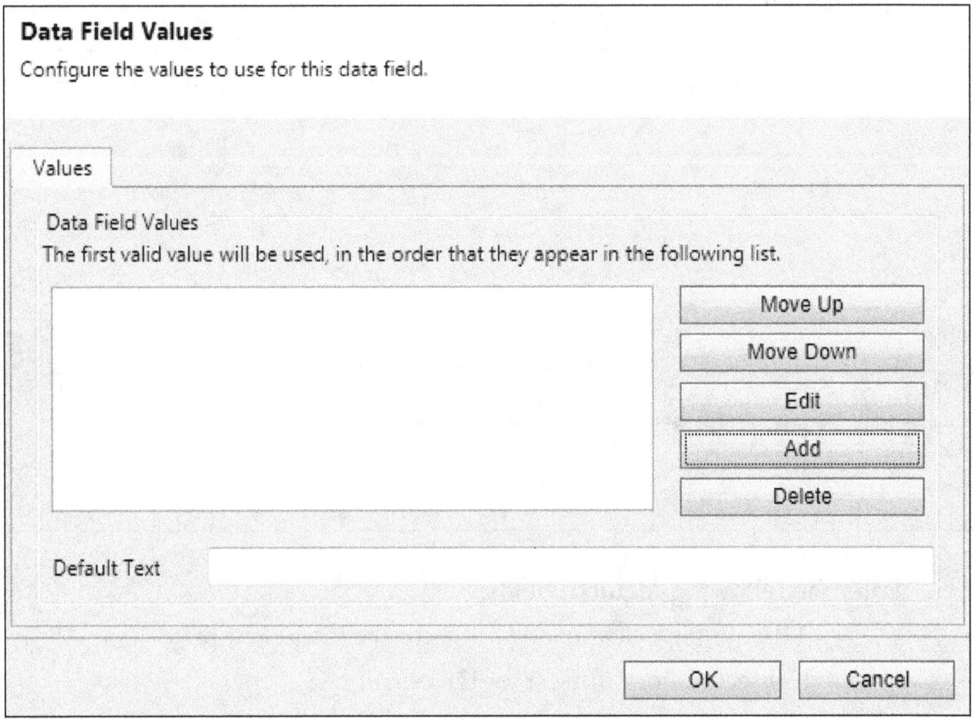

8. In the **Data Field Values** dialog box, click on **Add** to select fields from the entity or related entities selected in **Template Type**.
9. Click on **OK**.
10. Repeat steps 8 and 9 until all necessary placeholders have been added.
11. Click on **Save and Close**.

Once a template has been created, it can be used to send direct e-mails.

Direct e-mails using e-mail templates

Direct e-mails are e-mails that are sent directly to one or more records by using an e-mail template. For this example, we'll illustrate how to send a direct e-mail to a number of contacts. To send a direct e-mail, follow these steps:

1. Start CRM and click on the **Sales** module.
2. Click on **Contacts**.

3. Find and select one or more contacts to which you want to send an e-mail. You can use the view, or an advanced find, to help you search faster.

4. Click on **Send Direct E-mail** in the **Contacts** ribbon bar under the **Collaborate** group.

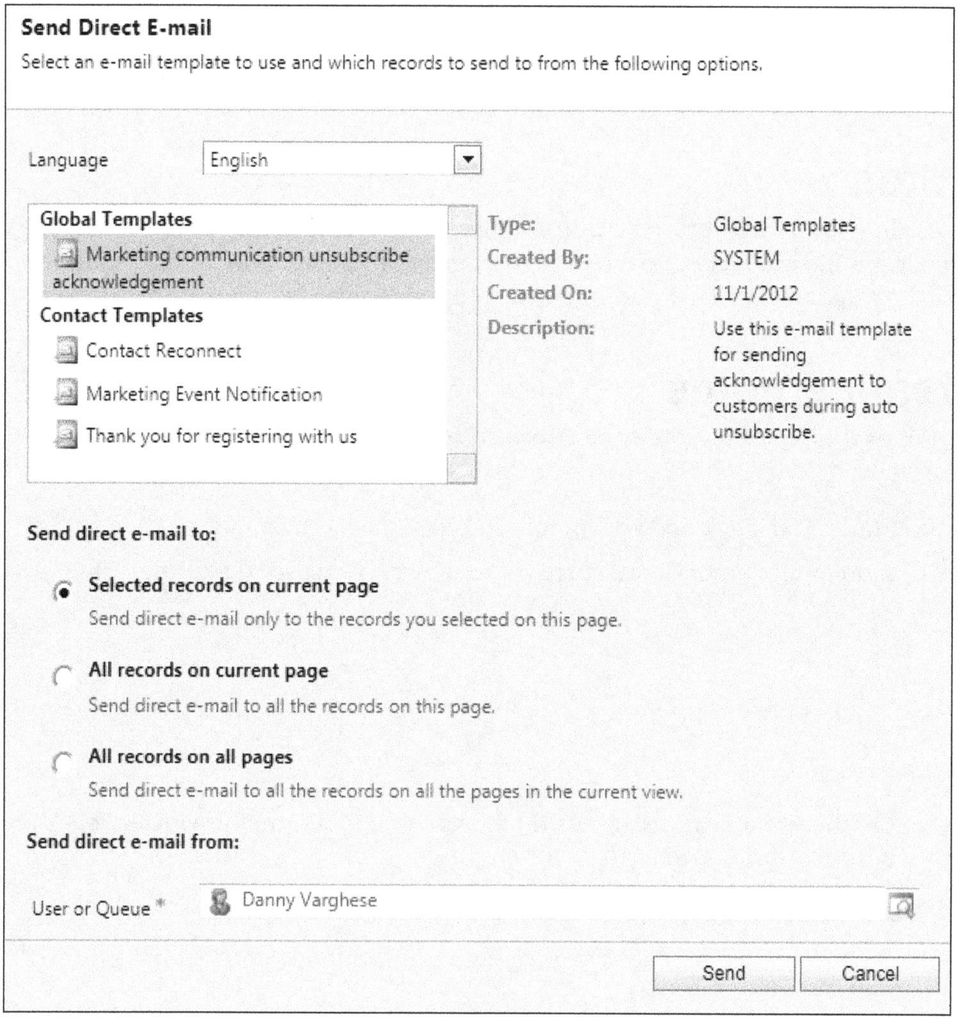

5. In the **Send Direct E-mail** dialog box, select the following information:
    i. **Language**: Select the language of the e-mail template, to filter the list of available templates.
    ii. **Template**: Select the type of template to use. In this case all global templates will be listed, and then any template with a template type of **Contact**.
    iii. **Send direct e-mail to**: Choose whether to an e-mail to records you selected on this page, all records on the page, or all records on all pages in the current view.
    iv. **Send direct e-mail from**: Select a user or queue to send the e-mail from.
6. Click on **Send**.

Another method for users in CRM to track interactions is the use of notes.

Notes

Notes allow users to capture free form notes about a record. In addition to text, whenever a file is attached to a record, it appears in the notes area. An example is a salesperson wanting to add notes to an opportunity that they are working on.

Creating notes

For this example, we use the contact record once again. To create a note, follow these steps:

1. Start CRM, click on **Workplace**, and then click on **Contacts**.
2. Find and open the contact record to which you wish to add the note.

3. On the ribbon bar, on the **Add** tabbed page, in the **Include** group, click on **Add Note**.

> You can also add notes if there is a **Notes** section on the form. Within the **Notes** section, you can enter text on the spot.

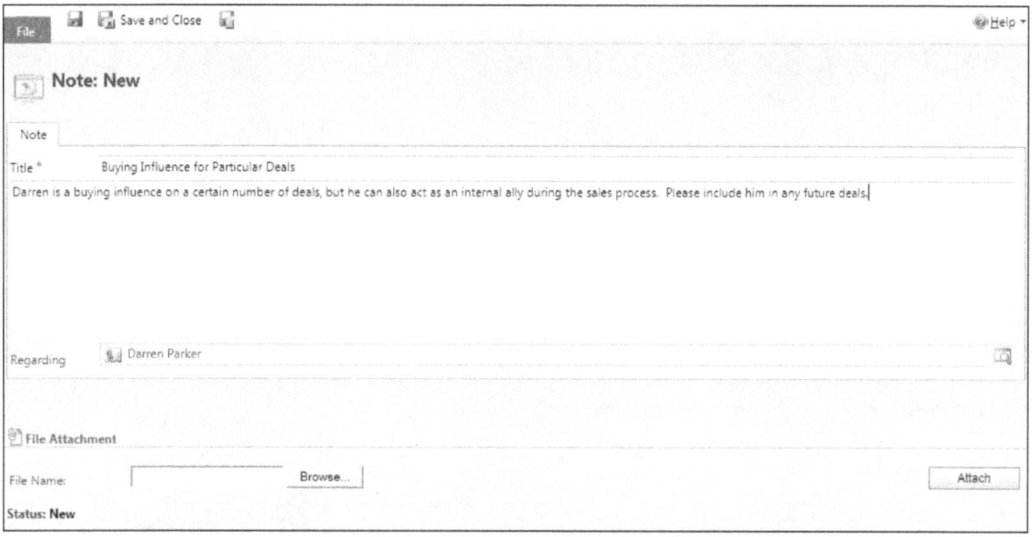

4. Enter the following field:
    i. **Title**: A clear, concise name for the note. This field is required.

    The **Regarding** field is not required, but it is worth mentioning that it will be auto-populated with the record from which you are creating the note.

5. Click on **Save and Close**.

Test your knowledge

Q. 1. Which of the following are valid activity types? (Choose all that apply.)

1. Task.
2. Recurring Task.
3. E-mail.
4. Phone Call.
5. Appointment.

Q. 2. Which of the fields below are common across all activities? (Choose all that apply.)

1. Recipient.
2. Regarding.
3. To.
4. Subject.

Q. 3. How is an e-mail is marked complete? (Choose all that apply.)

1. Using the **Complete** button.
2. Using the **Mark Complete** button.
3. Automatically, when the e-mail is saved.
4. Automatically, when the e-mail is sent.

Q. 4. What are the statuses of an activity?

1. Open.
2. Completed.
3. Scheduled.
4. Active.
5. Canceled.

Q. 5. If an entity has associated activities, and a user clicks on the Activities link in the left hand navigation of a record, what should he/she expect to see?

1. All activities.
2. Open and Canceled activities.
3. Open and Active activities.
4. Open and Scheduled activities.

Q. 6. Say there is an account that has contact records associated to it. Now let's say these contact records have activities. Where are all the places would you expect to see the contact's activities? (Choose all that apply.)

1. On the contact record.
2. On the account record.
3. On the contact's parent account record, assuming the contact has a parent account.
4. On the opportunity record.

Q. 7. All the places activities can viewed are: (Choose all that apply.)

1. On the record itself.
2. Within activity views.
3. On a record that has an activity's **Regarding** field set to it.
4. On a record that has activities.

Q. 8. What is required in order to send a direct e-mail?

1. Campaign template.
2. E-mail template.
3. Account template.
4. Bulk E-mail template.

Q. 9. Where do attachments appear on the form?

1. **Activities**.
2. **Attachments** tab.
3. **Notes**.
4. **General** section.

Q. 10. How can a user add notes?

1. By clicking on the **Add Notes** button.
2. By clicking on the **Add Attachment** button.
3. By clicking on the **Notes** section and clicking **Add a New Note.**
4. By clicking on the **Add One Notes** button.

Summary

Activities provide a way for an organization to track interactions with users in their own organization and with their customers. The different types of activities are:

- Task
- E-mail
- Phone call
- Letter
- Fax
- Appointment
- Recurring appointment
- Service activity
- Campaign response
- Custom activity

A custom activity allows an organization to track communication with other users or their customers, outside of traditional communication methods. Although these are becoming more common, some examples of custom activities are text messages and social media posts such as Facebook and Twitter.

Activities have several common attributes among the different record types, such as Subject, Owner and Regarding. Activity types such as e-mail, phone call, letter, fax and appointment have their own specific attributes. The aforementioned Regarding field is very important as it denotes the record related to the activity. This field is used to link the activity record to a record in the CRM system.

When an activity has been finished it can be marked completed. Once an activity is completed, certain parts of the activity form become read only, but notes can still be added, files can be attached, and the activity can be shared with other users or teams.

Activities can be seen on the "regarding" records via the activity associated view, through the activity roll-up functionality, or by using the activity views.

Notes can also be added to any entity that has the notes functionality enabled. Notes are yet another method for users to track interactions between other users and customers.

In the next chapter, you will learn how to create and manage marketing lists, campaigns, and campaign responses. You will also learn how to analyze marketing data in order to provide your organization with effective reporting.

3
Managing Marketing Automation Applications – Marketing Lists and Campaigns

In this chapter you will learn about:

- Marketing list core records
- Creating and managing marketing lists
- Creating and working with campaigns
- Creating and working with quick campaigns
- Managing campaigns
- Campaigns versus quick campaigns
- Reporting and analysis

Introduction to marketing list core records

As its name implies, a **core record** is a type of record that is central to Dynamics CRM. These record types may or may not be used, depending on the organization's needs. A **marketing list** is a group of three core record types: accounts, contacts, or leads. A few examples are a marketing list consisting of accounts with an address in the United States, contacts that belong to a company with an address in the United States, or leads entered into Dynamics CRM as a result of a recent trade show. A marketing list can only have *one type* of core record and that type is set at the time of creation of the list.

- A **lead** represents a prospective customer that a user can qualify or disqualify. These leads may come from website enquiry forms, trade shows, conventions, and so on.
- **Accounts** are essentially other organizations that your company has a business relationship with.
- **Contacts** represent individuals that your organization has a relationship with. These individuals can be related to accounts as well.

Creating and managing marketing lists

When creating marketing lists, there are three required fields that you must fill out:

- **Member type**: This defines which core record makes up the marketing list. A marketing list can only have one core record type, which can be account, contact, or lead. Once the member type is set on a marketing list, it cannot be changed.
- **List name**: This is a descriptive name for the marketing list. The name is shown on lookups for marketing lists, and is a primary field for the entity.
- **Type**: This can be either static or dynamic. The members of a static marketing list do not change unless updated manually. A dynamic marketing list is defined by a query, and the members are dynamically updated.

Let us take a look how to create static and dynamic marketing lists.

Creating static marketing lists

A scenario with our fictitious insurance company will give an example of how a static marketing list can be used.

Business scenarios

Race2Win Insurance Company is an organization that needs to market to their current customers that have an address in the United States. One option is to create a static marketing list with the following required fields filled out:

- **Member type** = Account
- **List name** = "Clients located in the United States."
- **Type** = Static

Once the marketing list is saved, the member type and marketing list type cannot be changed. At the time members are added to this list, the list remains static until a user manually manages the list. Even if more accounts are added to CRM with an address in the United States, this marketing list's members will remain the same.

Perform the following steps to create a static marketing list:

1. Start CRM, click on the **Marketing** module, and then click on **Marketing Lists**.
2. On the **Marketing List** ribbon, in the **Records** group, click on **New**.
3. Enter the following required fields:
    - **Name**: Enter a clear, concise description of the list
    - **Type**: Select **Static**
    - **Member Type**: Select either the **Account**, **Contact**, or **Lead** core record to determine what the list will comprise of

4. On the **Marketing List** ribbon, click on **Save**.
5. On the **Marketing List** ribbon, in the **Actions** group, click on **Manage Members**.
6. In the **Manage Members** dialog box, you can manage members by using the following options:
    - Use a lookup to find, select, and add members
    - Use an advanced find to add members
    - Use an advanced find to remove members
    - Use an advanced find to evaluate members that already exist on the list

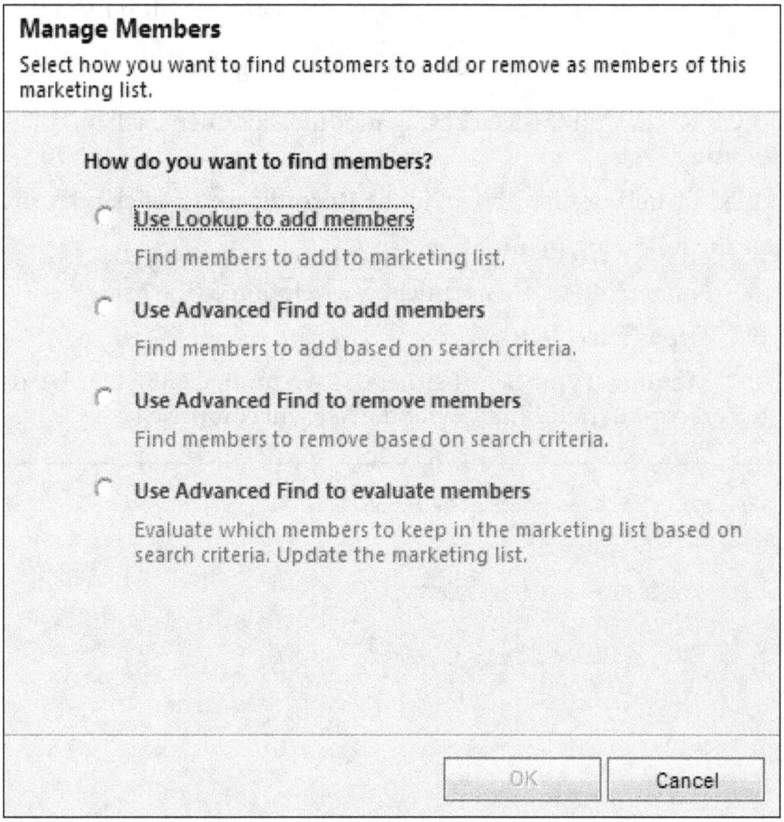

7. Select the method to add, remove, and manage members.
8. Click on **OK**.
9. Use either the lookup dialog box or advanced find to add or remove members.

Once members have been added or removed, you can view the members by clicking on **Marketing List Members** in the left-hand navigation pane. After members have been added, you can update static marketing lists in many different ways.

> This is the first time that **advanced find** is being introduced. According to `http://rc.crm.dynamics.com/rc/regcont/en_us/op/articles/vidAdvancedFind.aspx`, you can use advanced find to search for records given certain criteria. After you get the results of the search, you can analyze, edit, assign, or share one or more records. You can also save the search for future use as a personal view. An example of an advanced find is to search for all contacts that are tied to an account with a business address located in London, England. More about advanced find is given near the end of this chapter.

Managing members dialog box

As stated in the previous section, there are multiple ways to manage members in a marketing list. The first option is to use a lookup to add members; this displays a dialog box. The dialog box allows you to select one or more records of the marketing list member type (account, contact, or lead). The next two options allow the use of the advanced find feature to search for records to either add or remove. The last option uses an advanced find to update a marketing list by using the results from the query to determine which members to keep on the list. The options listed in the previous section are just a few ways in which you can manage marketing list members.

Updating static marketing lists

You can only add or remove members of the same type (defined when the marketing list was created). To add or remove leads, accounts, or contacts, use the following methods:

1. Click on the **Manage Members** button on the ribbon and use one of the options described in step 6 of the previous *Business scenarios* section.
2. If you're inside a lead, account, or contact record, you can click on the **Add to Marketing List** button.
3. If you're in a view of leads, account, or contacts, you can select one or more records and then click on the **Add to Marketing List** button on the ribbon.
4. From an advanced find list of leads, accounts or contacts, you can click on the **Add to Marketing List** button.

Let us now take a look how to create dynamic marketing lists.

Creating dynamic marketing lists

Perform the following steps to create a dynamic marketing list:

1. Start CRM, click on the **Marketing** module, and then click on **Marketing Lists**.
2. On the **Marketing List** ribbon, in the **Records** group, click on **New**.
3. Enter the following required fields:
    - **Name**: Enter a clear, concise description of the marketing list
    - **Type**: Select **Dynamic**
    - **Member Type:** Select either the **Account**, **Contact**, or **Lead** core record to determine what the list will comprise of

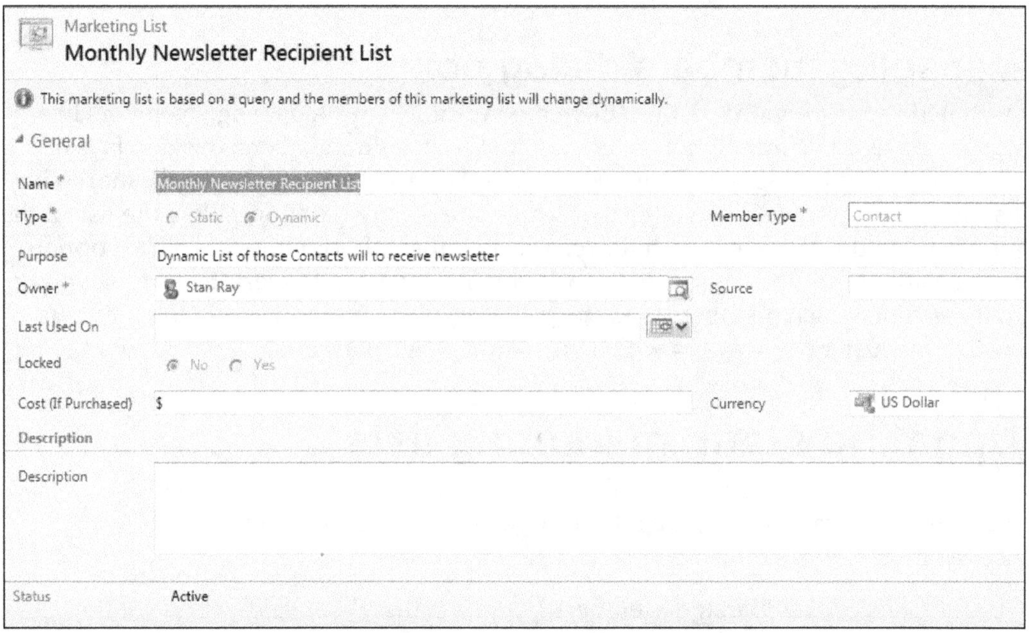

4. On the **Marketing List** ribbon, click on **Save**.
5. On the **Marketing List** ribbon, in the **Actions** group, click on **Manage Members**.
6. Use the advanced find feature to build a query to select the members of the marketing list. For example, you can use advanced find to build a query to retrieve all accounts with a business address in the city of Sydney and a country of Australia.

7. You can click on **Find** to preview the members that the query returns. Once you're satisfied with the query, click on the **Use Query** button to enable the marketing list to use this query.

The way dynamic marketing list works is that each time the list is used, the underlying query (built by using advanced find) is run, allowing the maintenance of its members to be automatic. Thus, if you need to manage the members of a dynamic marketing list, the advanced find query will need to be modified.

Business scenarios

The static marketing list Race2Win Insurance Company created for their clients with an address in the United States has outlived its usefulness. Business is excellent, and as they open more offices and gain more clients, they've found the effort needed to manage the static marketing list to be great. To meet their business need, the marketing team has decided to create a dynamic marketing list with the following required fields filled out:

- **Member type** = Account
- **List name** = "Clients located in the United States."
- **Type** = Dynamic

With this scenario, as more accounts are added with an address in the United States, the marketing list will reflect these additions. Because of this flexibility, there's no real need to manage these members on a regular basis.

We have walked through the creation and management of static and dynamic marketing lists. Let us now discuss how a dynamic marketing list can be copied to a static one.

Copying a dynamic marketing list to a static marketing list

A dynamic marketing list can be copied to a static marketing list, creating a snapshot and permanently adding the members to the list. To create this snapshot, perform the following steps:

1. Start CRM, click on the **Marketing** module, and then click on **Marketing Lists**.
2. Find and open the dynamic marketing list that you wish to copy to a static list.

3. Click on the **Copy to Static** button.

4. Click on **OK**.

The advanced find query will be executed to retrieve the list of members and then add these to a new static marketing list. The new list will be locked and have the same name as the dynamic marketing list plus a timestamp at the end. For example, if the dynamic marketing list is named "Target Accounts in Asia," the new static copy could be named "Target Accounts in Asia 1/1/2013 8:33:13 PM."

Copying a dynamic list to a static list allows organizations to keep a history of its lists at points in time. Another copy feature that CRM has is to copy members of one or marketing lists to another list.

Copying marketing lists

You can copy members *from* one or more dynamic or static marketing lists, but you can only copy the members *to* a static list. To copy a marketing list, perform the following steps:

1. Start CRM, click on the **Marketing** module, and then click on **Marketing Lists**.
2. Find the marketing list from which you want to copy the members.
3. Click on the **Copy to Static** button.
4. Click on **OK**.

Copying marketing lists acts as a way to merge marketing lists, as members are copied from one or more lists to another. What happens to the members of a marketing list if the list is deleted or deactivated?

Deleting and deactivating marketing lists

Deleting or deactivating a marketing list does not remove the accounts, contacts or leads that were part of that list from the system. For example, if a marketing list contains a list of leads created in 2012, and the marketing list gets deleted or deactivated, the list of leads will still exist in CRM. If a list is deactivated, it can be reactivated at any time, and will retain its list of members.

As reviewed earlier, marketing lists can be either static or dynamic. It is worth highlighting specific differences between the two.

Dynamic versus static marketing lists

There is a great comparison between dynamic and static marketing lists at `http://community.dynamics.com/product/crm/crmtechnical/b/crmbusiness/archive/2011/11/24/crm-2011-the-difference-between-dynamic-and-static-marketing-lists.aspx`. These differences are summarized in the table below:

	Dynamic list	**Static list**
Adding members	An advanced find query is associated to the marketing list. When the list is used, the query is run behind the scenes and members are added.	Members are manually added either using a lookup or an advanced find query.
Removing members	Automatically removed when the record doesn't meet the advanced find query.	Use advanced find to add or "evaluate" members.
Updating members	Updated automatically and deactivated members are automatically removed.	Updated manually.

Creating and working with campaigns

A marketing campaign represents an organization's marketing plans, activities, and lists over a period of time. Campaigns allows an organization to track activities to plan a campaign, activities during a campaign such as e-mails, phone calls, tasks, and any responses to the campaign.

One of the ultimate goals for a campaign is to help generate more revenue for a business. In order for an organization to track those returns on investment, Microsoft Dynamics CRM has a way to track financials on a campaign.

Business scenarios

With marketing lists created, Race2Win Insurance Company is ready to initiate a campaign for the fiscal year. Race2Win has introduced a new line of insurance products and would like to market them to their contacts in Canada.

Race2Win's marketing team starts by creating a **campaign** and associating a **marketing list** to it. The marketing list contains all of Race2Win's contacts that reside in Canada. They start the process by creating **planning activities** to track any planning efforts and costs associated with the campaign. The marketing team can tie the new insurance products as **targeted products** to the campaign. This enables the company to track their marketing efforts for certain products and potentially track **return on investment** (**ROI**).

The company decides to utilize its inside sales team to make cold calls to these contacts. Race2Win's marketing team creates phone call **campaign activities**. These campaign activities can be **distributed**, which is a process to create and associate a phone call activity to each contact on the marketing list. When an inside sales representative makes a phone call to a customer, they can record the interaction within the phone call activity.

If a customer on the phone asks for more information about a product, the representative can reference **sales literature** for marketing collateral or more information. If a customer shows interest in purchasing a product, a **campaign response** can be created to tie back the interest shown by the customer to the campaign. Campaign responses are one way of measuring campaign effectiveness.

Lastly, if needed, a campaign can be associated to other campaigns. An example of this is if Race2Win wants to launch a campaign of new products in North America. They can a launch one campaign for North America, and then several "child" campaigns for Canada, the United States, and Latin America.

As you can see from the business scenario we just discussed, there are several components that go into a campaign:

- Planning activities
- Campaign activities
- Campaign responses
- Targeted products
- Sales literature
- Marketing lists
- Related campaigns

Planning activities

Planning activities constitute any action taken to help plan a campaign. For example, your marketing team can start planning for a campaign by setting up appointments with various people, phone calls, e-mails and so on. These activities can be tracked as planning efforts for a campaign, and can help to quantify the time spent in planning a campaign.

Creating planning activities

To create a planning activity, perform the following steps:

1. Start CRM, click on the **Marketing** module, and then open the campaign you want to add the planning activity to.
2. In the left-hand navigation, click on **Planning Activities**.
3. On the **Activities List** tool tab on the **Campaign** ribbon, click on **Add New Activity**.

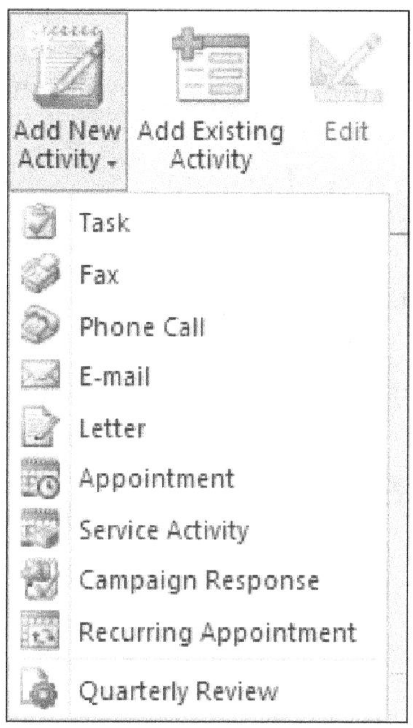

4. Select the appropriate activity that you want to associate to the campaign.
5. Click on **Save**.

The next step is to add one or more campaign activities so that once the campaign is launched it can be distributed to all of the core records in the target marketing lists.

Campaign activities

Campaign activities are much like standard Dynamics CRM activities, but they include financial tracking information. For example, if the activity is a letter, an organization can track the costs of paper, envelopes, and postage. These metrics can help track the cost of a campaign, much like how planning activities can track time spent on planning a campaign. Multiple campaign activities can be distributed per campaign, and each activity can use one or more marketing lists. When the cost of the activity is entered, it's rolled up into the overall cost of the campaign. Campaign activities can be used to distribute the following types of activities to the campaign's marketing list members:

- Appointment
- E-mail
- Fax
- Letter
- Phone call

Campaign activities are required in order for a campaign to be launched. Information about launching a campaign is mentioned later in this chapter.

Creating campaign activities

To create a campaign activity, perform the following steps:

1. Start CRM, click on the **Marketing** module, and then open the campaign that you want to add the planning activity to.
2. In the left-hand navigation, click on **Campaign Activities**.
3. On the **Campaign Activities List Tools** tab of the **Campaign** ribbon, click on **Add New Campaign Activity**.

4. Enter the following required fields:
    - **Parent Campaign**: This field will auto-populate with the name of the campaign the activity is being created from.

- **Subject**: Enter a clear, concise name for the activity.
- **Channel**: While this field is not required, this is an important field worth noting. This field captures the type of communication or activity to be used in this campaign. The following are the channel values:

  1. **Phone**
  2. **Appointment**
  3. **Letter**
  4. **Letter via Mail Merge**
  5. **Fax**
  6. **Fax via Mail Merge**
  7. **E-mail**
  8. **E-mail via Mail Merge**
  9. **Other**

  The channel values, except for **Other**, control the type of CRM activity that will be distributed to members of the marketing list tied to the campaign. For example, if you choose a channel of e-mail, when the campaign activity is distributed, an e-mail activity will be created for the members of the target marketing lists associated to the campaign.

- **Owner**: This field is auto-populated with the name of the user creating the record, but can be changed.

5. Click on **Save**.

Campaign responses

A campaign response is a way in which an organization can measure the success of a campaign by tracking its responses. Once campaign activities are distributed, if a customer responds to one or more activities, the response can be tracked using campaign responses. More about campaign responses is discussed later in this chapter.

Targeted products

If there are products being tracked in Dynamics CRM, then marketing campaigns can be used to promote certain products. This is a great way for an organization to track marketing efforts for various products and to measure marketing effectiveness for those products.

Adding targeted products

If an organization would like the campaign to focus on various products, they can do so by using the following steps:

1. Start CRM, click on the **Marketing** module, and then open the campaign that you want to add the product to.
2. In the left-hand navigation, click on **Targeted Products**.
3. On the **Campaign Activities List Tools** tab of the **Campaign** ribbon, click on **Add Existing Product**.

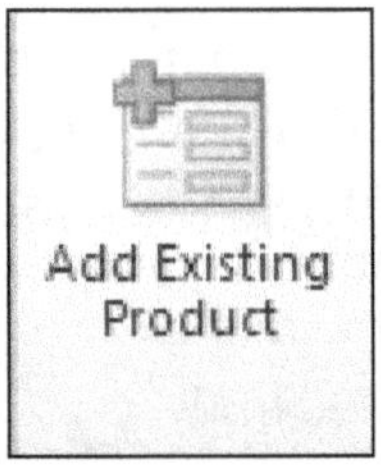

4. Use the lookup dialog box to locate and select an existing product, and then click on **OK**.

Once the products have been associated to a campaign, we can help out the sales and marketing folks by adding literature about these products in case questions arise, or they want to pass it along to customers.

Sales literature

Sales literature is documentation about items in the product catalog. The sales literature entity can help an organization educate its employees and customers about certain products.

Adding sales literature

To add sales literature to a campaign, perform the following steps:

1. Start CRM, click on the **Marketing** module, and then open the campaign that you want to add the sales literature to.
2. In the left-hand navigation, click on **Sales Literature**.
3. On the **Campaign Activities List Tools** tab of the **Campaign** ribbon, click on **Add Existing Sales Literature**.

4. Use the lookup dialog box to find and select an existing sales literature, and then click on **OK**.

The next component of a campaign is a required one in order for the campaign to be launched, and that is marketing lists.

Target marketing lists

Target marketing lists are essentially the marketing lists that an organization wants to target for a particular campaign. A campaign can have one or more target marketing lists and at least one is required in order for a campaign to be launched.

Adding marketing lists

Perform the following the steps to add a marketing list to a campaign:

1. Start CRM, click on the **Marketing** module, and then click on **Campaigns**. Select the campaign you want and open it.
2. In the left-hand side navigation, click on **Target Marketing Lists**.
3. On the **Campaign Activities List Tools** tab of the **Campaign** ribbon, click on **Add Existing Marketing List**.
4. Use the lookup dialog box to find the marketing list.
5. Select the marketing list and add it.

6. Within the **Add Marketing List to Campaign** dialog box, if you check the **Add the marketing lists to open undistributed campaign activities in the current campaign** checkbox, then the marketing list is automatically associated to all undistributed campaign activities.

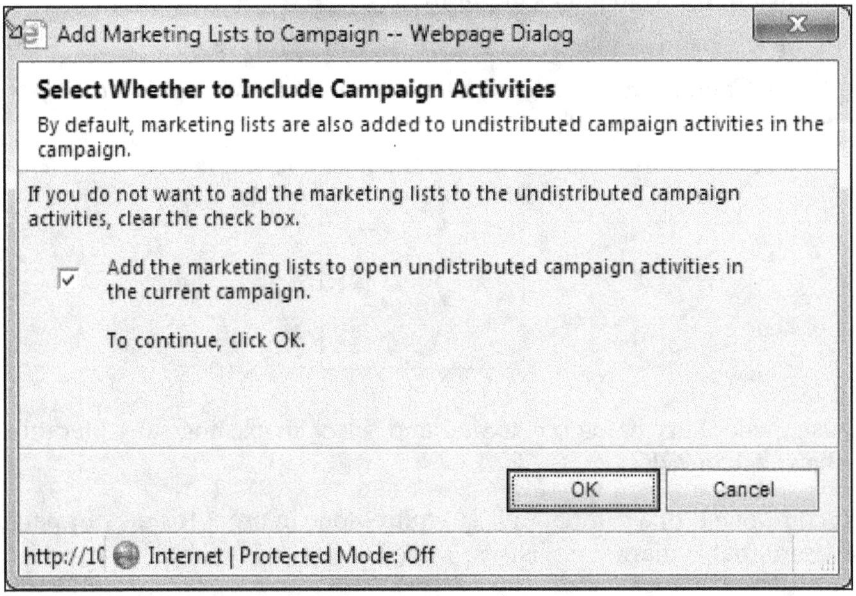

Related campaigns

A campaign can be added to other campaigns to help compare effectiveness against each other, and also to identify the campaigns as being part of a larger campaign.

Adding related campaigns

To add a related campaign, perform the following steps:

1. Start CRM, click on the **Marketing** module, and then open the campaign that you want to relate another campaign to.
2. In the left-hand navigation, click on **Related Campaigns**.
3. On the **Campaign Activities List Tools** tab of the **Campaign** ribbon, click on **Add Existing Campaign**.
4. Use the lookup dialog box to find and select the campaign, and then click on **OK**.

As you can see, there is quite a lot of complexity when setting up a full-fledged marketing campaign. You can track financials and ROI related to a campaign, create planning activities to track time and effort in planning a campaign, distribute multiple activities for a campaign, and associate products and sales literature to a campaign.

All of the above components can be part of the marketing campaign, but each is used depending on the business need. Let's now take a look at the steps to create a campaign.

Creating marketing campaigns

To create a campaign in Microsoft Dynamics CRM 2011, perform the following steps:

1. Start CRM, click on the **Marketing** module, and then click on **Campaigns**.
2. On the **Campaigns** ribbon, in the **Records** group, click on **New**.
3. Enter the following required fields:
    - **Name**: Enter a clear, concise name for the campaign
    - **Currency**: This field will be populated with the default currency of the system, but can be changed
    - **Owner**: This field defaults to the name of the user creating the record, but can be changed

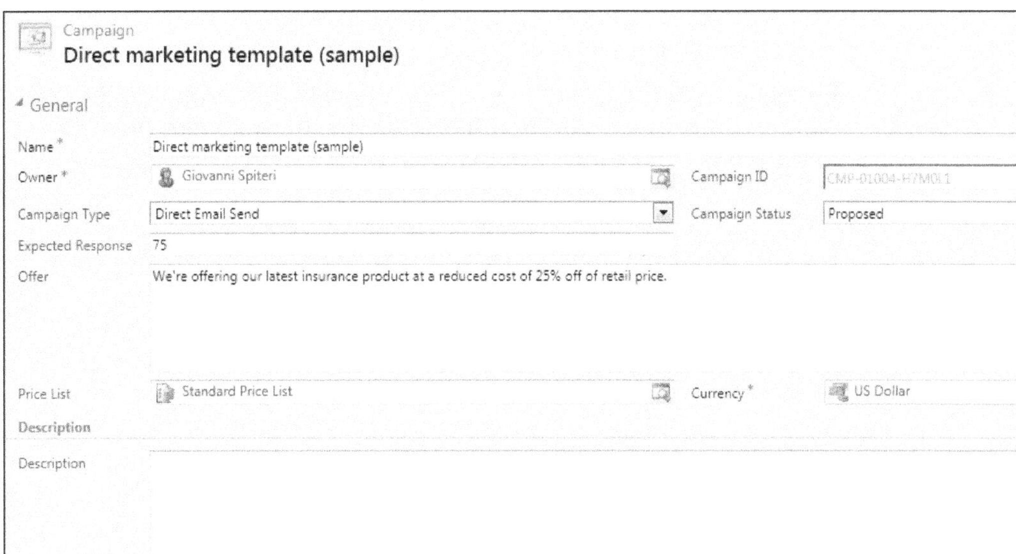

4. The following fields are not required, but are worth noting:
    - **Status Reason**: This field defaults to **Proposed**. The campaign status can have the following values:
        1. **Proposed**
        2. **Ready to Launch**
        3. **Launched**
        4. **Completed**
        5. **Canceled**
        6. **Suspended**
    - **Expected Response** (%): The expected percentage of responses for the campaign. This can be useful to track actual versus estimated response rates for a campaign.
    - **Price List**: If a price list is entered, then any opportunities generated from this campaign will inherit this price list.
    - **Proposed Begin Date**: The date on which the owner of the campaign is proposing to begin the campaign.
    - **Proposed End Date**: The date on which marketing is proposing the campaign will end.
    - **Actual Begin Date**: The date the campaign actually started.
    - **Actual End Date**: The date the campaign actually ended.
    - **Financials section**: Enter any relevant financial information that you want to track. A more in-depth explanation of campaign financial information can be found in the next section.

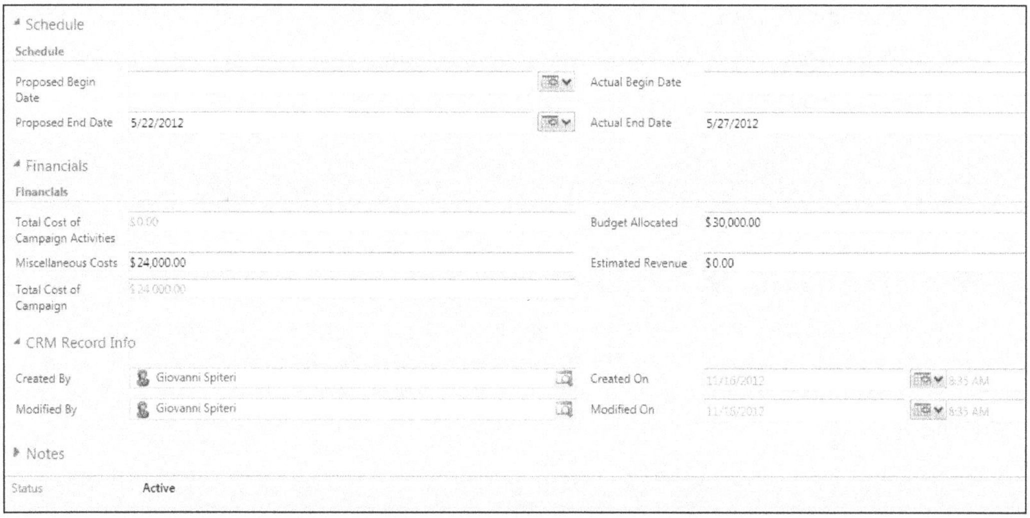

5. Click on **Save**.

Campaign financial metrics

Financial metrics can be tracked on a campaign to assist in tracking ROI. The campaign costs are stored on the campaign activities, and the campaign stores budgetary information and the sum of all costs of the activities.

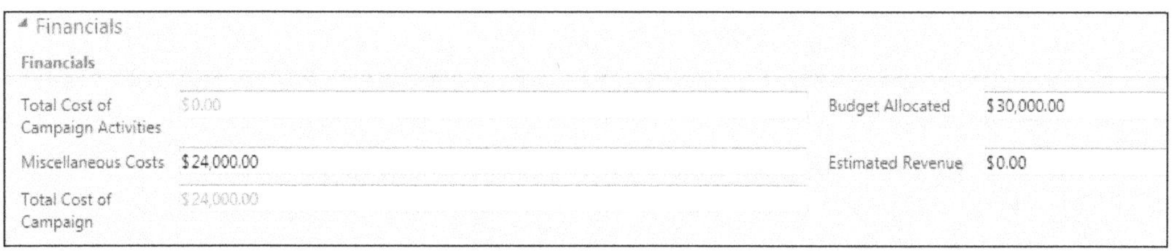

An explanation of the fields is as follows:

- **Total Cost of Campaign Activities** is the sum of the costs entered on all of the campaign activities
- **Miscellaneous Costs** are costs not being tracked by the campaign activities
- **Total Cost of the Campaign = Total Cost of Campaign Activities + Miscellaneous Costs**

- **Estimated Revenue** is the revenue expected to be generated by the campaign
- **Budget Allocated** is the amount of money allocated for the campaign
- **Expected ROI** is the expected return on investment for this campaign
- **Actual ROI** is the actual return on investment for this campaign

Creating and working with quick campaigns

A quick campaign can be defined as a communication method that creates a single campaign activity for distribution to members of a marketing list. A regular campaign is different in that it supports end-to-end marketing programs that have multiple activities.

Quick campaigns can be created by using a wizard in Dynamics CRM 2011. There are several key differences between a campaign and quick campaign:

- You cannot create any planning activities for a quick campaign
- You can only distribute one activity type with a quick campaign
- You cannot associate products or sales literature to a quick campaign

Quick campaigns are meant for low-weight, quick results with minimal time spent setting them up. The core records that comprise a quick campaign can be selected by using three methods:

- Using existing marketing lists in the marketing lists grid; you can select a list and then click on the **Create Quick Campaign** button. This will launch the quick campaign wizard.
- Use advanced find to search for core records such as leads, accounts, or contacts and then, when the results are displayed, click on the **Quick Campaign** button.
- In any view of leads, accounts, or contacts, you can select one or more core records and then click on the **Quick Campaign** button.

For the purposes of this example, let's walk through an example of how to create a quick campaign by using a marketing list.

Creating quick campaigns

To create a quick campaign from a marketing list, perform the following steps:

1. Start CRM, click on the **Marketing** module, and then click on **Marketing Lists**.
2. Select a marketing list from which to generate a quick campaign. You can only select one marketing list at a time for which to run the quick campaign wizard.
3. On the **Marketing List** ribbon bar, in the **Actions** group, click on the **Create Quick Campaign** button.
4. Click on **Next**.

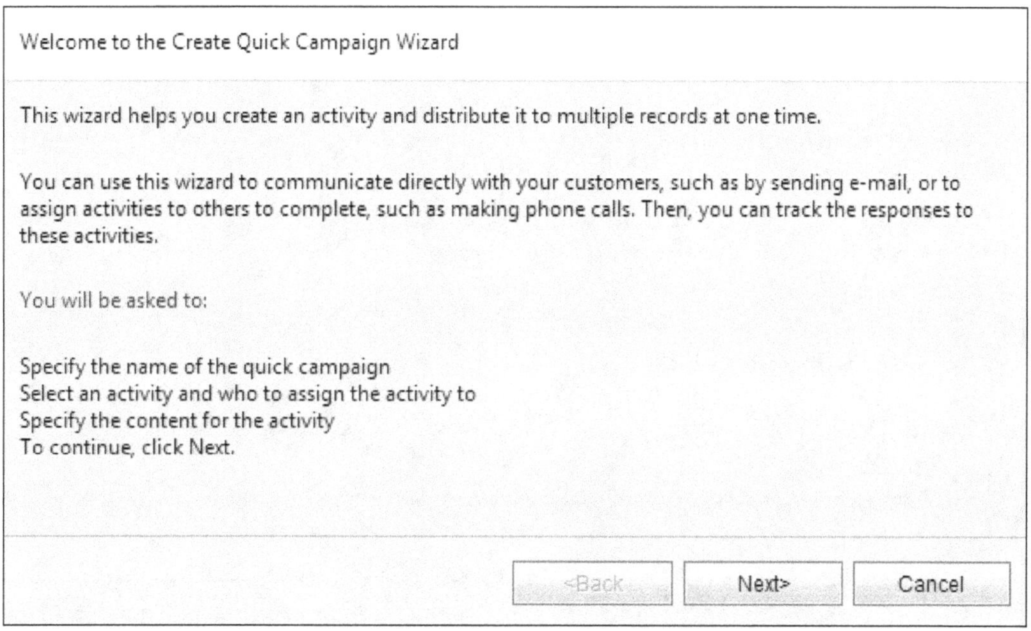

5. Enter a clear, concise name for the quick campaign, and then click on **Next**.
6. Select the **Activity Type** for the campaign.
7. Choose how to assign these activities—whether they should be assigned to you, to the owners of the records selected in the marketing list, or to another user or team.
8. Select the **Add the created activities to a queue** checkbox if you'd like the activities to be added to a particular queue.

9. Select the **Mark e-mail messages to be sent and close corresponding e-mail activities.** checkbox to automatically send e-mails if they are being created.
10. Click on **Next**.

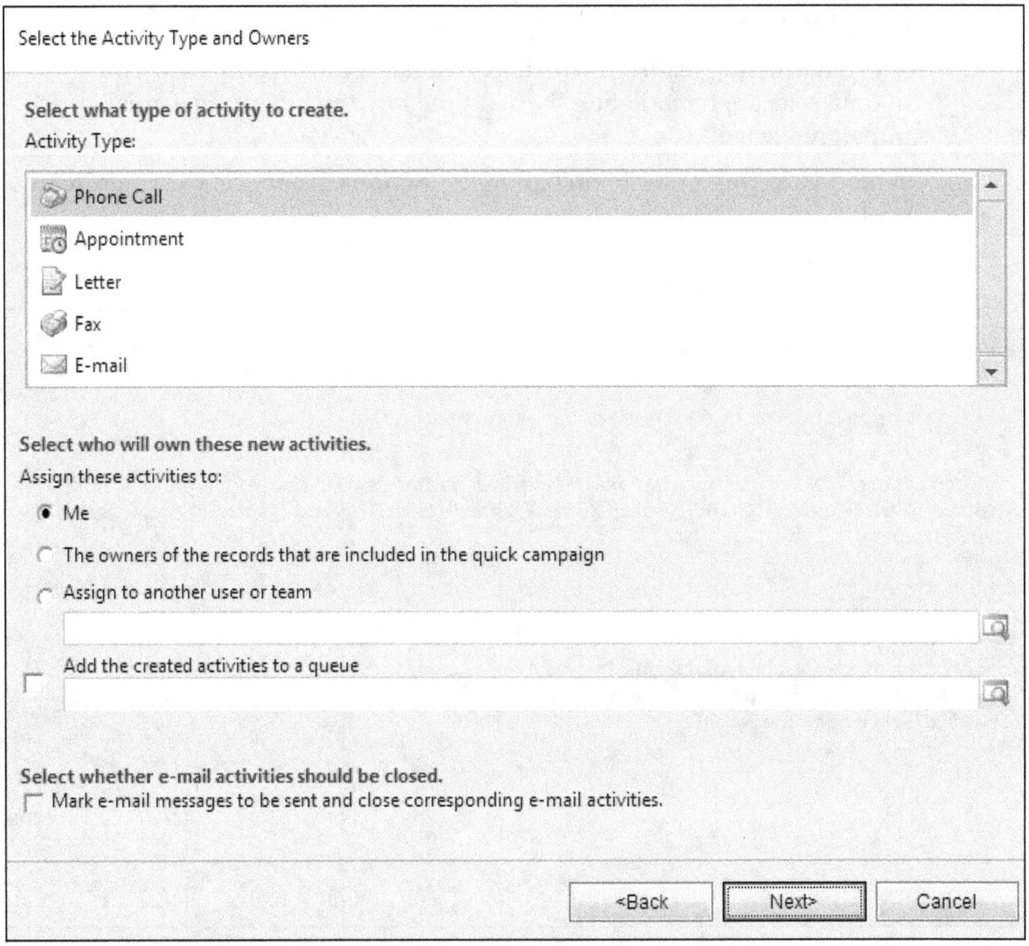

11. Fill out the form depending on the activity type chosen.
12. Click on **Next**, and then review the information about the quick campaign. When satisfied, click on **Create**.

The steps to create a quick campaign are drastically reduced compared to the normal full-blown marketing campaign. While that can be advantageous from a cost and time savings perspective, it's important to know the limitations of quick campaigns.

Scope of a quick campaign

It is valuable to understand the scope of a quick campaign. Quick campaigns:

- Can distribute only one type of activity
- Cannot track financial information
- Have no built-in reports
- Cannot create planning activities
- Cannot associate target products or pricelists
- Cannot be saved as or created from a template

Managing campaigns

Once you have created a campaign, set up the planning activities and campaign activities, added optional products and sales literature, associated one more marketing lists and potentially other related campaigns, it's time to distribute the campaign activities.

Distributing campaign activities pushes out activities to each member found on the marketing list. Let's review a few concepts that we covered earlier. After creating a campaign, you can associate one or more marketing lists. When creating the campaign activity, we had to set the **Channel** field. This **Channel** field dictates the type of activity that will be created for each member on the marketing list(s). For example, if the campaign activity channel is phone, then when the campaign is distributed, CRM will create a phone call activity for each member on the marketing list(s).

Distributing campaign activities

Use the following steps to distribute campaign activities:

1. Start CRM, click on the **Marketing** module, and select **Campaigns**.
2. In the view, select and open the campaign for which you want to distribute activities.
3. In the left-hand navigation, click on **Campaign Activities**.
4. In the view, select and open the activity that you want to distribute.
5. On the **Campaign Activity** ribbon bar, in the **Actions** group, click on **Distribute Campaign Activity**.

   Doing this will open up a form for the activity type selected when creating the campaign activity. For example, if the campaign activity type was a phone call, then a phone call activity form will appear.

6. Click on **Distribute**.

7. In this example, a phone call activity is being distributed. The dialog asks you how ownership should be set. You have the following options:
    - **The owners of the records in the target marketing lists**: Whoever owns the leads, accounts, or contacts on the targeted marketing lists will own the activity that is being distributed
    - **I will own the new Phone Calls**: The currently logged-in user will own the activities
    - **Assign to another user or team**
    - There is an option to assign this activity to a **queue** (queues are explored when we talk about the CRM Service module in *Chapter 7, Managing Service Management Applications*)

  - If the activity is an e-mail, you have the option to automatically send the e-mail when these steps are completed

8. Click on **OK**.

When the campaign activity is distributed, Microsoft Dynamics CRM 2011 will create an activity for each member of the marketing list(s). However, the system is smart enough to take into account the **customer preferences** set by an organization.

> Customer preferences are fields on the account or contact which store communication preferences for a customer. For example, if a contact does not wish to have e-mails sent to him/her, then the system can store that preference on the contact record.

With these steps, your organization has now set up a marketing campaign and distributed its activities. It's now time to learn how to track responses to this campaign.

Campaign responses

As stated earlier, campaign responses allow an organization to measure the success of a campaign by tracking responses to the campaign. Once campaign activities are distributed, and a customer responds to one or more of these activities, these responses can be tracked by using campaign responses. There's a few ways in which responses can be created:

- Manually create a campaign response. An example of this is if a mailing campaign was initiated with reply-back cards. If someone is interested, they send a reply card back to an organization and someone within the company can record that as a response.
- Convert a distributed campaign activity into a campaign response.
- If e-mail tracking is enabled, an e-mail campaign was initiated. If an individual responds to that e-mail, a response can be automatically created.
- Imported using the Data Import Wizard in Microsoft Dynamics CRM 2011.

Creating a campaign response manually

To create a campaign response manually, perform the following steps:

1. Start CRM, go to the **Marketing** module, and click on **Campaigns**.
2. In the view, select and open the campaign to add a response to.
3. In the left-hand navigation, click on **Campaign Responses**.

4. On the **List Tools Campaign Responses** ribbon, in the **Records** group, click on **Add New Campaign Response**.
5. Enter the following required fields:
    - **Parent Campaign**: This will auto-populate with the campaign that the response is being created from
    - **Subject**: Enter a clear, concise name for the campaign response
    - **Owner**: This will auto-populate with the user currently logged in, but can be changed

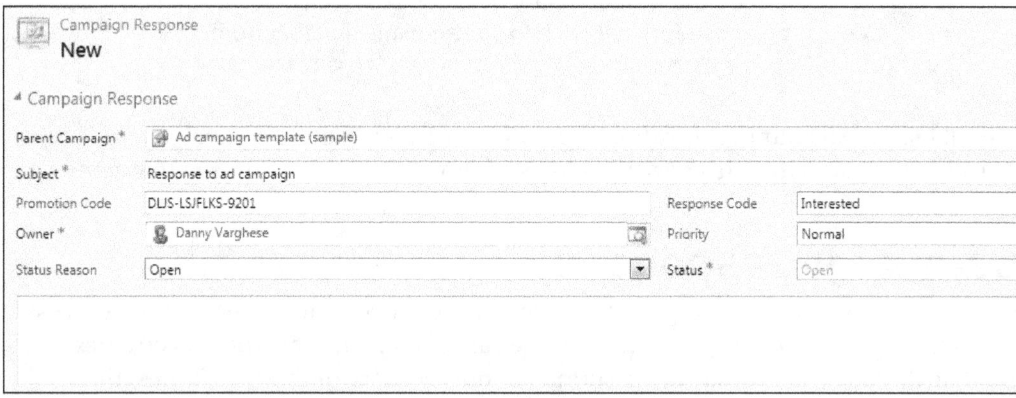

6. Click on **Save and Close**.

Another method to create a campaign response is to promote an activity that was distributed from a campaign to being a response.

Converting an activity to a campaign response

In order for an activity to be promoted to a campaign response, the activity must be distributed from a campaign. To promote an activity to a campaign response, perform the following steps:

1. Start CRM, go to the **Marketing** module, and then click on **Campaigns**.
2. In the view, select and open a campaign with campaign activities that have been distributed.
3. In the left-hand navigation, click on **Campaign Activities**.
4. In the view, select and open a distributed **Campaign Activity**.
5. In the left-hand navigation, click on the navigation link specified for the activities created. For example, if phone call activities were distributed, the left-hand navigation would read **Phone Calls Created**.

6. Select and open the activity that was created for this campaign activity.
7. On the **Activity** ribbon bar, in the **Convert Activity** group, click on **Promote Activity**.
8. Edit any of the information on the form, including the **Subject** field, in order to make it more descriptive about the response.

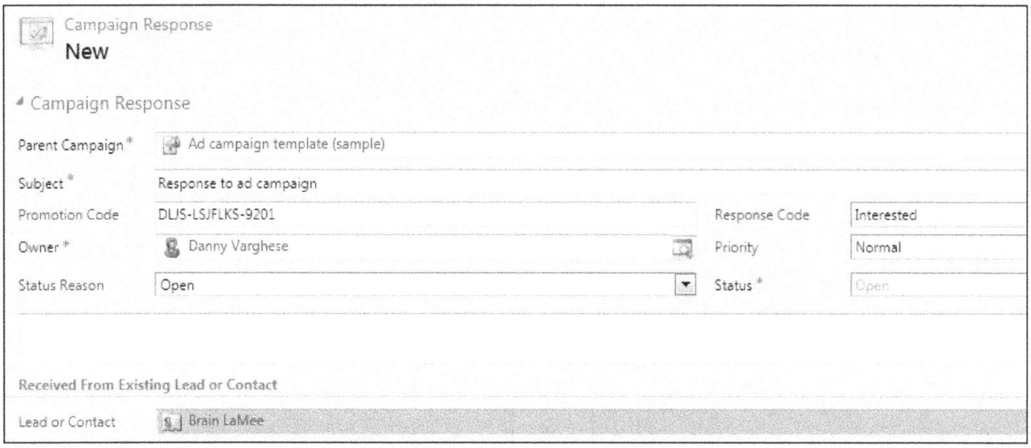

9. Click on **Save and Close** to create the campaign response.
10. Click on **Save and Close** to close the activity record.
11. Click on **Save and Close** to close the campaign activity.
12. Click on **Save and Close** to close the campaign.

Once the campaign response has been created, you can convert it to a lead, opportunity, quote, or another entity. This allows an organization to track the response or result of a campaign throughout an entire sales cycle.

Converting a campaign response

To convert a campaign response, perform the following steps:

1. Start CRM, click on the **Marketing** module, and then select **Campaigns**.
2. In the view, select and open the campaign for which you wish to convert the response.
3. On the left-hand navigation page, click on **Campaign Responses**.
4. Select the campaign response that you wish to convert.
5. On the **Campaign Response** ribbon bar, in the **Actions** group, click on **Convert Campaign Response**.

6. In the dialog, select one of the following options:
    - To create a new lead, select **Create New lead**
    - To use an existing lead, click on **Convert an existing lead**
    - To create a new opportunity, select **Create new record for a customer**, and select **Opportunity** as the record type
7. To open the newly converted record, select the **Open newly created records** box.
8. Click on **OK**.

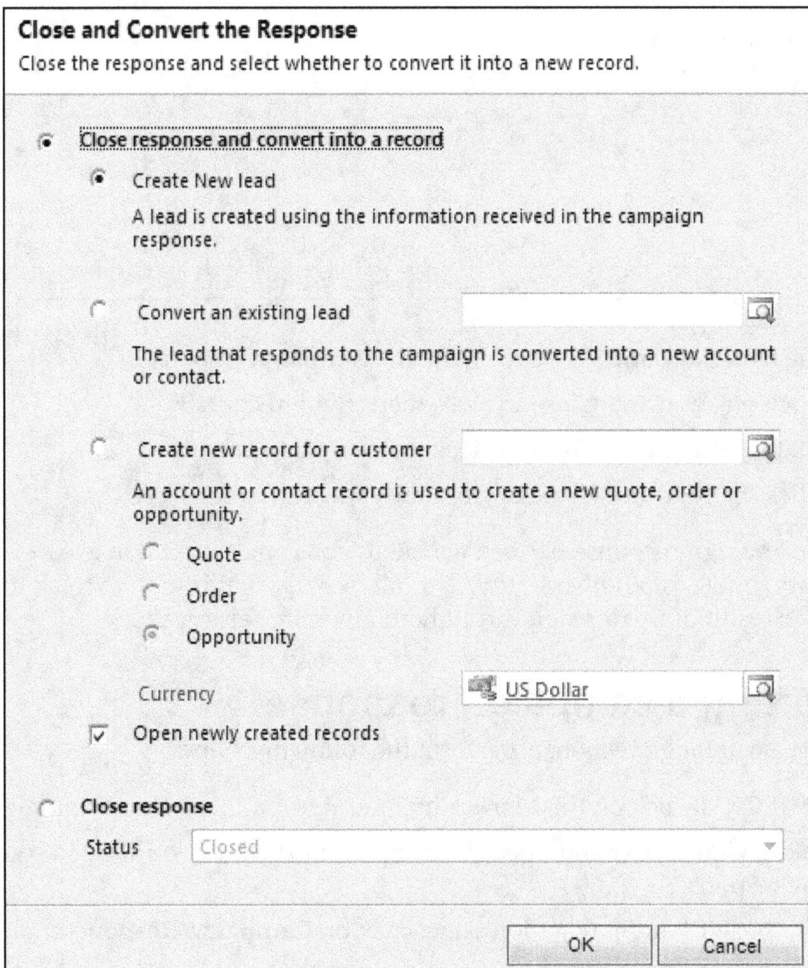

9. Enter the required information to fill out the form, and then click on **Save and Close**.

Besides creating a campaign response, you can also close a campaign response.

Closing a campaign response

When a campaign response is created, it has a status of open. You can close a campaign response with a status of closed or canceled. When it's closed, the record becomes deactivated, but can be re-opened at any point in time. To close a campaign response manually (that is, not converting the response), perform the following steps:

1. Start CRM, click on the **Marketing** module, and then select **Campaigns**.
2. In the view, select and open the campaign for which you wish to close the response.
3. On the left-hand navigation page, click on **Campaign Responses**.
4. Select the campaign response that you wish to close.
5. Click on **Close Campaign Response**.
6. Select the status that you wish to close the response with.
7. Click on **Save and Close**.

As you can see, there can be a large amount of effort in managing marketing campaigns. Many times, an organization may run very similar campaigns. In these cases, campaign templates can be used to reduce the time it takes to enter the data for a campaign.

Campaign templates

You can create a campaign, add campaign related records, and then save it as a template for use later. Campaign templates can have the following related entities:

- Marketing lists
- Targeted products
- Sales literature
- Planning activities
- Campaign activities

Campaign templates can be created manually or from an existing campaign.

Creating campaign templates

To create a campaign template, perform the following steps:

1. Start CRM, go to the **Marketing** module, and then click on **Campaigns**.
2. In the **Campaign** ribbon bar, click on **New Template**:

3. In the marketing campaign form, enter the necessary information.
4. Click on **Save and Close**.

Creating campaign templates from an existing campaign

To create a campaign template from an existing campaign, perform the following steps:

1. Start CRM, go to the **Marketing** module, and then click on **Campaigns**.
2. Select and open the campaign from which you wish to create the template.
3. In the **Campaign** ribbon bar, click on **Copy as Campaign**.

4. Enter a new name for the campaign.
5. Click on **Save and Close**.

Campaigns versus quick campaigns

The process for setting up campaigns can vary depending on the type of campaign (campaign versus quick campaign), and also what type of records a user wants to associate to a campaign (products, sales literature, planning activities, and so on). To better understand the flow of a campaign, see the following illustration:

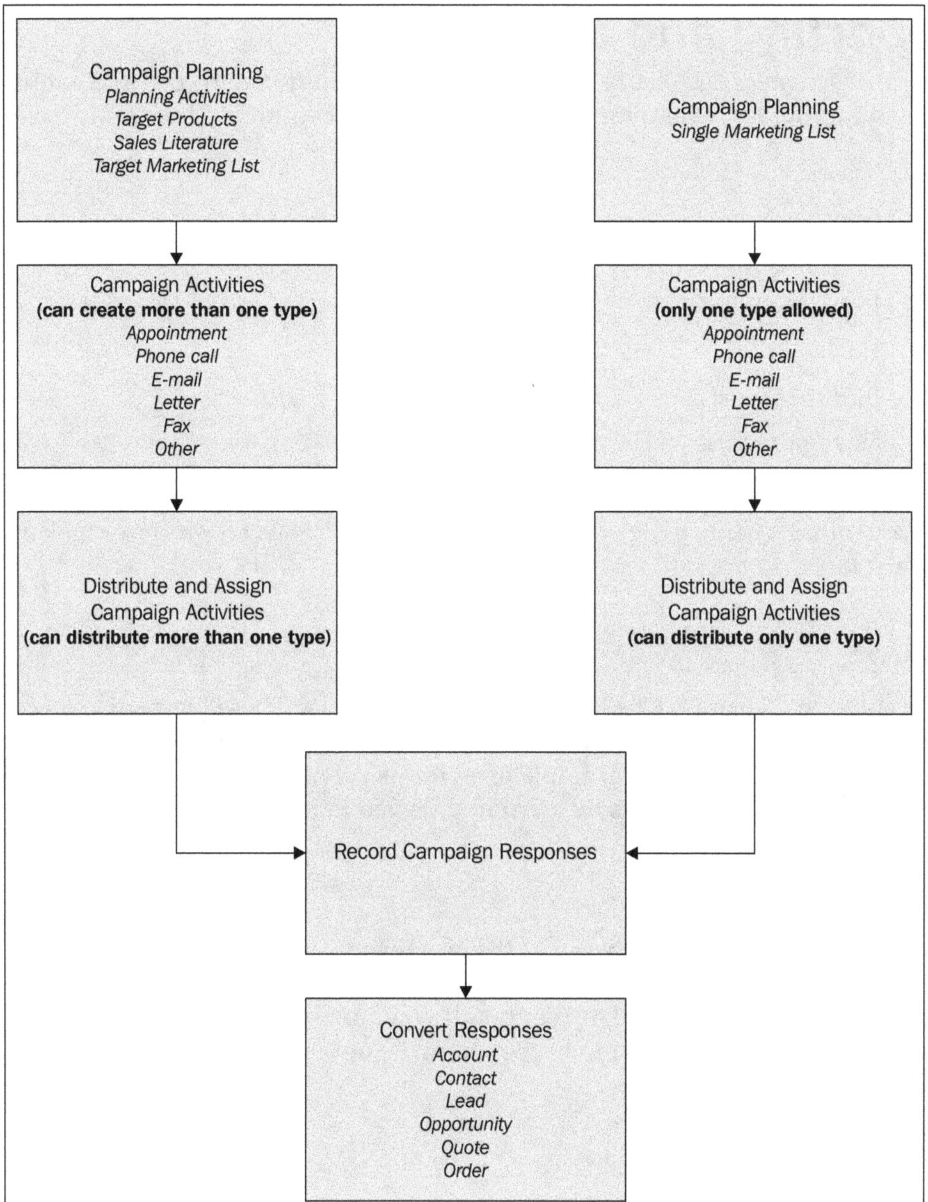

With marketing efforts under way, the next feature that Microsoft Dynamics CRM 2011 offers is analysis of the data and responses. Any good analysis of campaign and/or marketing data is completely contingent on good data. There's an old adage, "trash in, trash out," so it's critical that all information is being captured about the campaign, and that the responses are accurately recorded.

Reporting and analysis

Microsoft Dynamics CRM 2011 is not only a robust solution to record and capture data, but it provides several tools to analyze the data captured. These tools include:

- Views
- Charts
- Advanced find
- Export to Excel
- Dashboards
- Built-in reports
- Custom reports

Goals can also be considered a tool of CRM that allows users to analyze data, but we'll cover that when we cover sales. For this chapter, let us take a closer look at the standard tools.

Views

Every entity in Dynamics CRM 2011 has pre-built views. These views display certain columns of data. Columns can be added or removed from these views to display more or less information. An example of a view is "My Campaigns", which is a list of campaigns where the owner is the currently logged in user.

Charts

Accessing charts is straightforward as the charts show up on the right-hand side of a view. **Charts** are a graphical representation of records in a view. In any view, the chart selection is collapsed, by default. If you move the mouse over to the right-hand side, and expand the chart section, the out of the box charts for each entity are displayed.

There are two types of charts:

- **Personal chart**: This is created by a user and can only be seen by the creator unless it is shared with other users
- **System chart**: This can be created by a user or can be pre-built, but it is visible to all users

The interaction with the charts and views are contextual as well, much like the Dynamics CRM 2011 ribbon bar. When a chart is expanded, and a specific area is selected on the chart, the view automatically filters to show the results based on the selection of the chart. This ability provides a rich user experience and a quick way to analyze data.

Advanced find

Microsoft Dynamics CRM 2011 allows you to perform queries that are more complex than simply searching on views. These searches can search on the columns of a particular entity and related entities as well. Advanced finds can be saved for later use, and can also shared with other users and teams.

Creating an advanced find

To create an advanced find, perform the following steps:

1. Start CRM.
2. Click on **Advanced Find** on the ribbon bar:

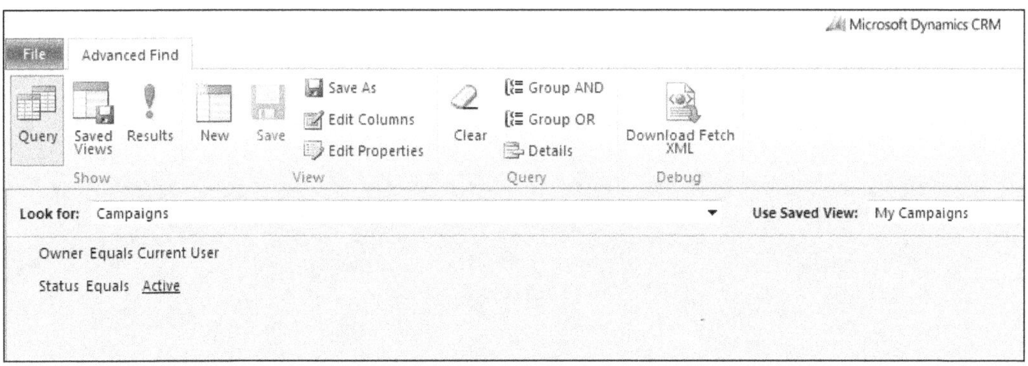

3. In the **Look for** drop down field, select the entity that you want to perform a search on.
4. Click on **Details** to enable the ability to add more filters.
5. Add the necessary search parameters.

6. Click on **Results**.
7. Once you are satisfied with the results, click on **Save** or **Save As** to save this advanced find as a personal view.

An advanced find saved for later use is called a **personal view**. Personal views cannot be exported to different environments. If you want this view to be exported to other CRM implementations, you must create a public view.

Once an advanced find is created or you use an out of the box CRM view, the results can be exported to Excel for analysis.

Export to Excel

Microsoft Dynamics CRM 2011 allows you to export the results of a view to Microsoft Excel. To export results to Excel for a view or advanced find, click on **Export to Excel** on the ribbon bar.

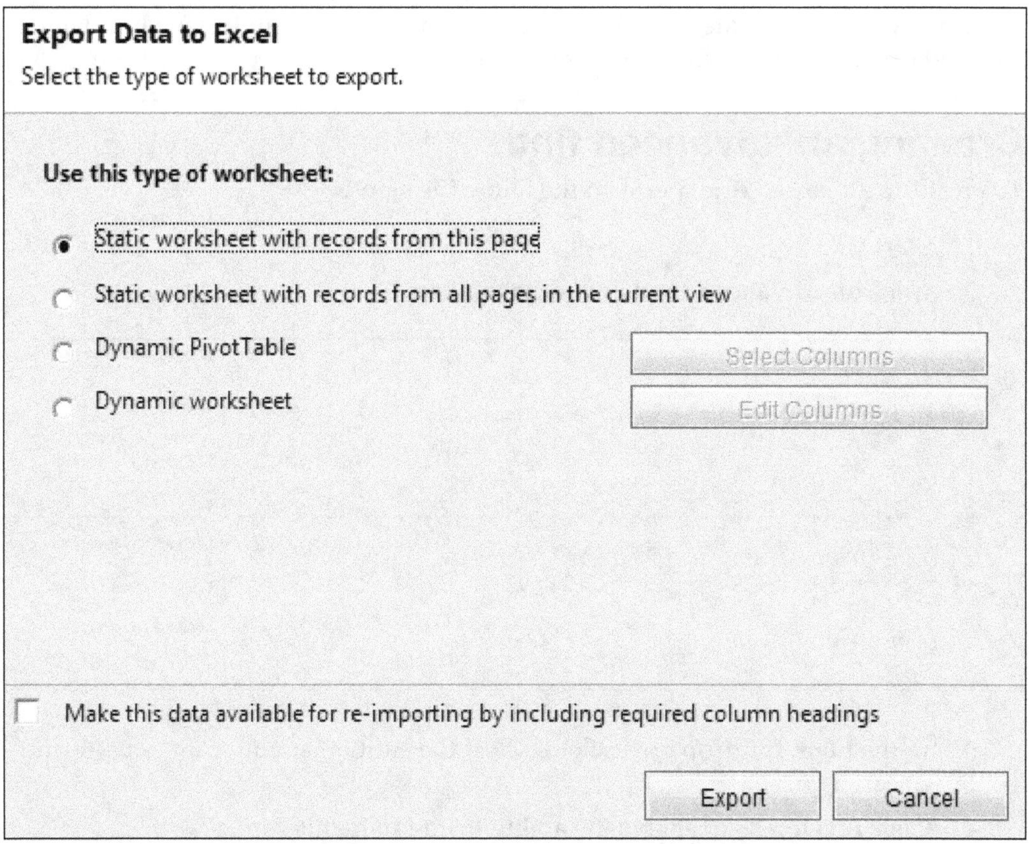

The options are described as follows:

- **Static worksheet with records from this page**: Only records on the current page are exported into a static Microsoft Excel worksheet. The columns exported will be the columns in the view.
- **Static worksheet with records from all pages in the current view**: All records on all pages in the current view are exported to a static Microsoft Excel worksheet.
- **Dynamic PivotTable**: The results are exported into a Microsoft Excel worksheet into a pivot table with an active connection to Dynamics CRM 2011. Selecting this option allows users to re-open the Excel spreadsheet at a later time and the data will be refreshed automatically.
- **Dynamic worksheet**: The results are exported into a Microsoft Excel worksheet with an active connection to Dynamics CRM 2011. Selecting this option allows users to re-open the Excel spreadsheet at a later time and the data will be refreshed automatically.
- If the checkbox for **Make this data available for re-importing by including required column headings** is selected, then CRM will export all columns in the current view plus any additional required fields needed for re-import, including a hidden column with the unique ID of each record.

Dashboards

Microsoft Dynamics CRM 2011 introduces the concept of dashboards. A dashboard is a collection of charts or graphs all on one page. Dashboards allow users to see the most important data all at once to enable organizations to make important business decisions easier. Similar to views and charts, Dynamics CRM comes with pre-built dashboards, and dashboards can be created by users as well. They can be categorized into two types:

- **Personal dashboard**: It can be created by any user and is visible only to the user that created it, unless they share the dashboard
- **System dashboard**: It can be created by a user, but Dynamics CRM comes with several pre-built ones, and they are visible to all users

Marketing dashboards

Speaking of pre-built dashboards, Dynamics CRM 2011 comes with a marketing dashboard that contains the following:

- Campaigns by type
- A comparison of budgeted versus actual costs for a campaign
- Leads by source campaign
- Revenue generated by campaigns

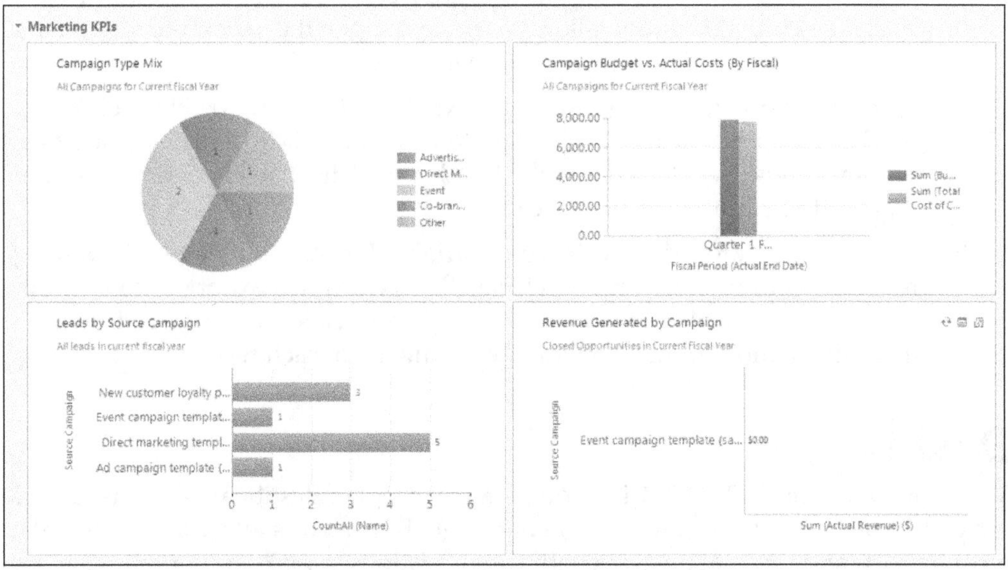

Another highlight of dashboards is that the data reflected is the most recent and does not have issues of stale data. That is, when data is updated in CRM, the results are reflected in the dashboards (if the user is viewing a dashboard, he/she may have to refresh the dashboard to see the latest results).

Creating a personal dashboard

To create a personal dashboard, perform the following steps:

1. Start CRM, click on **Workplace**, and then click on **Dashboards** in the left-hand navigation.
2. On the CRM ribbon bar, in the **Dashboards** tab, click on **New**.
3. In the **Dashboards Layout** dialog, select the appropriate layout, such as **3-Column Regular Dashboard** or **2-Column Regular Dashboard**.

4. Click on **Create**.

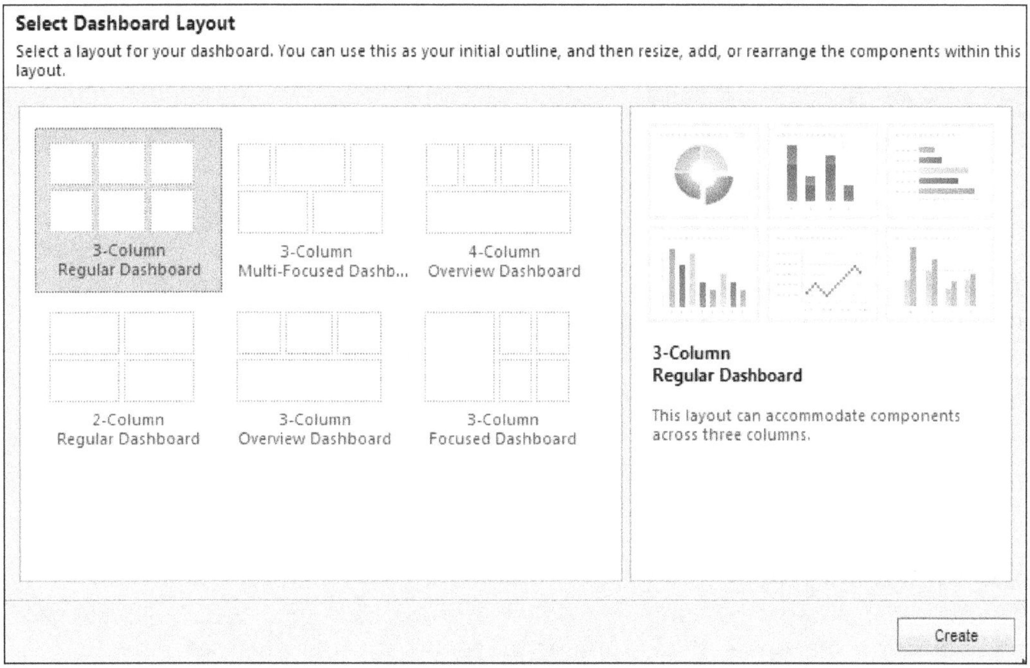

5. Enter a name for the dashboard.
6. On the **Dashboard** tab, in the **Insert Image** section, click on **Chart**.
7. Select the entity containing the data for the chart in the **Record Type** drop-down list.
8. Select the appropriate view in the **View** drop-down list.
9. Select the chart in the **Chart** drop-down list.
10. Click on **OK**.
11. Repeat steps 5 to 10 for each section.

When a personal dashboard is created, only the user that created it can see the dashboard, unless the user specifically shares it. Users can also create a public chart which can be available for the entire organization and can be exported as part of a solution.

System reports

Microsoft Dynamics CRM 2011 has several canned or built-in marketing reports to help an organization analyze its marketing efforts:

- Campaign activity status
- Campaign comparison
- Campaign performance
- Lead source effectiveness

A closer look at each of these reports can help you determine which to use when measuring the effectiveness of an organization's marketing tactics.

Campaign activity status

This report displays a summary for each campaign activity, including the parent campaign's details. By default, this report displays only campaigns with activities or notes that were created within the dates specified by the person running the report.

Campaign comparison

This report compares two campaigns based on parameters such as cost effectiveness and number of responses. When running the report, the user must select the campaigns to compare.

Campaign performance

This report tracks the status and progress of campaigns, including all of the campaign dates, targets, definitions, responses, and financial returns. By default, this report displays only campaigns modified in the last 30 days, but this can be changed by the user.

Lead source effectiveness

This report displays all leads and compares how effective your lead sources are at creating opportunities. The report lists the percentage of qualified leads, and leads that generate revenue for each lead category.

Running marketing reports

To run any of the reports described above, perform the following steps:

1. Start CRM, click on the **Workplace** module, and then click on **Reports** in the left-hand navigation.
2. Locate the report that you want to run in the list, and double-click on it to run the report.

3. If necessary, set the appropriate search criteria and filters.
4. Click on **Run Report**.

Report wizard

While Dynamics CRM offers many canned reports that are powerful, often organizations may want to create custom reports tailored to their needs. To enable this, you can use the **report wizard**. The report wizard allows the following features:

- Grouping and aggregation of data, such as grouping campaigns by campaign type. For example, if several campaigns are launched around a new product line, while others are launched around new services offered, these can be grouped in a custom report.
- Filtering allows report data to be pared down.
- Graphs and charts can be used to represent data visually.
- Drilldown reports can be added. This is where rows of data can be drilled down on, in order to retrieve more specific data.

Creating reports

To create a custom report, perform the following steps:

1. Start CRM, click on the **Workplace** module, and then click on **Reports** on the left-hand navigation.
2. Click on **New**.
3. In the **Report** dialog box, click on the **Report Wizard** button.

4. Click on **New**.
5. Specify a clear and concise **Report Name**.

6. Select **Primary Entity Type**.
7. Click on **Next**.
8. In the **Report Filtering Criteria** section, click on **Clear**.
9. Enter the filtering criteria or parameters for the report.
10. Click on **Next**.
11. Add any groupings and columns that you want to display.
12. Click on **OK**.
13. Select a report format (chart, table, or graph).
14. Click on **Next**.
15. Click on **Finish**.

The report created can now be run by the individual that created the report. This means that the report cannot be seen by anyone else in the organization unless they explicitly share the report or change the report properties called **Viewable By** to **Organization**.

In addition to creating reports, you can schedule reports to run at a specific time so that you have a snapshot at a specific moment in time.

> The ability to schedule reports is only available for on-premise instances and is not available for CRM online.

Snapshot reports

A report snapshot captures the report query results at a specific point in time. Report snapshots can be created in two ways:

- On-demand
- Scheduled

When snapshot reports are created on-demand, the query is run against the latest data in the system and a snapshot is created and then stored on the report server. When a report is scheduled, the query is run on a schedule and then the data and layout is saved to the report server. To schedule a report, perform the following steps:

1. Start CRM, go to the **Workplace** module, and then click on **Reports**.
2. Find and select the report that you wish to schedule.
3. In the **Reports** ribbon, select **Schedule Reports**.
4. In the **Report Scheduling Wizard**, select the type of snapshot that you wish to create. In this case, select **On a schedule**, to set up a scheduled report.

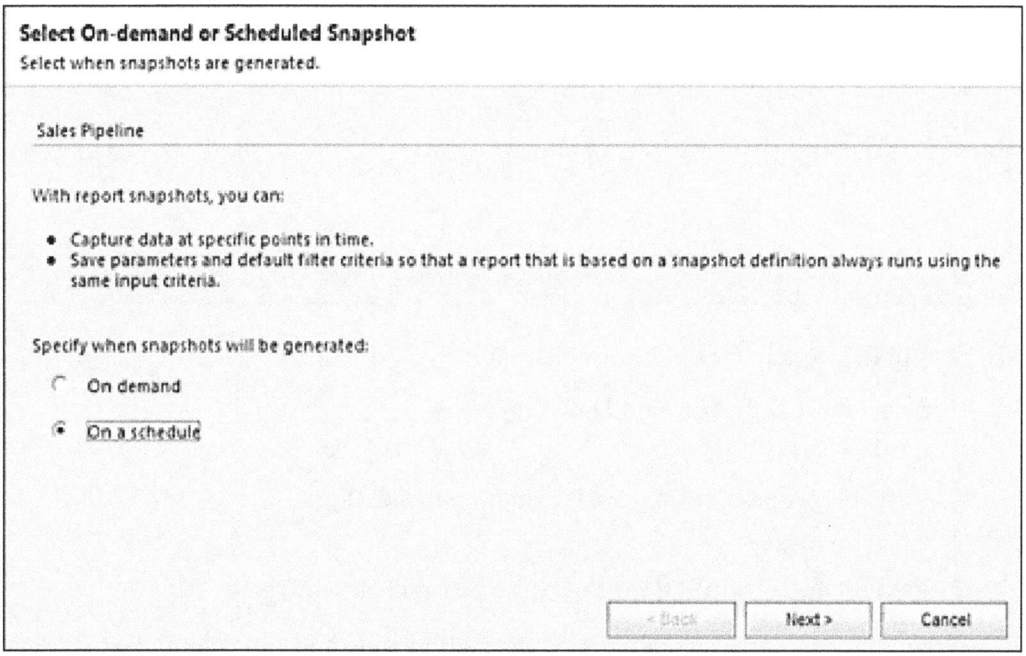

5. Click on **Next**.

6. Select the frequency with which to generate the report.

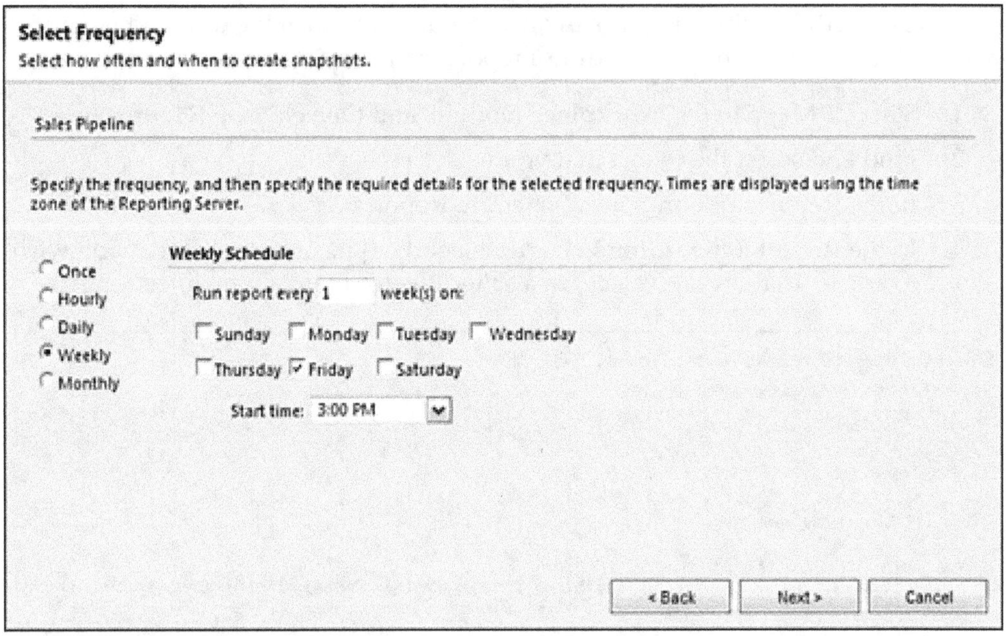

7. Click on **Next**.
8. Select **Start Date** and **End Date** if necessary.
9. Click on **Next**.
10. If the report has parameters, set them in this dialog.
11. Click on **Next**.
12. Review the scheduling summary, and then click on **Create**.

When the report is run, a snapshot is created with a date and timestamp. For example, if you were to schedule the Campaign Activity Status report, when the report is scheduled and run, a new report will be created and accessible in the reports grid view. The new report will have a name such as "Campaign Activity Status - Scheduled Snapshots 1_1_2013."

Test your knowledge

Q.1. What are the core record types that can be associated to a marketing list? (Choose all that apply.)

1. Account.
2. Contact.
3. Opportunity.
4. Lead.
5. Marketing list.
6. Campaign.

Q.2. What are the differences between static and dynamic marketing lists when adding members? (Choose all that apply.)

1. For dynamic marketing lists, an advanced find query is associated to the marketing list. For static marketing lists, members are added manually via a lookup or advanced find.
2. For dynamic marketing lists, members are added manually via a lookup or advanced find. For a static marketing list, an advanced find query is associated to the marketing list.
3. For dynamic and static marketing lists, members are added manually via a lookup or advanced find.
4. For dynamic and static marketing lists, an advanced find query is associated to the marketing list.

Q.3. What are components that can be associated to a marketing campaign? (Choose all that apply)

1. Sales literature.
2. Accounts.
3. Contacts.
4. Leads.
5. Products.

Q.4. What are the differences between a campaign and quick campaign? (Choose all that apply.)

1. Quick campaigns can only have one target marketing list while campaigns can have one or more target marketing lists.
2. Quick campaigns usually last for one day while campaigns can last much longer.
3. Quick campaigns can only distribute on activity type while campaigns can distribute multiple activity types.
4. A quick campaign can have one product associated to it while a campaign can have multiple products tied to it.
5. Quick campaigns do not allow the recording of campaign responses while campaigns do.

Q.5. What are the types of campaign activities? (Choose all that apply.)

1. Planning activities.
2. Tasks.
3. Phone calls.
4. Appointment.
5. Service appointment.

Q.6. State true or false: A marketing list must be associated to a campaign before the campaign can be launched.

Q.7. State true or false: When data is updated in CRM and the chart is refreshed, the data is not reflected automatically in a chart.

Q.8. What is a dynamic worksheet when exporting data to Excel?

1. The results will be exported into a Microsoft Excel worksheet into a pivot table with an active connection to Dynamics CRM 2011. Selecting this option allows users to re-open the Excel spreadsheet at a later time and the data will be refreshed automatically.
2. The results will be exported into a Microsoft Excel worksheet with an active connection to Dynamics CRM 2011. Selecting this option allows users to re-open the excel spreadsheet at a later time and the data will be refreshed automatically.
3. All records on all pages in the current view are exported to a static Microsoft Excel worksheet.
4. None of the above.

Q.9. What are the marketing system reports? (Choose all that apply.)

1. Campaign activity.
2. Campaign activity status.
3. Lead source effectiveness.
4. Campaign overview.
5. Campaign performance.

Q.10. State true or false: Custom reports are not allowed in Microsoft Dynamics CRM 2011.

Summary

Marketing lists can be used to group accounts, contacts, or leads, and can be used as part of a marketing campaign. There are two different marketing list types: static and dynamic. Members are added, removed, and updated manually in a static marketing list. With a dynamic marketing list, members are added via an advanced find query, and then removed or updated automatically. Dynamic marketing lists can also be copied to create a static one. You can manage marketing lists in other ways as well. You can copy members from one or more marketing lists (whether dynamic or static), but you can only copy members to a static list. Deleting or deactivating a marketing list does not remove the accounts, contacts, or leads that were part of that list from the system. Marketing lists are also an integral part of marketing campaigns.

A marketing campaign represents an organization's marketing plans, activities, and lists over a period of time. There are several related entities that can be associated to a campaign: planning activities, campaign activities, campaign responses, targeted products, sales literature, marketing lists, and related campaigns. There is quite a bit of effort around campaigns, and what if an organization would like to spin up a campaign quickly, with very little effort/time? Dynamics CRM comes to the rescue once again with quick campaigns. Using the quick campaign wizard, users can create simple campaigns that have one marketing list and that distribute one type of activity. Both types of campaigns can effectively promote your organization's products and services, and can help you to align your marketing department's goals with any strategic initiative that your organization is looking to undertake.

One of the first actions to take when you launch a campaign is to distribute the campaign activities. Distributing campaign activities pushes out activities to each member found on the marketing list. Once campaign activities are distributed, and a customer responds to one or more activities, these responses can be tracked using campaign responses. Campaign responses can be created manually, converted from a distributed campaign activity, or imported using the data import wizard. If e-mail tracking is enabled, an e-mail campaign was initiated, and an individual responds to that e-mail, a response can be automatically created. Lastly, campaign responses can be closed with a status of closed or canceled.

CRM is not only a robust solution for recording and capturing data, but it provides several tools to analyze the data captured. These tools include: views, charts, advanced find, export to Excel, dashboards, built-in reports, custom reports. Views display columns of data, while charts graphically represent the data found in a view. Advanced find is a tool that allows you to perform queries that are more complex than searching on views. Export to Excel is a function that exports the results of a view to Microsoft Excel. Microsoft Dynamics CRM 2011 introduces the concept of a dashboard, which is a collection of charts or graphs all on one page. Among the several pre-built dashboards available in CRM, a marketing dashboard exists, which contains the following charts: campaigns by type, a comparison of campaign budgeted versus actual costs, leads by source campaign, and revenue generated by campaigns.

In the next chapter, we introduce you to the sales module of Microsoft Dynamics CRM 2011. The topics covered include creating and managing leads, accounts, contacts, opportunities, competitors, and goals. Lastly, we will dive into sales reporting and analysis.

4

Managing Sales Applications

In this chapter you will learn about:

- Creating and managing leads
- Creating and managing accounts and contacts
- Creating and managing opportunities
- Creating competitors
- Creating and managing goals
- Reporting and analysis

Creating and managing leads

Let us take a look at a business scenario relating to leads.

Business scenarios

Race2Win Insurance Company set up a booth at a trade show to market to potential customers. The marketing team present at the show took down information about each person that visited the booth and expressed interest in one or more of Race2Win's insurance products or services. This information included the visitor's name, address, phone numbers, and information about the company they worked for.

The trade show has ended, and as part of Race2Win's marketing strategy, they will now enter the information collected into their Dynamics CRM system as leads. The people that showed interest are all potential customers.

The marketing team can now pass these leads on to the various inside sales people to make phone calls following up on the interest expressed at the trade show. As mentioned in *Chapter 2, Activities and Notes*, these phone calls can be tracked as activities in order to help track all interactions with potential customers.

Creating leads

To create a lead, follow these steps:

1. Start CRM, click on the **Sales** module, and then click on **Leads**.
2. On the **Leads** ribbon bar, in the **Records** group, click on **New**.

3. Enter the following required fields (some fields are not for input, but are listed here for explanation):
    i. **Topic**: Enter a clear and concise description of the topic that the lead is interested in
    ii. **Last Name**
    iii. **Company Name**

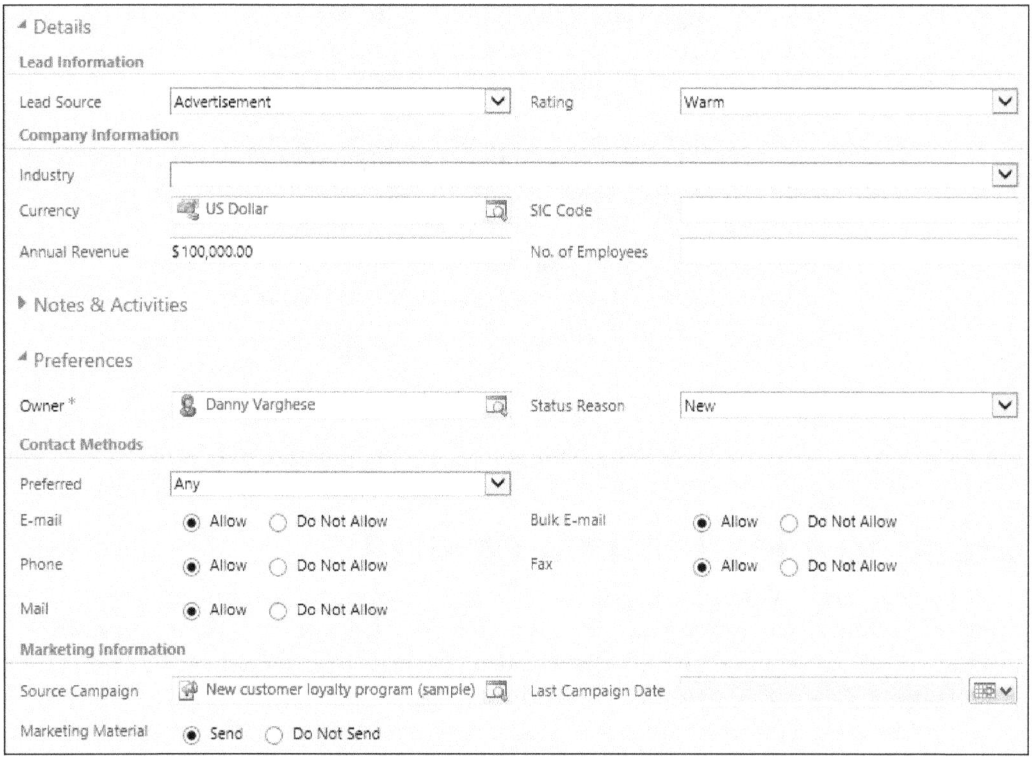

    iv. **Owner**: Defaults to the user creating the record, but can be changed.

4. The following fields are not required, but are worth mentioning:
    i. **Preferred**: Preferred method of communication to the lead. Possible values are **Any**, **E-mail**, **Phone**, **Fax**, and **Mail**.
    ii. Select the Marketing preferences as follows:
        a. **E-mail**: Selecting **Allow** allows all e-mail, including e-mail-related to campaign activities, to be sent to the lead. Selecting **Do Not Allow** does not allow e-mails to be sent to this lead.
        b. **Phone**
        c. **Mail**
        d. **Bulk E-mail**: Selecting **Allow** allows e-mail as part of a bulk e-mail process, including bulk e-mail related to campaign activities, to be sent. Selecting **Do Not Allow** does not allow bulk e-mails to be sent to this lead.
        e. **Fax**

iii. **Last Campaign Date**: Date on which the lead was last involved in a campaign. This is a read-only field that is set automatically when any marketing communication is sent to the addresses for the record.

iv. **Marketing Material**: If you select **Send**, marketing material (such as e-mails or letters) that corresponds to campaigns is allowed to be sent. If you select **Do Not Send**, marketing materials are not sent, and activities related to the sending of marketing materials cannot be created for the record.

v. **Currency**: Set to the system default value, but can be changed.

5. Click on **Save**.

A lead record can also be created by converting an e-mail activity record.

Creating a lead from an e-mail

A business example would be if someone is browsing the corporate website of Race2Win Insurance company and wants to get more information about a certain product. If that user sends an e-mail expressing interest to someone within the organization, Race2Win would want to add that person in as a lead with a lead source set to **Web**. For rapid entry of a lead, CRM allows an e-mail to be converted into a lead by using the following steps:

1. Start CRM, go to the **Workplace** module, and then click on **Activities**.
2. Find and open the e-mail that you wish to convert.
3. On the **Lead** ribbon bar, in the **Covert Activity** group, click on **To Lead**.

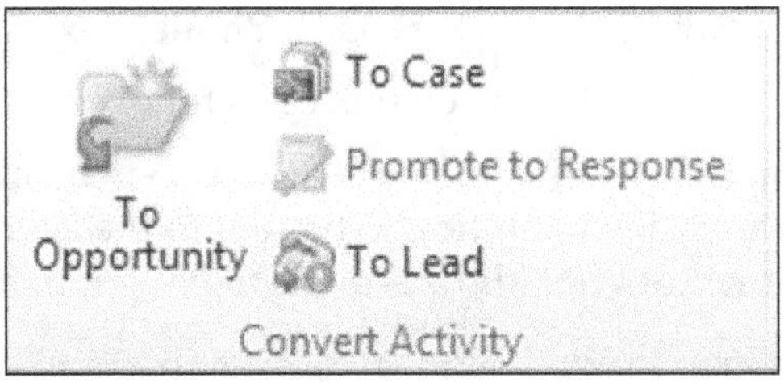

4. In the **Convert E-mail to Lead** dialog box, enter the following information:
    - **First Name**
    - **Last Name**
    - **Company**

- ◦ **E-mail Address**

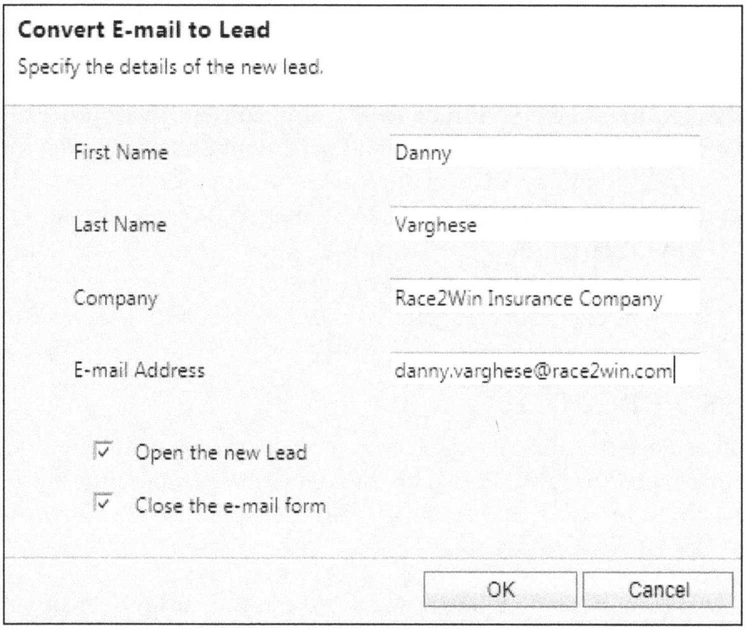

5. Click on **OK**.

Lead status

A lead record can have various statuses and status reasons that help to define the state that the record is in. For each status, there are various status reasons. **According to MSDN, the various statuses are displayed in the following table**:

Status	Associated Status Reason
0 Open	1 New * 2 Contacted
1 Qualified	3 Qualified *
2 Disqualified	4 Lost * 5 Cannot Contact 6 No Longer Interested 7 Canceled

Once leads are created, most organization start a **lead qualification** process.

Managing leads

Lead qualification is a process in which an organization determines if a company or individual is displaying the intent, and has the ability to make a purchase within a certain timeframe. In Dynamics CRM, qualifying a lead changes the status of the lead, but it also requires the creation of an account, contact, or opportunity (at least one must be created). This is because in most organizations, once a lead is qualified, the company or individual is ready to purchase a product or service. If they're ready to purchase a product or service, they can be managed like a customer (account or contact) and begin to start having sales opportunities. Typically, the qualification process varies between organizations and is dependent on various business rules. An example of these business rules are demonstrated in the following business scenario.

Business scenarios

A salesperson at Race2Win Insurance Company has a lead on selling one of their insurance products to an individual. This salesperson needs to find out if this individual is truly interested, and to do so, the salesperson will follow the lead qualification process set forth by Race2Win.

Race2Win is using the **BANT** method, which stands for B**udget, Authority, Need, and Timeframe**. This is not covered in the certification exam, but is being used as an example of a process an organization might use to qualify a lead. The salesperson analyzes the lead to see if the lead has the budget to purchase the product, the authority to make the buying decision, whether they truly have the need for the product, and finally if they're looking to buy within a given timeframe.

Using this process has helped this salesperson determine that the lead he/she is working on is ready to be qualified.

Qualifying or disqualifying a lead

To qualify a lead, follow these steps:

1. Start CRM and go to the **Marketing** module.
2. Find and open the lead that you wish to qualify.

3. In the **Lead** ribbon bar in the **Actions** group, click on **Qualify**.

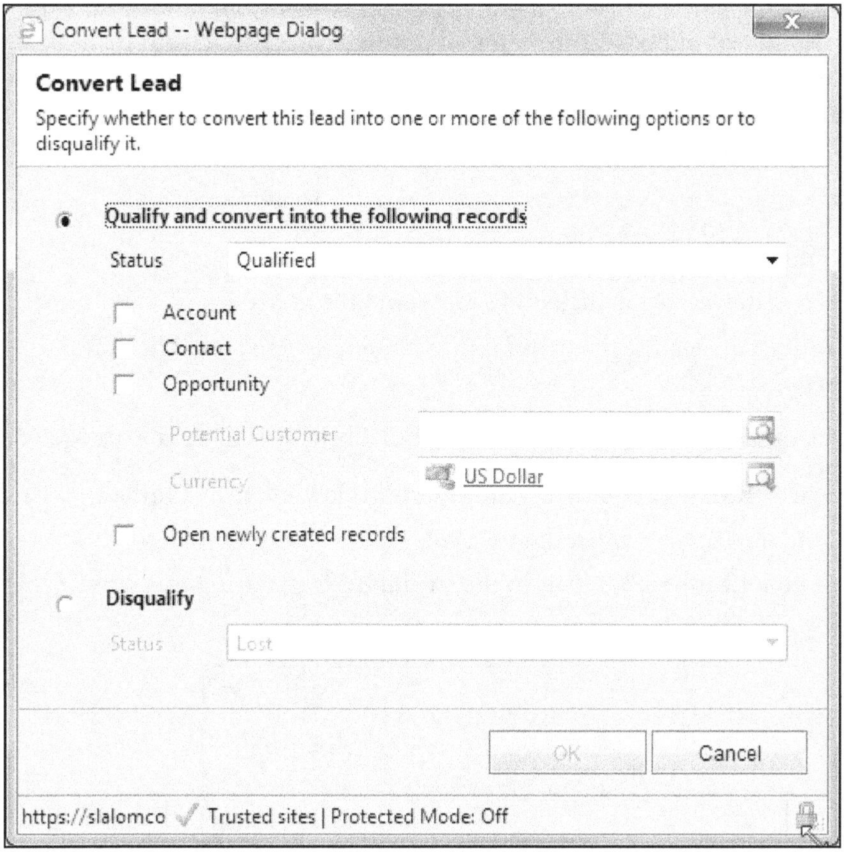

4. In the convert lead dialog, you can choose whether to qualify and convert a lead into an account, contact, and/or opportunity record, or disqualify the lead.
5. If you choose to qualify a lead, the lead will be deactivated with a status of **Qualified**. Furthermore, an account, contact, or opportunity must be created (at least one of them must be chosen, but more than one can be selected). If only an opportunity is chosen to be created from a lead, a potential customer (either an account or a contact) must be selected. If an account and/or contact are both selected with an opportunity, the potential customer for an opportunity becomes the account or contact. If an account and contact is selected with an opportunity, the potential customer becomes the account. The **potential customer** is an attribute of the opportunity record.
6. If you choose to disqualify the lead, you will have to choose from a list of statuses—**Lost**, **Cannot Contact**, **No Longer Interested**, or **Canceled**. When a lead is disqualified, the record becomes deactivated.

Assigning leads

Besides creating and qualifying them, leads can be assigned or shared. A business example of this would be if, through marketing efforts, Race2Win Insurance Company produced a large number of leads. Their marketing department can assign leads to various inside sales people so that they can begin the lead qualification process.

There are multiple ways in which a lead can be assigned. You can:

- Open the lead record and change the owner field
- Open the lead and click on the **Assign** button
- Within the lead view, select one or more record(s) and click on the **Assign** button

For this example, let us explore how to assign a lead within the **Leads** view.

1. Start CRM, go to the **Sales** module, and then click on **Leads**.
2. Find and select the lead(s) that you wish to assign.
3. On the **Leads** ribbon bar, in the **Collaborate** group, click on the **Assign** button.

4. In the **Assign** dialog box, select whether you wish to assign the record(s) to yourself, or to another user or team.

5. Click on **OK**.

Sharing leads

An example of sharing a lead is if an inside sales person needed help in qualifying a lead, they can share the record with someone to get their input.

To share a lead, follow these steps:

1. Start CRM, go to the **Sales** module, and then click on **Leads**.
2. Find and select the lead(s) that you wish to share.
3. On the **Lead** ribbon, inside the **Collaborate** group, click on **Share**:

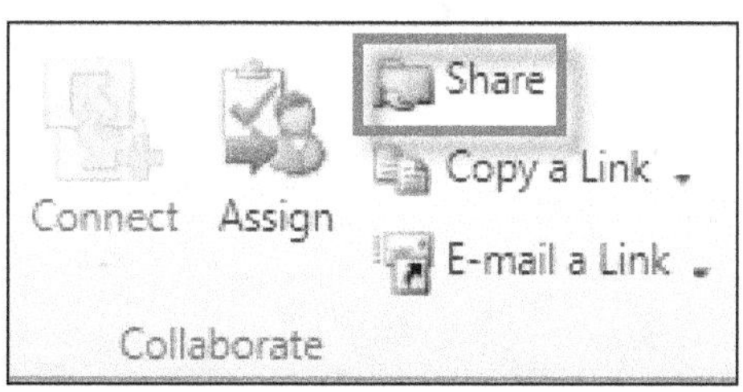

4. In the **Common Tasks** section, click on **Add User/Team**.

5. A lookup dialog appears allowing you to select one or more user(s) or team(s).
6. Click on **Add** to add the user(s) or team(s) to the lookup dialog box.
7. Click on **OK** to add the user(s) or team(s) to the sharing dialog box.
8. Within the sharing dialog box, select which permissions you want to grant to the users. You can choose from **Read**, **Write**, **Delete**, **Append**, **Assign**, and **Share**.

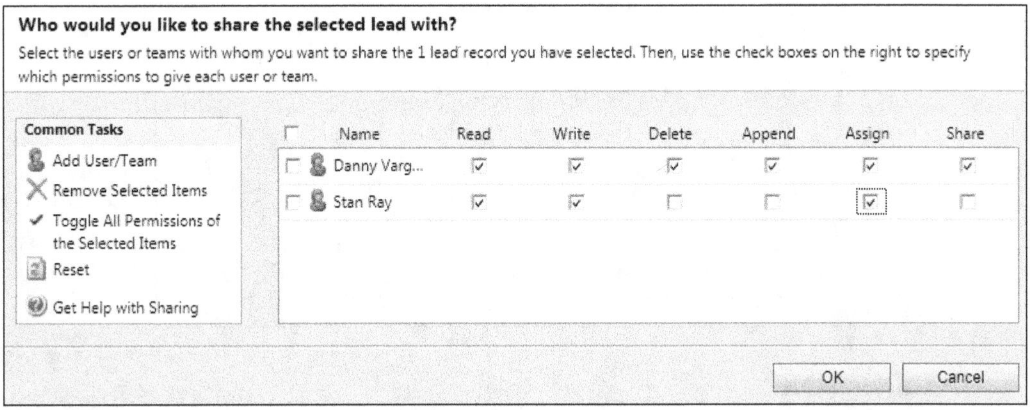

9. Click on **OK**.

Activating a lead

When a lead is disqualified, it becomes inactive. Sometimes, that company or individual may express interest again, and instead of creating a new lead, you may choose to reactivate the lead. To activate a lead, follow these steps:

1. Start CRM and go to the **Marketing** module.
2. Find the lead that you wish to reactivate. If the lead is inactive, it may show up in a different view, such as **Closed Leads**.
3. You have two options here. The first option is to select the lead from the view, and on the **Leads** ribbon bar, in the **Records** group, click on **Activate**.

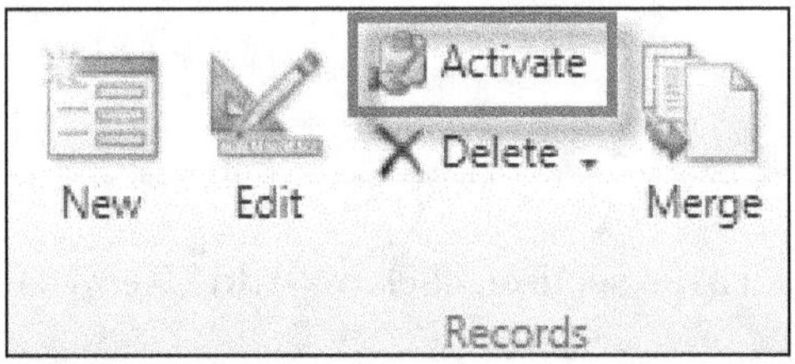

4. The second option is to open the record and, on the **Lead** ribbon bar in the **Actions** group, click on **Reactivate Lead**.

5. For either option, click on **OK**.

Creating and managing accounts and contacts

Accounts and contacts are collectively known as customers in CRM. Understanding how to create and manage these customers in CRM is essential, and necessary before tracking sales.

Accounts

The account entity is one of the central components of a CRM system and is essential in managing customers that are organizations. Opportunities, sales, and service-related items for an organization can all be tracked by using the account entity.

According to MSDN, the account entity can be a parent to almost any other entity, including another account. An account can only have one parent account, but can have multiple child accounts and/or child contacts.

Business scenarios

An inside sales representative at Race2Win Insurance Company went through a qualification process on a lead. Using their company's business rules, the sales representative qualified the lead and converted it to an account.

The inside sales representative has now handed the account over to a sales representative that manages accounts in that organization's sales territory. The sales representative can begin collecting demographic and industry information in order to gather more insight into the organization to which they are trying to sell to.

Methods to create accounts

An account can be created in any of the following ways:

- Using the CRM Data Import Wizard. The Data Import Wizard is beyond the scope of the certification exam, and thus will not be covered in this book.
- In the **Account** view, in the **Records** group, click on the **New** button.

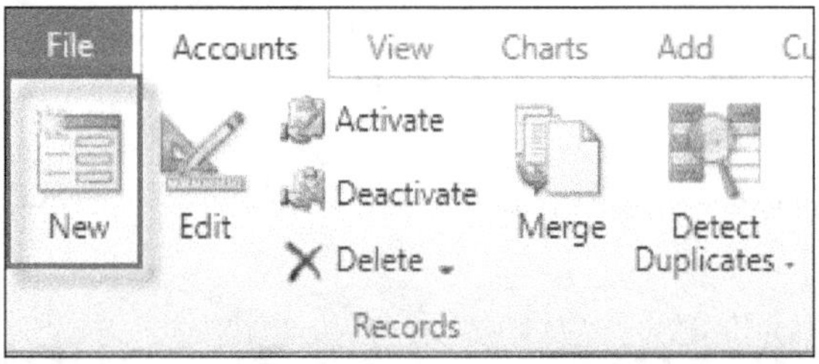

- On the ribbon bar, in the **File** tab, click on **New Record**, and then select **Account**.

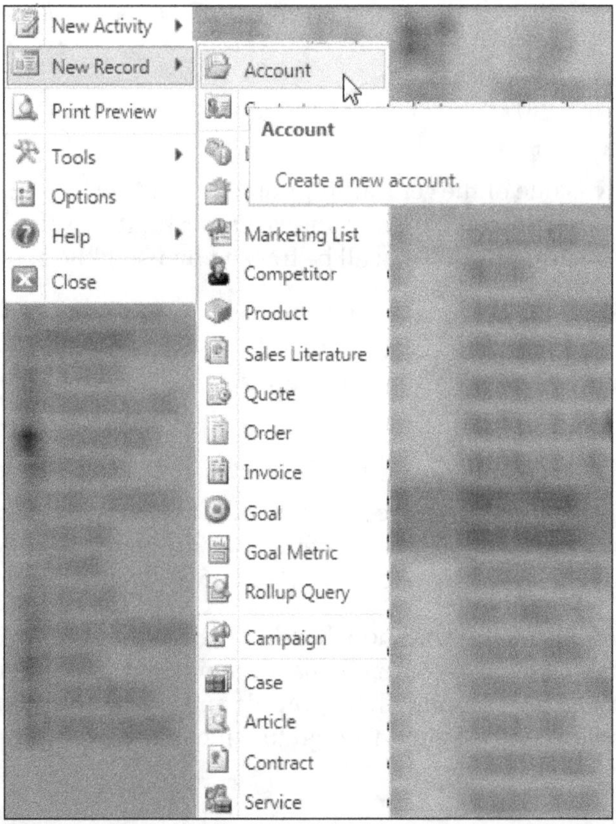

- In the **Account Lookup** dialog, click on **New**. A lookup to the account entity appears on the account form itself as the parent account field.

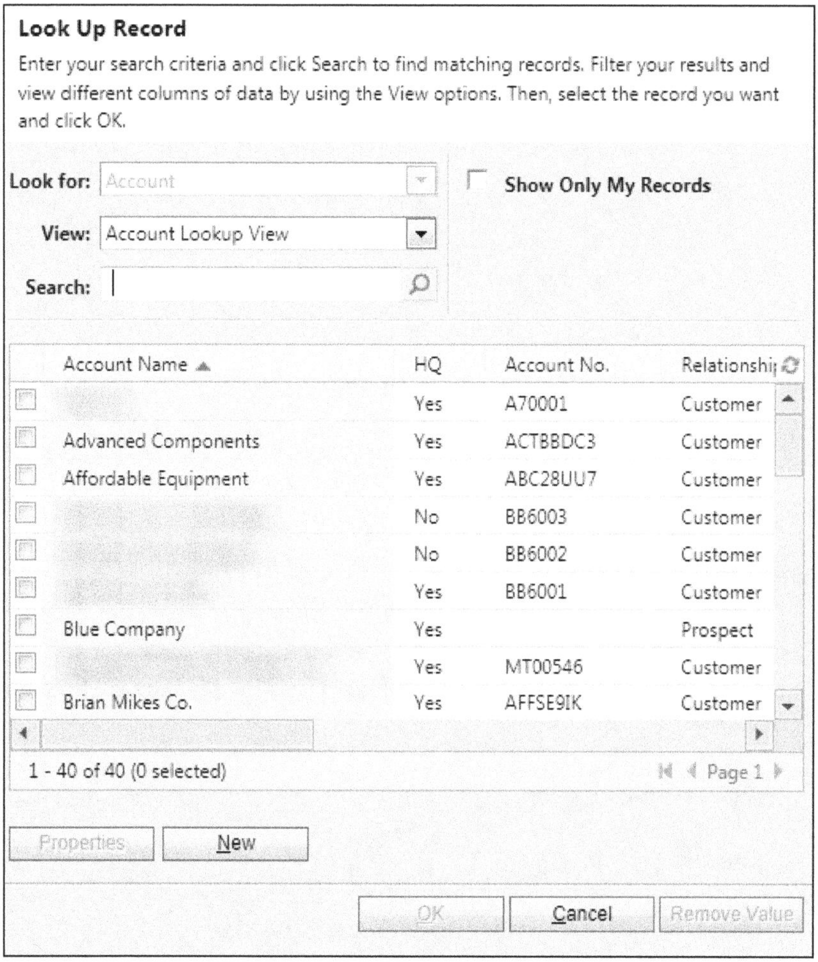

Creating accounts

An account can be created in different ways, from converting a lead into an account, to creating one manually. For this scenario, we'll cover how to create an account manually. To create an account manually, follow these steps:

1. Start CRM, go to the **Sales** module, and then click on **Accounts**.

2. In the **Accounts** ribbon bar, in the **Records** group, click on the **New** button.

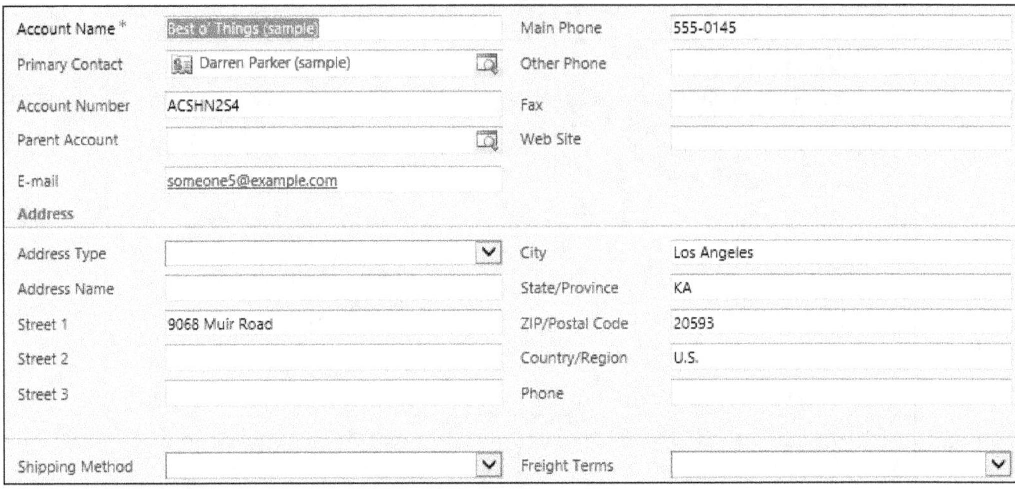

3. Enter the following required fields:
   i. **Account Name**: Enter a clear, concise name for the account.
   ii. **Owner**: This is a required field; however it's pre-populated with the user creating the record.

The following screenshot shows the shipping and **Details** section of the account form:

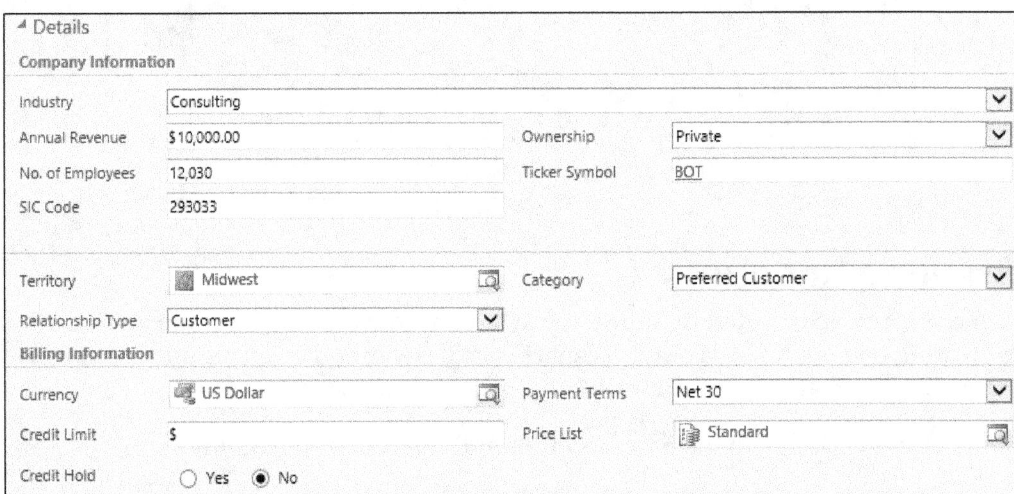

The following screenshot shows the industry and marketing information of the account form:

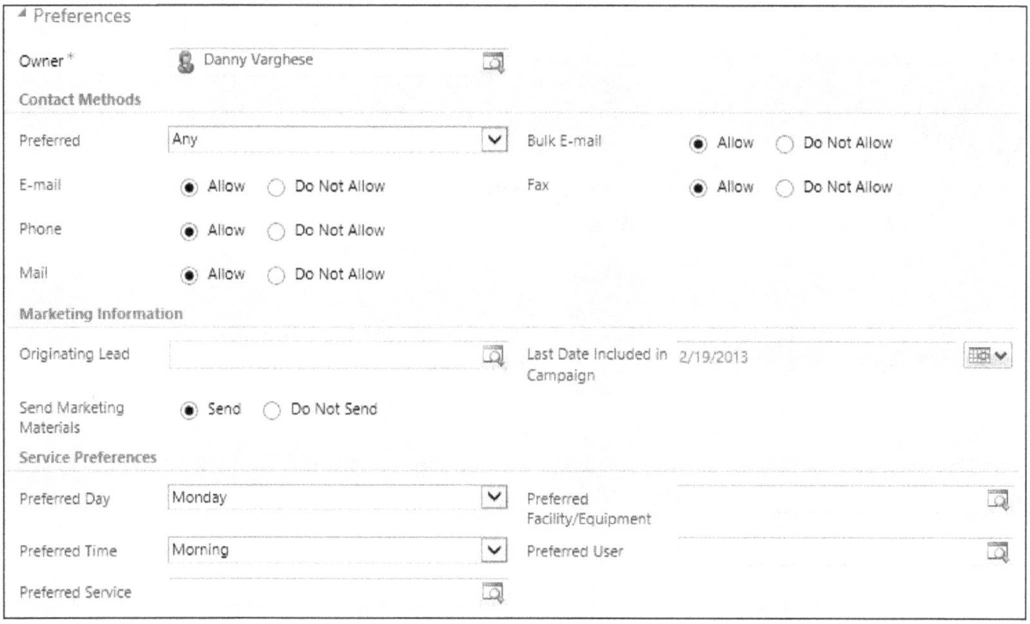

4. Click on **Save**.

Contacts

The contact entity is also one of the central components of a CRM system and is essential in managing customers that are individuals. Opportunities, sales, and service-related items for an individual can all be tracked by using the contact entity.

According to MSDN, the contact entity can be a parent to every other entity except accounts and contacts, and a contact can have only one account as its parent.

Business scenarios

A sales representative at Race2Win Insurance Company has successfully sold some products to an account that they are managing. Throughout the selling process, the sales representative met key players within the organization. Race2Win use Dynamics CRM to track these individuals as contacts for the organization.

Within the contact record, the sales representative tracks information such as their role within the organization, and personal information such phone numbers, birthday, and anniversary. This allows the sales representative to keep in touch with these individuals and helps them to build meaningful relationships. The sales representative is hoping that these interactions can help bring him/her future opportunities.

Creating contacts

Contacts can be created in multiple ways, similar to how the account can be created. An additional way in which a contact can be created is within the contact's associated view on an account.

> When a contact is added via an associated view, the relationship between the contact and the account is automatically set. That is, the parent customer field on the contact is set.

For the purpose of this book, we'll focus on creating a contact by going to the contact view. To create a contact via the contact view, follow these steps:

1. Start CRM, go to the **Sales** module, and then click on **Contacts**.
2. In the **Contacts** ribbon bar, in the **Records** group, click on the **New** button.

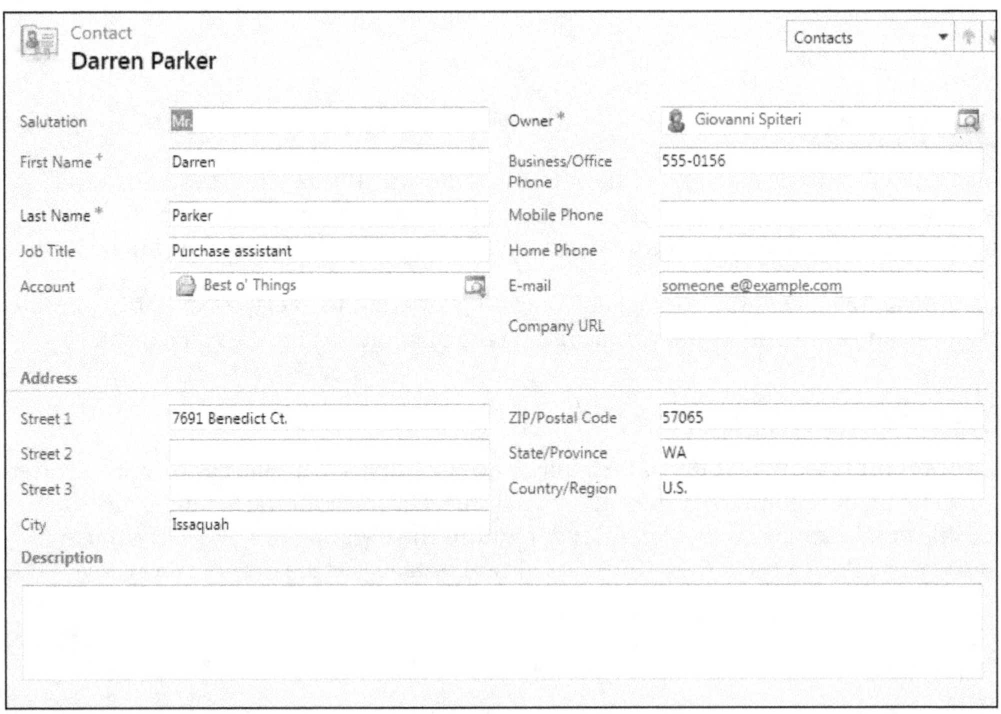

3. Enter the following required fields:
    i. **Last Name**
    ii. **Parent Customer**: This is not a required field, but it is worth noting that a contact can have an account or a contact as a parent.
    iii. **Owner**

    The following screenshot shows the rest of the contact form.

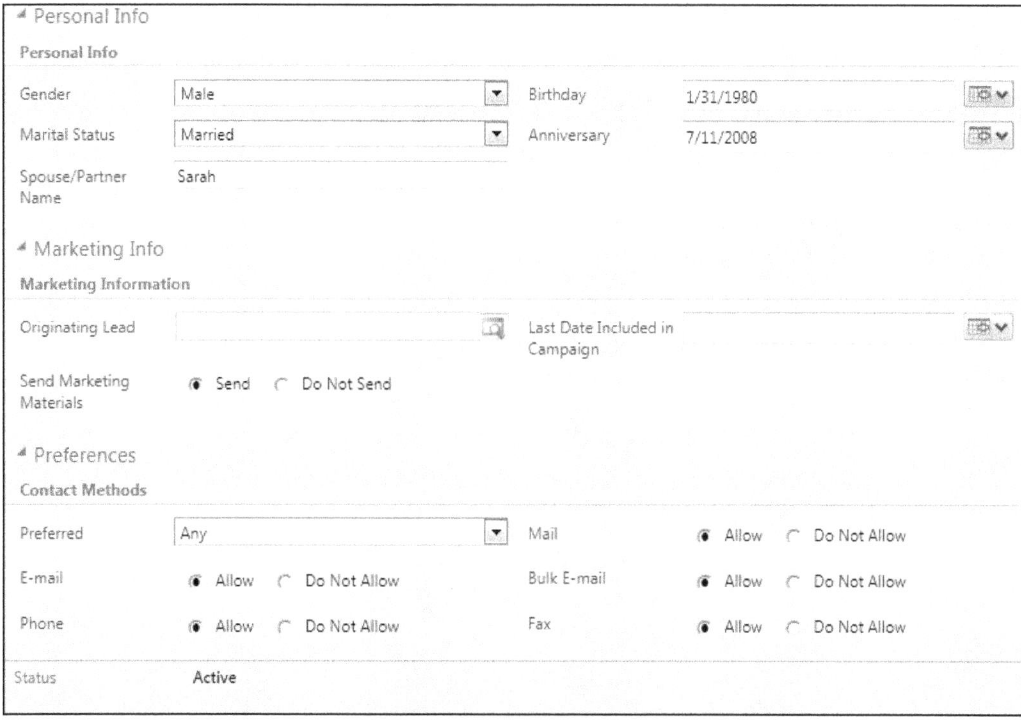

4. Click on **Save**.

Account and contact records can be shared, assigned, deactivated, activated, and merged.

Managing accounts and contacts

Like many entities in CRM, accounts and contacts can be shared with user(s) or team(s). They can also be assigned to a user or team. The process for sharing and assigning accounts and contacts is the same as outlined earlier in this chapter, in the *Assigning leads* and *Sharing leads* sections.

An account or contact can be deactivated at any time as well. For example, if one of Race2Win Insurance Company's accounts decides to do business elsewhere, they can choose to deactivate the account in case the client ever decides to do business with Race2Win again. To activate an account or contact, follow the steps outlined earlier in this chapter, in the *Activating a lead* section.

Accounts and contacts have an added functionality that comes in handy, especially when CRM may become full of duplicate accounts and/or contact records. To help alleviate some of the data cleanup, CRM allows the merging of records of these types.

Merging accounts and contacts

Many CRM systems experience cases of duplicate accounts or contacts. This can be from poor data management strategies, incorrect data entry, or even in a new system after a data migration from another system. Whatever the case, the ability to merge duplicate records of the same type can help save time.

When two records are merged, one is considered the master record, and the other a duplicate record. To merge two records (let us use two accounts for this scenario), follow these steps:

1. Start CRM, click on **Sales**, and then click on **Accounts**.
2. Find and select the two account records that you want to merge.

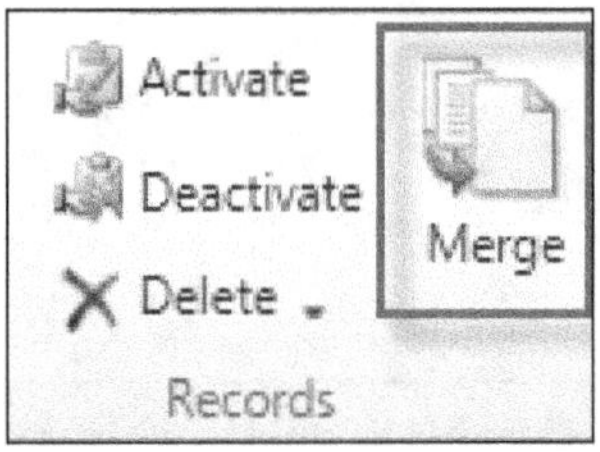

3. On the **Accounts** ribbon bar, in the **Records** group, click on the **Merge** button.

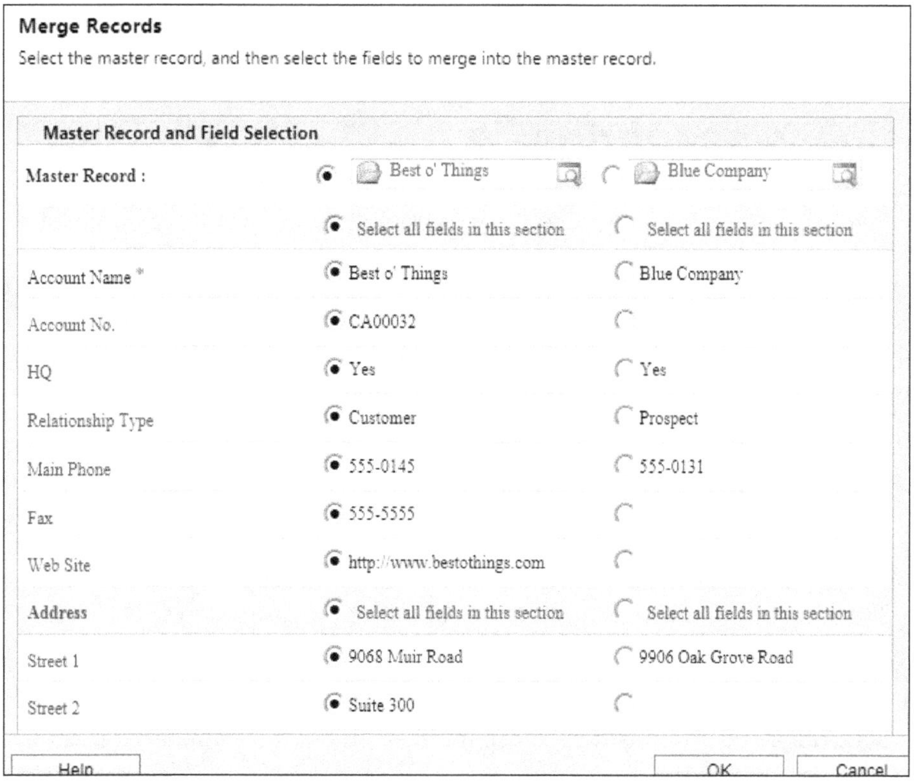

4. In the **Merge** dialog box, choose the master record by selecting the radio button next to the appropriate account record.
5. Go through each field and determine which value you wish to use in the master record.
6. Click on **OK**.

Based on your selection in the merge dialog box, for each field, CRM will either keep the value the master record, or copy the value from the duplicate record to the master record. It will then deactivate the duplicate record, and associate all related records (activities, opportunities) to the master record. Even though the duplicate record is deactivated, a user can reactivate it at any time.

> Reactivating a merged record does not re-associate any of the related records.

Creating and managing opportunities

An opportunity in CRM represents a potential sale. The sales process varies between organizations, which is why Dynamics CRM provides various ways to manage opportunities.

Business scenarios

The sales team at Race2Win Insurance Company is focused on efforts to drive revenue for the company. They also want to track these efforts, as revenue has a direct impact on their salary. CRM allows a sales representative to create and track sales opportunities. These opportunities can have activities, which can help a representative to track interactions with his/her customers. The sales representative can also add products in the form of opportunity products, in order to get more accurate pricing and estimated revenue information.

Race2Win Insurance Company has their own selling process in place, and various sales stages that are used to track milestones for an opportunity. For example, the opportunity may start off in a stage of open, but if a customer experiences serious interest, the opportunity may move to the next stage of alignment which then tells the sales person to take a different course of action to move it to the next stage, and so on. Tracking of the stages is another feature of opportunities in CRM.

Race2Win would also like the ability to track all opportunities in the system, and be able to manage their pipeline and perform sales forecasting. The use of opportunities, along with reporting and dashboard capabilities, gives an organization the tools to do just that.

Creating opportunities

Opportunities can be created in a few different ways by: converting an activity to an opportunity, by converting a lead to an opportunity, or by using the CRM user interface. Let's explore each of these methods at greater length.

Converting an activity to an opportunity

For this particular example, let's convert a task activity to an opportunity. To convert an activity to an opportunity, follow these steps:

1. Start CRM, go to the **Workplace** module, and then click on **Activities**.
2. In the view selector, click on **Tasks**, and then click on **All Tasks**.

3. Find and open the task that you wish to convert.

4. In the **Task** ribbon bar, in the **Convert Activity** group, click on the **To Opportunity** button.

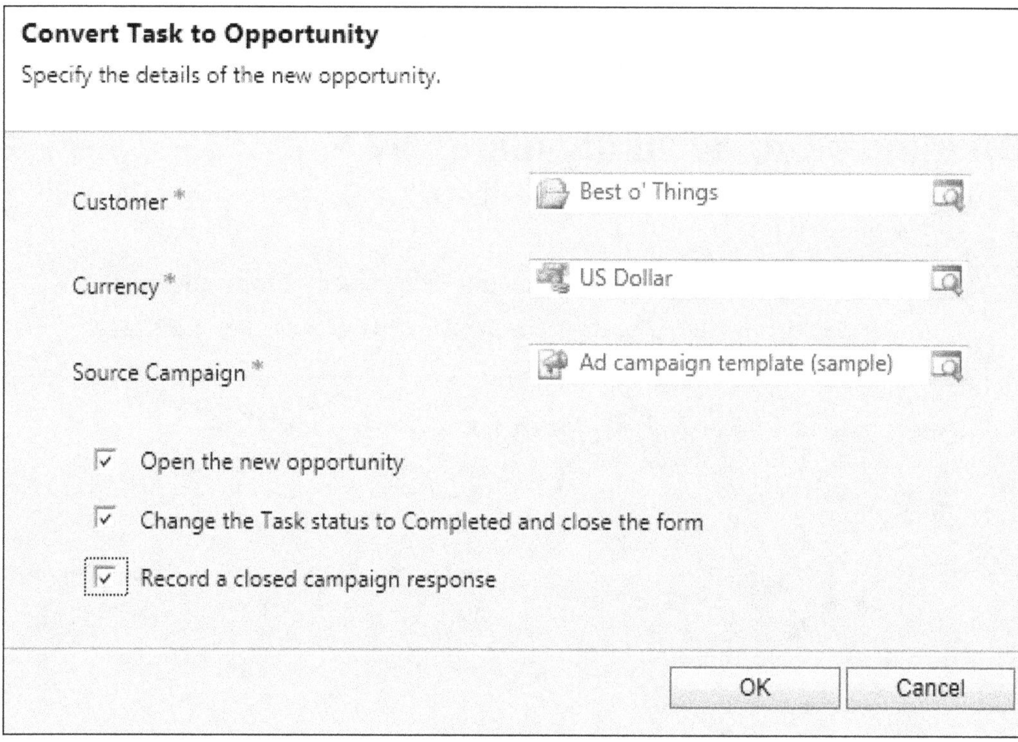

5. In the **Convert Task to Opportunity** dialog box, enter the following information:
   i. **Customer**
   ii. **Currency**: This is set to the default currency of your Dynamics CRM system, but you have the ability to change it here
   iii. **Source Campaign**: If you want to link a campaign to the opportunity in order to help track ROI, you can do so here

iv. **Open New Opportunity**: Select this checkbox if you want the new opportunity to be opened after clicking on **OK**

v. **Change the Task status to Completed and close form**: Select this checkbox if you want the activity to be completed and the form closed

vi. **Record a closed campaign response**: Selecting this checkbox makes the source campaign field required

6. Click on **OK**.

Converting a lead to an opportunity

To convert a lead to an opportunity, see the steps outlined earlier in this chapter under the *Managing leads* and *Qualifying or disqualifying a lead* sections.

Creating an opportunity manually

Yet another way to create an opportunity is through the Dynamics CRM UI. To do this, follow these steps:

1. Start CRM, go to the **Sales** module, and then click on **Opportunities**.
2. In the **Opportunities** ribbon bar, in the **Records** group, click on **New**.

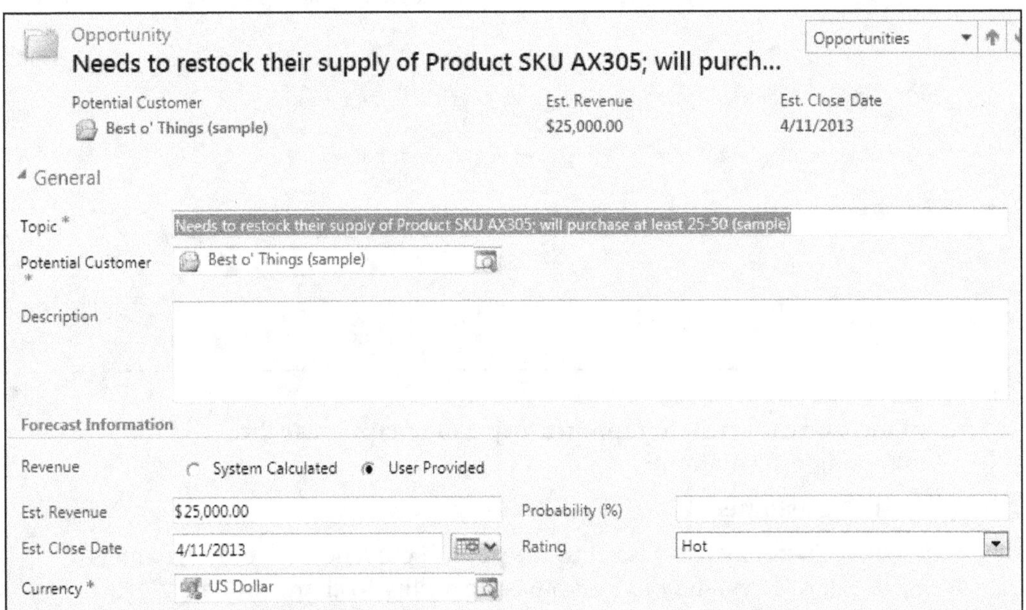

3. Complete the following required fields on the form:
    - i. **Topic**: Enter a clear, concise description of the opportunity
    - ii. **Potential Customer**: This can be either an account or a contact
    - iii. **Currency**: This field will auto-populate with the system default currency but can be changed
    - iv. **Owner**
4. The following fields are not required, but are worth mentioning:
    - i. **Revenue**: Choose either **System Calculated**, in which case if opportunity products are added (we'll be discussing this further in the chapter), the system will automatically calculate the estimated revenue, or choose **User Provided**, in which case the estimated revenue field will become enabled for you to enter an estimate.
    - ii. **Est. Revenue**: Enter the amount of revenue estimated to be recognized, if the opportunity is won.
    - iii. **Est. Close Date**: Select the estimated date on which the opportunity could potentially be closed.
    - iv. **Probability %**: Enter the probability of closing the opportunity (as a percentage).
    - v. **Rating**: Select from **1 - Hot**, **2 - Warm**, or **3 - Cold**.

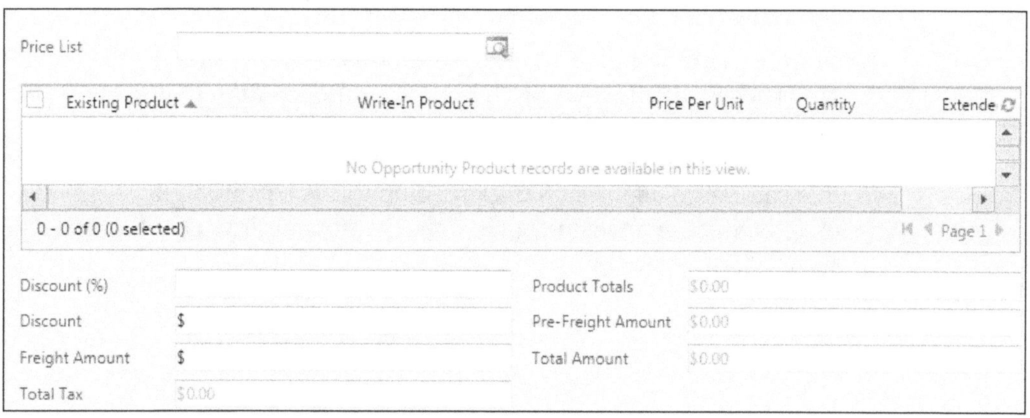

- vi. **Price List**: If the revenue method chosen is **System Provided**, select a pricelist to be applied to all of the opportunity's products.
- vii. **Discount %**: If you choose to apply a discount percentage to the whole opportunity, you can do so here.

viii. **Discount**: If the user chooses to apply a discount amount to the whole opportunity they can do so here.

ix. **Freight Amount**: If an additional freight amount is to be added to the total amount of the opportunity, it can be added here.

x. **Total Tax**: Total amount of tax applied to each of the products tied to the opportunity. Opportunity products will be discussed later in this chapter.

xi. **Product Totals**: Total net price of the products tied to the opportunity.

xii. **Pre-Freight Amount**: Total price of products tied to the opportunity plus all applicable taxes.

xiii. **Total Amount**: Total price of products toed to the opportunity, including taxes and freight.

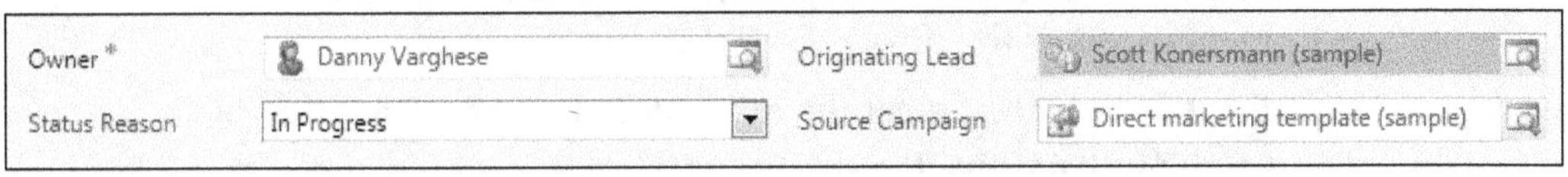

xiv. **Status Reason**: The opportunity status is explained below.

xv. **Originating Lead**: If a lead is converted to an opportunity, this lookup will be set to the lead who converted it; otherwise you can select the lead that originated this opportunity

xvi. **Source Campaign**: If a campaign response is converted to an opportunity, this field will be set to the campaign that the response came from. Alternatively, you can perform a lookup to find the campaign record. Being able to convert an opportunity to a campaign enables an organization to track campaign effectiveness by measuring how many opportunities came from a particular campaign.

5. Click on **Save**.

Opportunity status

The status of an entity, such as opportunity, defines the overall state of the entity. Status reason is a sub-category of status. For each status value, there may be one or more status reasons that further explain the status. According to MSDN, the table of status to status reason values is as follows:

State	State value	Status	Status value
Open	0	In Progress	1
Open	0	On Hold	2
Won	1	Won	3
Lost	2	Canceled	4
Lost	2	Out-Sold	5

Opportunity products

Products are discussed in the next chapter, but here we'll give a brief overview of how opportunities are tied to products. An opportunity can have multiple products associated to it. These are known as opportunity products and allows a user to add products to an opportunity that could be potentially sold to the customer.

> Opportunity products cannot be added unless a price list has been set on the opportunity itself. This is because the price of the product for that opportunity must come from the price list. Price lists will also be discussed in the next chapter.

Creating opportunity products

To create an opportunity product follow these steps:

1. Start CRM, click on the **Sales** module, and then click on **Opportunities**.
2. Find and open the opportunity to which you wish to add opportunity products.
3. Within the form, click inside the **Line Items** sub-grid.
4. On the **List Tools Opportunity Products** ribbon, in the **Records** group, click on **Add New Opportunity Product**.

> A price list must be set on the opportunity before an opportunity product can be added.

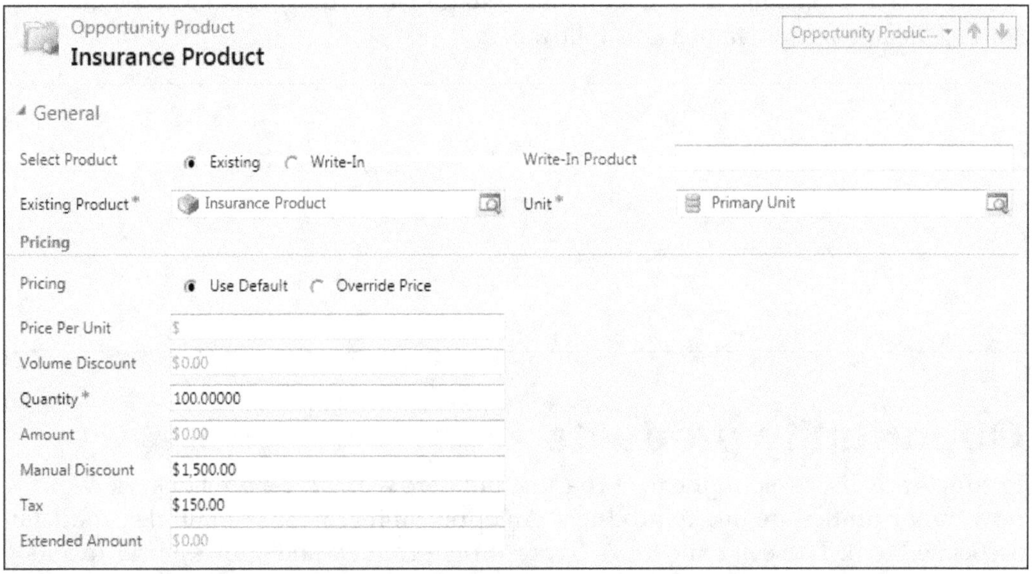

5. Enter the following required fields:

    i. **Select Product**: This is not a required field per se, but the field is defaulted to **Existing**. If you choose **Existing**, the **Existing Product** lookup will be enabled allowing the user to select a product from the product catalog. If you choose **Write-In,** the **Write-In Product** text field will become required, the **Pricing** field will automatically be set to **Override Price**, and the **Price Per Unit** field will become enabled.

    ii. **Existing Product** (if necessary).

    iii. **Write-In Product** (if necessary): A write-in product is a way for users to add a product to the opportunity that may not exist in the product catalog (the product catalog is explained in great detail in the next chapter). Also, many organizations may not keep a product catalog in CRM, but rather in some back-end accounting system like Microsoft Dynamics GP or AX. In these cases, write-in products offer flexibility to add a product to the opportunity.

    iv. **Unit**: If an existing product is required, the default unit is required for selection.

6. The following fields are not required, but are important to understand:
    i. **Pricing**: If **Use Default** is selected, on save of the record, the price is pulled from the price list and entered on the opportunity. If **Override Price** is selected, all the price fields will become enabled for you to enter your own price for the product.
    ii. **Price Per Unit**: Inherited from price list or manually entered. Note that you are allowed to enter a negative value to reflect a credit to the customer.
    iii. **Volume Discount**: If the product is taken from the product catalog and there is a volume discount for the product, it will be automatically applied here.
    iv. **Quantity**
    v. **Amount**: This is equivalent to (price per unit - volume discount) * quantity.
    vi. **Manual Discount**
    vii. **Tax**
    viii. **Extended Amount**: This is equivalent to Amount - Manual Discount + Tax
7. Click on **Save**.

Once an opportunity is created, there are several ways to manage them.

Managing opportunities

Opportunities can be managed like many other entities in CRM by having the ability to assign and share opportunity records. The steps to assign or share an opportunity is similar to the steps taken in assigning or sharing a lead, mentioned earlier this chapter.

At the end of a sales process, it will be the ultimate goal of the sales group to close the opportunity. Ideally, all opportunities would be closed as a "won" opportunity, but we all know sometimes life isn't always that easy.

Closing opportunities

When an opportunity is created, its status defaults to **Open**. When an organization's sales cycle is completed, the opportunity can be closed with one of two statuses—**Won** or **Lost**. By closing an opportunity, the record gets deactivated, and an opportunity close activity is created. This entity is used to store information about the revenue, why you closed the opportunity, the close date, and competitor information (if applicable). It also contains information about the user that created the opportunity.

To close an opportunity, follow these steps:

1. Start CRM, click on the **Sales** module, and then click on **Opportunities**.
2. Find and select the opportunity you wish you close.

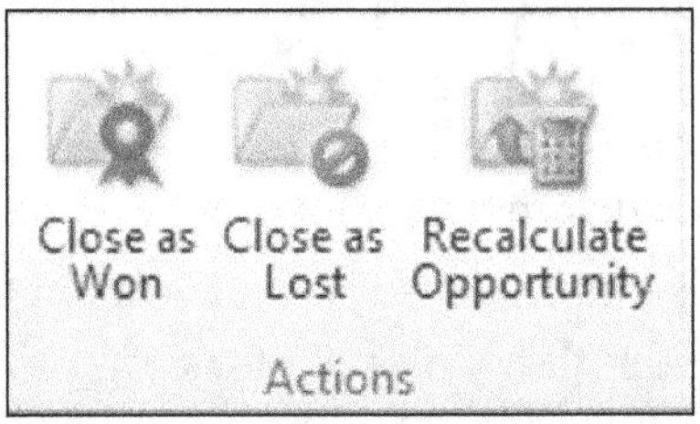

3. On the **Opportunities** ribbon bar, in the **Actions** group, click on either **Close as Won** or **Close as Lost**.

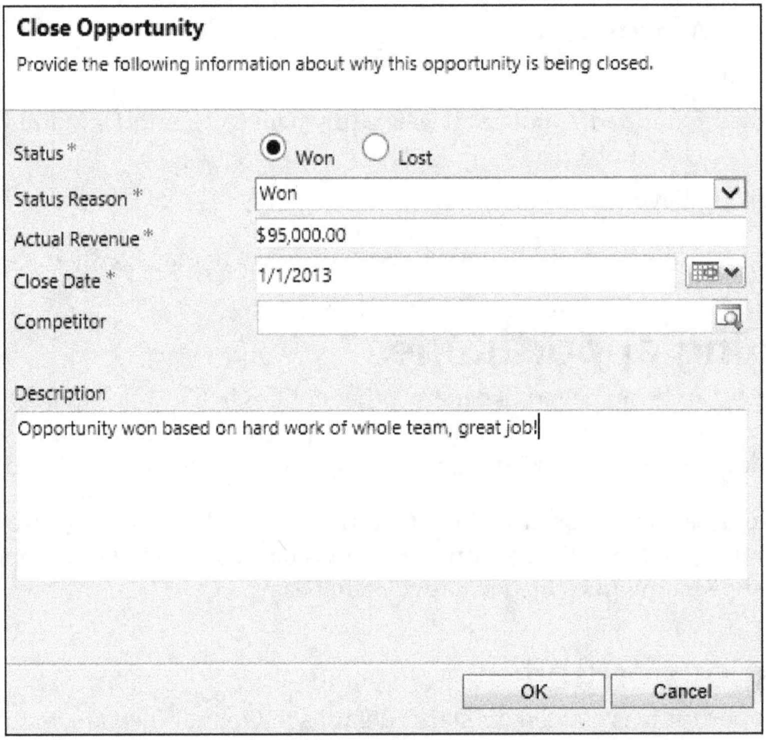

4. In the **Close Opportunity** dialog, enter the following required fields:
    i. **Status**: If you click on the **Close as Won** button, the status will be defaulted to **Won**, otherwise if you click on **Close as Lost** the status will be defaulted to **Lost**.

   ii. **Status Reason**: Based on the selection of **Status**, the **Status Reason** will change to indicate the reason for the opportunity being won or lost. The values for the status and status reason are listed in the section about **Opportunity Status**.

   iii. **Actual Revenue**: If the opportunity was won, the actual revenue will be defaulted to the estimated revenue from the opportunity, with the ability to change the value. If the opportunity is lost, the actual revenue will be set to $0.00.

   iv. **Close Date**: This will default to the current date.

5. Click on **OK**.

Microsoft Dynamics CRM does allow an opportunity to be re-opened after it has been closed. An example of why an organization would want to re-open an opportunity is if the opportunity was originally lost and then the customer expresses interest in the sale again.

Reopening opportunities

To reopen an opportunity record, follow these steps:

1. Start CRM, click on the **Sales** module, and then click on **Opportunities.**
2. Find the opportunity you wish to reopen and open the record.

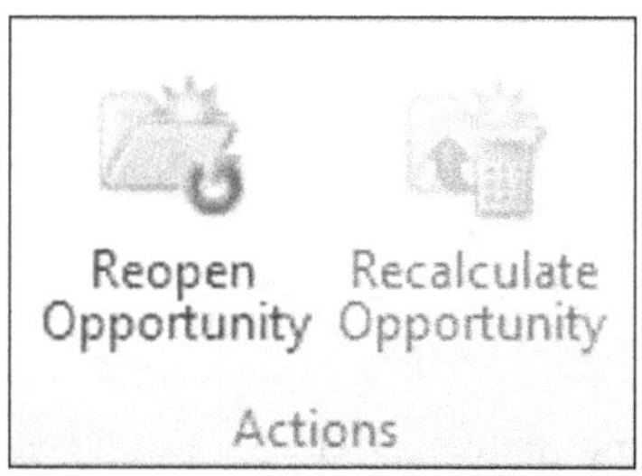

3. On the **Opportunity** ribbon bar, in the **Actions** group, click on **Reopen Opportunity**.
4. Click on **OK**.
5. In addition to reopening an opportunity, the record, while active, can have the totals recalculated at any time.

Recalculating an opportunity

The recalculate opportunity functionality is only available if the revenue field on an opportunity is set to **System Calculated** (as opposed to **User Provided**). The button to recalculate the opportunity is enabled, but if the **Revenue** field is set to **User Provided**, the record is simply saved and the form is refreshed. As opportunity products (or line items as they are displayed on the opportunity form) are added, the estimated revenue field on the opportunity is not updated. When the **Recalculate Opportunity** button is clicked, the sum of the total amount on all opportunity products are placed in the estimated revenue field in the opportunity.

Multi-currency and opportunities

CRM is a multi-currency system, which means each record with money fields can have a different currency. This feature allows an organization to create and manage opportunities (among other entities such as quotes, orders, and invoices) with multiple currencies.

When CRM is initially installed, a **base currency** is set for the system and cannot be changed. All other currencies are known as **transaction currencies**. For example, a system might have a base currency of United States Dollars (USD), and transaction currencies like the British Pound (GBP) and the Indian Rupee (Rs). The exchange rate in CRM is the value in the transaction currency equivalent to one base currency. For example, the exchange rate in the system might be 45 Rs to 1 USD.

As it relates to opportunities, the currency field defaults to the base currency. However, it can be changed as long as there are no opportunity products, quotes, orders, or invoices associated to it. If an opportunity does not have any of these related records associated to it, then the currency can be changed up until the opportunity is closed. If a currency is changed on the opportunity, then a price list with the same currency must also be set.

Every record with monetary fields has a field for the transaction currency amount and another for the base currency amount. For example, the **Estimated Revenue** field on an opportunity is a money field representing the transaction currency selected for the opportunity. There is a corresponding base currency field called **Estimate Revenue (Base)** which uses the defined exchange rate and displays the base currency amount. Let's say the base currency of CRM is US dollar (USD), the currency selected on the opportunity is Rupees (Rs.), and the exchange rate is set to 1 USD = 45 Rs. If the **Estimated Revenue** amount is 45 Rs, then the Estimated Revenue (Base) amount is 1 USD.

This is important to note in case an opportunity has been created with a currency different than that of the base system currency. If the exchange rate is changed, then opportunities created before the change will not be updated, and the base currency amounts will not be changed to reflect the new exchange rate. The reason for this is that CRM preserves the exchange rate at the time the opportunity was created, so fluctuations in rates won't affect the organization or customer unfairly.

Viewing opportunities

There are a number of out of the box views that enable an organization to intelligently search for data. Samples of the views available for opportunities are:

- **Closed Opportunities**: Lists all opportunities that are closed, with a status of either won or lost.
- **Closed Opportunities in Current Fiscal Year**: Lists all opportunities that were closed in the current fiscal year, either with a status of won or lost.
- **My Closed Opportunities**: Lists all closed opportunities owned by the current logged in user.
- **My Closed Opportunities in Current Fiscal Year**: Lists all opportunities closed in the current fiscal year and that are owned by the current logged in user.
- **Open Opportunities**: Lists all open opportunities.
- **Won Opportunities**: Lists all closed opportunities with a status of won.
- **Lost Opportunities**: Lists all closed opportunities with a status of lost.

Creating competitors

To create a competitor, follow these steps:

1. Start CRM, go to the **Sales** module, and then click on **Competitors**.

2. On the **Competitors** ribbon bar, in the **Records** group, click on the **New** button.

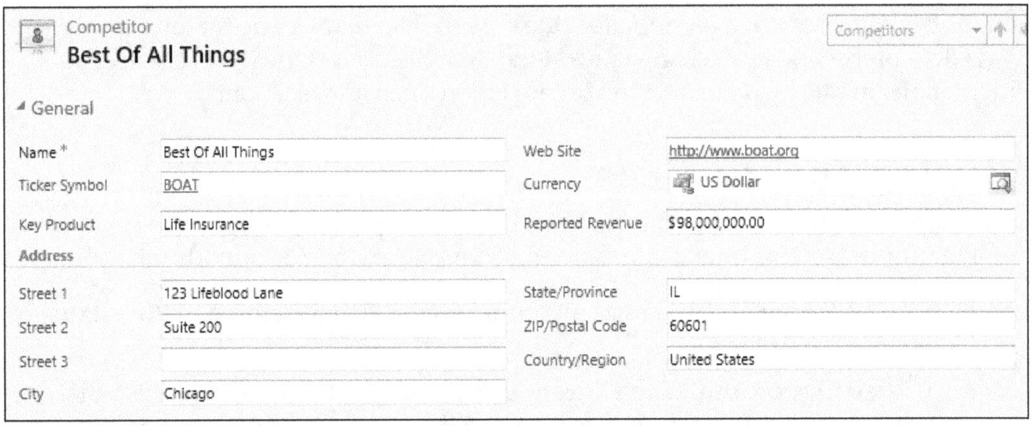

3. Fill out the following required fields:
   i. **Name**
4. The following fields are not required, but worth mentioning:
   i. **Ticker Symbol**: This is an abbreviation used to uniquely identify a publicly traded company. For example, the ticker symbol for Microsoft is MSFT.
   ii. **Key Product**: A product that the competitor is known for, potentially a product that differentiates themselves from your organization.

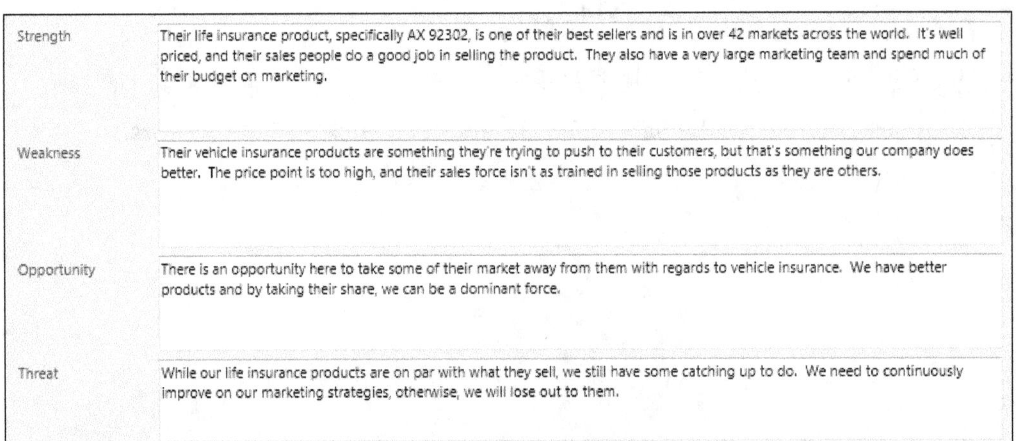

   iii. **Strength**: Key strengths to note about your competitor.

  iv. **Weaknesses**: Areas where your organization might have a competitive advantage over.
  v. **Opportunity**: Areas where there is an opportunity to win business from this competitor.
  vi. **Threat**: Areas where your organization might lose business to the competitor

5. Click on **Save**.

Tracking competition on an opportunity can help sales people engage their customers more effectively throughout the selling process. As opportunities are created and managed, it's essential that sales people and their managers can track progress of an individual's or team's goals.

Creating and managing goals

Microsoft Dynamics CRM 2011 enables an organization to track goals for an individual or a team. These goals can be rolled up by a manager to see how a certain group of individuals is progressing.

Business scenarios

Race2Win Insurance Company's sales teams have been working their opportunities and progressing them through the various sales stages. Each sales person within the company has a sales quota to meet by the end of the year. Each fiscal quarter, the sales manager meets with each member of the sales team to review progress towards the quota. One of the key metrics the sales managers follow is the amount of actual revenue generated from won (closed) opportunities.

Race2Win was able to accomplish this by using a feature called goals. First, a **goal metric** was created to specify whether to measure a *count* or an *amount* of something. Next, a **rollup field** on the goal metric was created to apply the metric on a specific field. In this case, Race2Win wanted to track the total amount (metric) of actual revenue of an opportunity that is closed as won (rollup field). Next, a **rollup query** was created to search for opportunity records to measure the goals against. Lastly, a **goal** was created to tie the metric and rollup query to a specific **target** and time period.

Setting up goals can be tricky, so let us take a look at each step in order.

Goal metric

The first step in the process of setting up a goal is to create a goal metric. Goal metrics are a way to measure the goal and include some sort of metric for a specific entity. For example, with marketing, a goal metric could be a count of the number of campaign responses received. In this case the metric is the actual count of something, and the count is applied to the campaign response entity. Another example is the total actual revenue of all won (closed) opportunities.

Creating a goal metric

To create a goal metric, follow these steps:

1. Start **CRM**, go to the **Sales** Module, and then click on **Goal Metrics**.
2. On the **Goal Metrics** ribbon bar, in the **Records** group, click on **New**.

3. Complete the following fields:
   i. **Name**: Enter a clear, concise name for the goal metric.
   ii. **Metric Type**: Choose **Count** or **Amount**. Count should be used when you want to count the number of records selected by the goal metric. Amount should be used when you want to sum the amount of a selected field within the records selected by the goal metric.
   iii. **Amount Data Type**: If the metric type is set to **Amount**, this field will be enabled giving the user choices of *Money*, *Decimal*, or *Integer*.
4. The **Track Stretch Target** field is not required, but if this checkbox is selected, then on the goal record there will be two target fields shown. If not selected, then only one target field will be shown. The target field is explained more when we cover the *Creating goals* section.
5. Click on **Save**, but do not close the record.

Once the goal metric has been created, the next step is to create rollup fields for the goal metric.

Rollup fields

Rollup fields are used to define which entities and fields will be used to calculate the value of the target. There are three types of rollup fields:

- **Actual**: Measures the current value of the target. For example, measuring the actual revenue on a closed opportunity that has been won.
- **In Progress**: Measures the value of what is in progress for the target. For example, the estimated revenue of all open opportunities.
- **Custom**: An example of this is to count the number of opportunities lost.

Creating rollup fields

To create a rollup field, follow these steps:

1. Continuing from the steps outlined in the *Creating a goal metric* section, click inside the **Rollup Fields** sub-grid, and then on the **Rollup Fields** ribbon bar, inside the **Records** group, click on **Add New Rollup Field**.

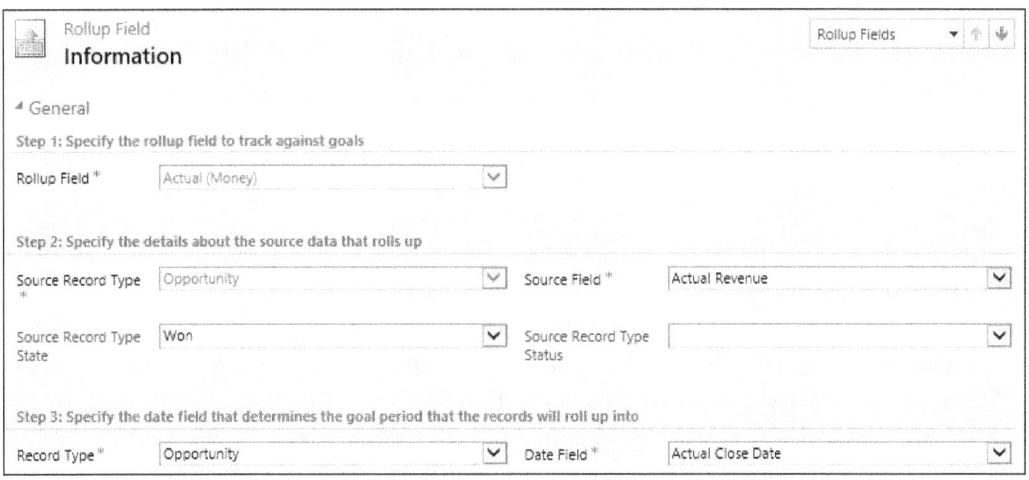

2. Complete the following fields:
   i. **Rollup Field**: Choose from **Actual, In Progress**, and **Custom**.
   ii. **Source Record Type**: The type of record to define the rollup field for. In the examples we've been using, we would set this value to **Opportunity**.

iii. **Source Record Type State**: The state that the record should have in order to be included in this specific rollup value. For example, if we wanted to track the actual revenue of opportunities we've won, then this field would be set to **Won**.

iv. **Source Field**: The field used to measure the **Actual, In Progress** or **Custom** value on. An example here would be *Actual Revenue*. Note that this field is only required when the metric type on the goal metric is set to **Amount**.

v. **Source Record Type Status**: The status reason that the record should have in order to be included in this specific rollup value.

vi. **Record Type**: Type of record used to define the date field that determines the goal period that the records will roll up into. An example of this would be Opportunity.

vii. **Date Field**: Date field that determines the goal period records will roll up into. For example, if the goal is to measure the actual revenue of closed opportunities in a fiscal year, then the system needs a date to check to see if it's in the current fiscal year. In the example we've been using, this date would be the *Actual Close Date*.

3. Click on **Save and Close**.
4. Repeat steps 1 to 3 until all of the necessary rollup fields have been created.
5. Click on **Save and Close** to save and close the goal metric.

The next step is to create a rollup query that will pull in all of the records that you want to measure against.

Rollup query

Rollup queries help you gather data about a goal and all child goals. Thinking back to the business scenario about goals, Race2Win's sales managers wanted sales people on their team to track individual goals. A rollup query can be used to gather the data to measure the goals against. For example, the query could search for all opportunity records with a status of closed and a closed date in the current fiscal year.

Creating rollup queries

To create a rollup query, follow these steps:

1. Start CRM, go to the **Sales** module, and then click on **Rollup Queries**.
2. On the **Rollup Queries** ribbon bar, in the **Records** group, click on **New**.

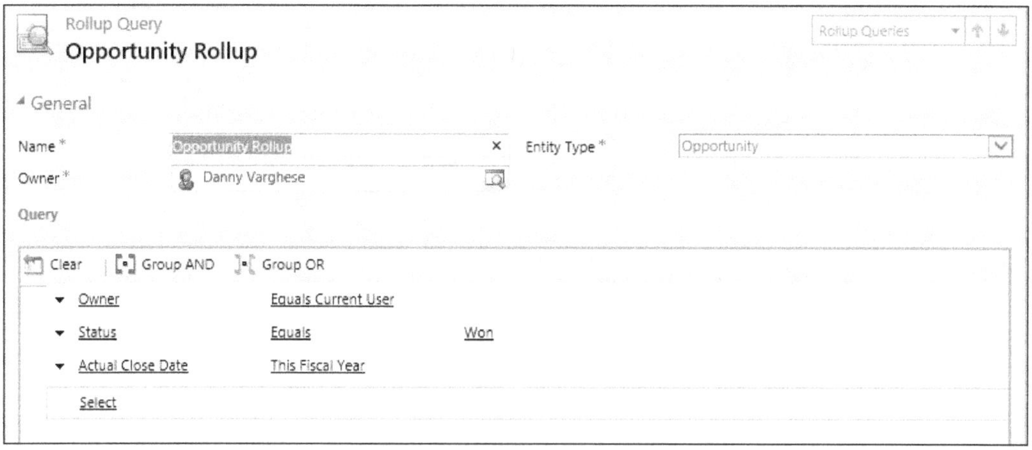

3. Enter the following required fields:
   i. **Name**: Enter a clear, concise name for the rollup query
   ii. **Owner**: Defaults to the currently logged in user
   iii. **Entity Type**: Define the entity for which this query will be run
4. Under **Query**, use the controls to add the criteria for your query. The criteria that you can add depends on the entity type you have chosen.
5. To test the query, click on **View Records**.
6. Click on **Save and Close**.

The next step is to create the actual goal itself.

Creating goals

To create a goal, follow these steps:

1. Start CRM, go to the **Sales** module, and then click on **Goals**.
2. On the **Goals** ribbon bar, in the **Records** group, click on **New**.

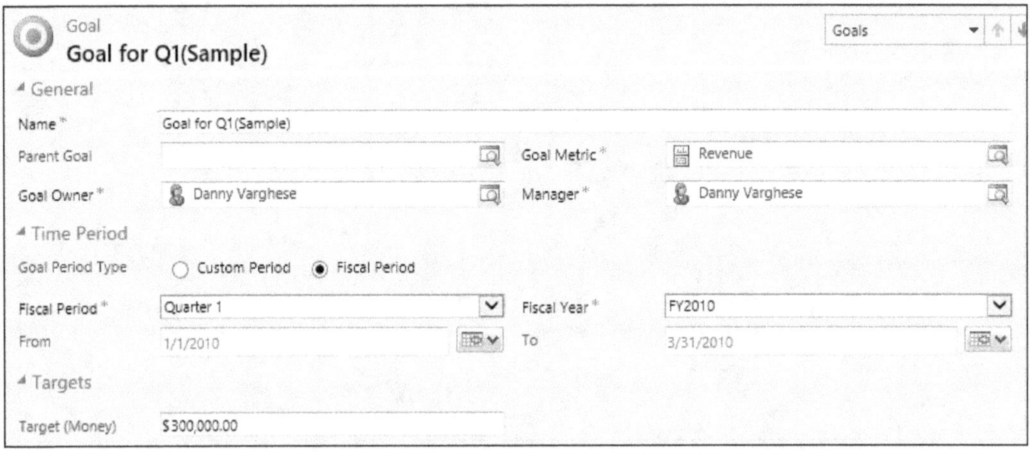

3. Complete the following required fields:
    i. **Name**: Enter a clear, concise name for the goal.
    ii. **Goal Owner**: The user for whom the goal is being tracked.
    iii. **Manager**: The goal manager is defaulted to the user creating the goal, and this person has full access to the record. An example of where the manager would be different than the owner is if a sales manager creates a goal for one of his team members. As soon as a goal is created, the goal record gets shared with the goal owner. Whenever this goal has a parent goal associated to it, the manager of the parent goal also has access to see this goal.
    iv. **Goal Period Type**: Select either **Custom Period** or **Fiscal Period**. If **Custom Period** is selected, then **Fiscal Period** and **Fiscal Year** on the form are disabled, and the **From** and **To** dates are enabled. The opposite is true if **Fiscal Period** is selected, in which case the **From** and **To** fields are auto populated with the **Fiscal Period** start and end dates.
    v. **Fiscal Period** (if applicable)
    vi. **Fiscal Year** (if applicable)
    vii. **From** (if applicable)
    viii. **To** (if applicable)

ix. **Roll Up Only from Child Goals**: If **Yes** is selected, then the values from the child goals only are rolled up.

x. **Record Set for Rollup**: If **Owned by goal owner** is selected, then the records that satisfy the rollup query and have the same owner as the goal will be evaluated, otherwise all records that satisfy the query criteria will be evaluated.

4. The following fields are not required, but are important to mention:

   i. **Parent Goal**: If you are creating a child goal, then you can attach the parent goal here. In the business scenario for goals, above, a manager is trying to roll up all of his team's goals into one goal. His team member's goals will each have this field set to one parent goal, which is owned by the manager.

   ii. **Target**: This is a specific value for the goal metric over a given period of time. For example, if the goal metric is to measure the sum of actual revenue on opportunities that were won, the target could be 1,000,000.00 USD in the current fiscal period.

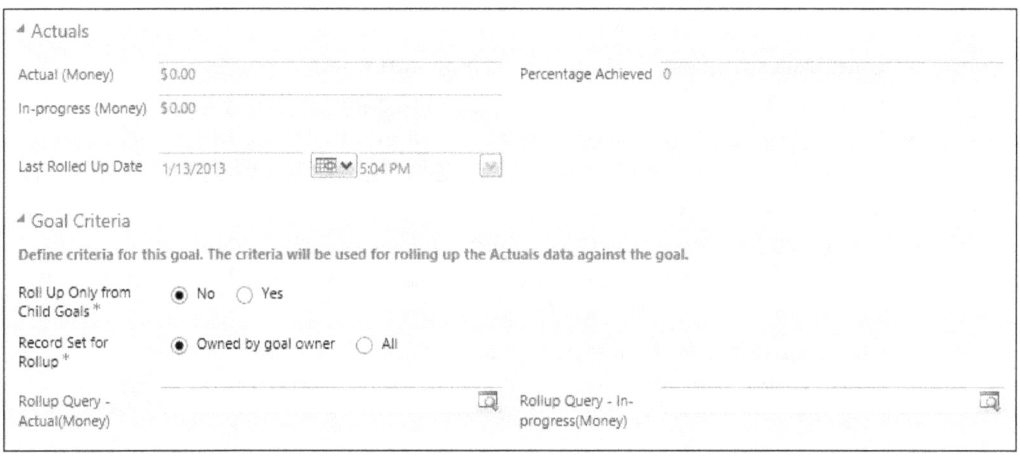

   iii. The **Actuals** section of the form is not for user entry. The fields here display the actual values of the goal metrics since the last time the goal was recalculated. The **Last Rolled Up Date** is the date on which the goal was last recalculated.

   iv. **Rollup Query - Actual**: Select the rollup query to be used to evaluate the actual values of the goal metric.

   v. **Rollup Query – In-progress**: Select the rollup query to be used to evaluate the in-progress values of the goal metric.

Reporting and analysis

In regards to sales data, there are specific out of the box views, charts, reports, and dashboards to help an organization analyze and make educated decisions around sales. Let's take a closer look at the system reports and dashboards around sales.

Reporting

CRM comes with the following out of the box reports:

- **Account Distribution**: This report examines the top revenue-generating accounts by using two charts. The earned revenue chart displays the earned revenue grouped by product, territory, or industry. The accounts count chart displays the amount of earned revenue using the same grouping as the earned revenue chart. This report uses opportunities that are closed as won.
- **Account Overview**: This report displays a one-page overview of an account, including related contact information, summaries of opportunities, and case data.
- **Account Summary**: This report displays the history of an account, and what is scheduled to occur in the future. It shows a chronological summary for an account, including service and sales data, and notes.
- **Competitor Win Loss**: This report is used to compare your sales team against your competitors. It displays a list of competitors, with data on open, closed (won and lost) opportunities for each. The report only pulls in opportunities with competitors associated to it.
- **Lead Source Effectiveness**: This report shows all leads, along with which leads generate opportunities. It the percentage of qualified leads, and leads that generate revenue for each lead category.
- **Neglected Accounts**: This report lists accounts that have not been communicated with recently. The report displays a chart with accounts that have had no activities completed within a specified number of days.
- **Neglected Leads**: This report lists leads that have not been communicated with recently. It displays a chart with leads that have had no activities completed within a specified number of days.
- **Progress Against Goals**: This report displays sales progress against the organization's sales goals. It displays a chart with the target and actual values of the goals.
- **Sales History**: This report shows a history of sales performance by sales representative. It displays a chart of both lost revenue (from lost opportunities) and won revenue (from won opportunities).
- **Sales Pipeline**: This report displays a chart of potential sales grouped by user, sales territory, customer territory, date, products, rating, or sales stage.

Dashboards

Dashboards offer a visual representation of data in the form of charts, HTML pages, web sites and other sources. CRM comes with the following out of the box dashboards to help represent sales data:

- Sales Activity Dashboard
- Sales Performance Dashboard

Sales Activity Dashboard

The Sales Activity Dashboard displays the following charts:

- **Sales Pipeline**: A funnel chart displaying a sum of the estimated revenue of open opportunities owned by the current logged-in user, grouped by pipeline phase.
- **Percentage Achieved of Goals**: A line graph displaying the percentage of each goal owned by the current logged-in user that has been achieved.
- **My Open Leads by Source**: A pie chart of open leads owned by the current logged-in user, grouped by lead source.
- **My Top Opportunities**: A bar chart of opportunities owned by the current logged-in user, displayed in order of estimated revenue, largest to smallest.
- **Top Customers**: A bar chart of accounts or contacts that have opportunities, ordered by customers with the highest estimated revenue.

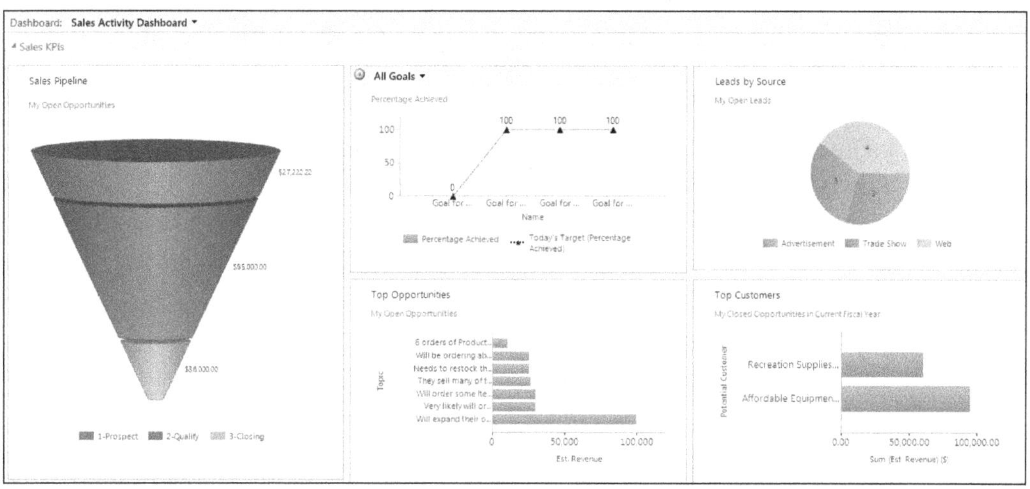

The dashboard also contains a view of open activities owned by the currently logged-in user.

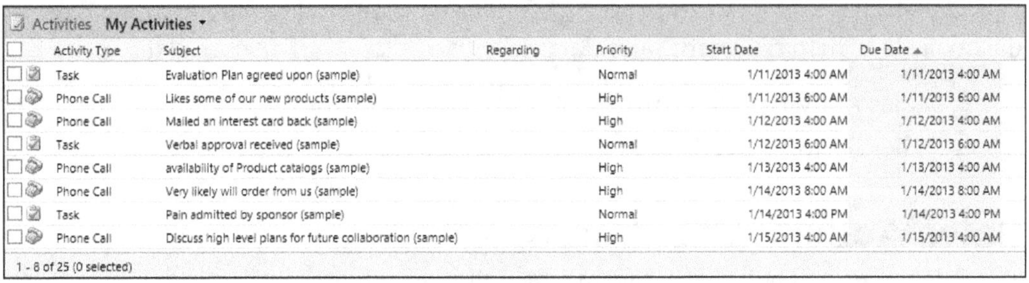

Activities **My Activities** ▾

Activity Type	Subject	Regarding	Priority	Start Date	Due Date ▲
Task	Evaluation Plan agreed upon (sample)		Normal	1/11/2013 4:00 AM	1/11/2013 4:00 AM
Phone Call	Likes some of our new products (sample)		High	1/11/2013 6:00 AM	1/11/2013 6:00 AM
Phone Call	Mailed an interest card back (sample)		High	1/12/2013 4:00 AM	1/12/2013 4:00 AM
Task	Verbal approval received (sample)		Normal	1/12/2013 6:00 AM	1/12/2013 6:00 AM
Phone Call	availability of Product catalogs (sample)		High	1/13/2013 4:00 AM	1/13/2013 4:00 AM
Phone Call	Very likely will order from us (sample)		High	1/14/2013 8:00 AM	1/14/2013 8:00 AM
Task	Pain admitted by sponsor (sample)		Normal	1/14/2013 4:00 PM	1/14/2013 4:00 PM
Phone Call	Discuss high level plans for future collaboration (sample)		High	1/15/2013 4:00 AM	1/15/2013 4:00 AM

1 - 8 of 25 (0 selected)

Sales Performance Dashboard

The Sales Performance Dashboard contains the following charts:

- **Sales Pipeline**: A funnel chart displaying a sum of the estimated revenue of open opportunities owned by the current logged-in user, grouped by pipeline phase.
- **Goal Progress – My Goals for the Period**: A stacked bar chart displaying the progress of goals (in terms of goal metric count or amount) owned by the currently logged-in user.
- **Goal Progress – My Groups Revenue Goal for this Period**: A stacked chart displaying the progress of goals (in terms of goal metric count or amount) where the goal manager is the current logged-in user.
- **Percentage Achieved - My Groups Revenue Goal for this Period**: A stacked chart displaying the percentage achieved where the goal manager is the current logged-in user.
- **Sales Leaderboard**: A bar chart displaying the users with the highest total of actual revenue for opportunities.

- **Deals Won vs. Deals Lost by Current User**: A bar chart comparing the opportunity revenue won with the opportunity revenue lost by the current logged-in user.

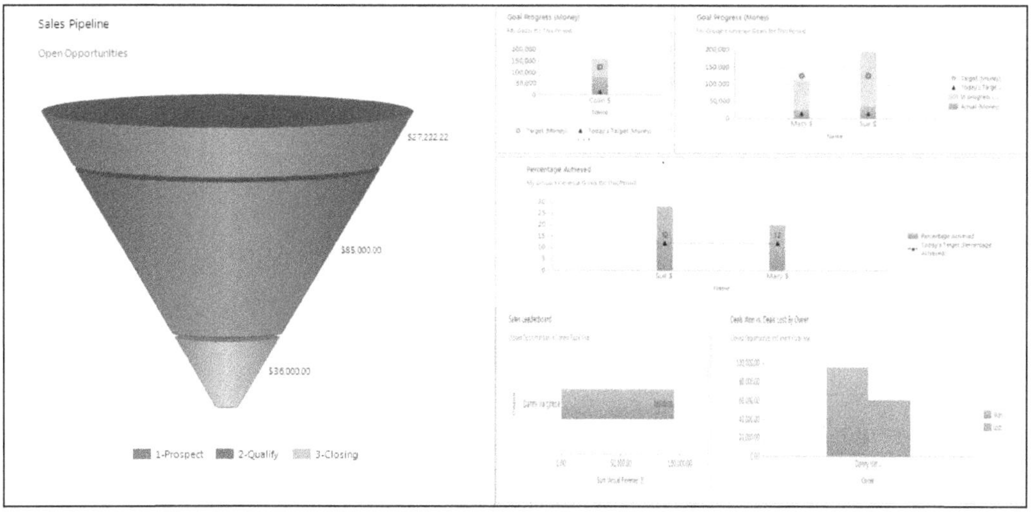

Test your knowledge

Q. 1. What are the statuses for a lead?

1. Open, New, Contacted.
2. Open, Qualified, Disqualified.
3. Lost, Cannot Contact, No Longer Interested, Canceled.
4. New, Contacted, Qualified.

Q. 2. Leads can be: (Choose all that apply.)

1. Qualified.
2. Disqualified.
3. Won.
4. Lost.
5. Assigned.
6. Shared.

Q. 3. What happens when account records are merged?

1. Account records cannot be merged; that only applies to contacts.
2. A master and duplicate record are created.
3. Field values selected in the merge dialog are copied to the master record, and the duplicate record is deactivated.
4. Field values selected in the merge dialog are copied to the master record, and the duplicate record is deleted.

Q. 4. What are the different ways an opportunity can be created?
(Choose all that apply.)

1. Converting an activity.
2. Converting a case.
3. Converting a lead.
4. Manually.

Q. 5. State whether true or false: Once an opportunity is closed, it can be re-opened.

Q. 6. After creating an opportunity, the sales person realized the incorrect currency was set. What is the best approach to changing the currency?

1. Change the system default currency.
2. Open the opportunity and change the default currency even if there are orders tied to it.
3. Open the opportunity and change the default currency, only if there are no opportunity products, quotes, orders or invoices associated to it.
4. You cannot change the currency once the opportunity is created, so you must clone the opportunity and then change the currency on the clone record.

Q. 7. What happens in relation to opportunities with a specific currency, when the exchange rate for that currency is changed?

1. The new exchange rate is reflected on all open opportunities with that currency.
2. The new exchange rate is reflected on all open and closed opportunities with that currency.
3. The new exchange rate is reflected only on closed opportunities with that currency.
4. The new exchange rate is reflected only on any new opportunities created with that currency.

Q. 8. What is a goal metric? (Choose all that apply.)

1. A way to measure a goal.
2. A way to measure a goal over time.
3. A way to measure the count of something.
4. A way to measure the count or amount of something.

Q. 9. Describe the security that exists around the goal manager field.

1. The goal manager has access to the current goal only.
2. The goal manager has no additional security associated with it.
3. The goal manager has access to the current goal and all child goals.
4. None of the above.
5. All of the above.

Q. 10. What is the Sales History report?

1. This report shows past sales performance by sales representative.
2. This report displays a chart of past sales grouped by user, sales territory, customer territory, date, products, rating, or sales stage.
3. This report shows a history of sales by account or contact.
4. This report shows a history of sales for the entire organization.

Summary

Leads are organizations or individuals that can potentially do business with an organization. Leads can be created manually, but an added feature in CRM is the ability to create a lead from an e-mail. Throughout the life-cycle of a lead, the record can be assigned to a user or team, shared with one or more users or teams and deactivated or reactivated. Many organizations go through a lead qualification process to determine if that lead will in fact result in the purchase of a product or service. Lead records have various statuses based on if the lead is open, qualified, or disqualified. When a lead record is qualified, a new account, contact and/or opportunity is created.

Accounts and contacts are two central components of any CRM system as they enable an organization to manage their customers. They can both be created in multiple ways, such as through the file menu on the ribbon, within a lookup dialog, or for a contact through an associated view. Account and contact records can be shared, assigned, deactivated, activated, and merged. Merging two records will deactivate the duplicate record, and associate all related records (activities and opportunities) to the master record.

When a customer is interested in purchasing products or services, an organization can track these by using opportunities. Opportunities in CRM are a way to track potential sales. Opportunity records can be created by converting an activity, converting a lead, or manually creating an opportunity. Opportunities, like all other entities, have a status field that defines the state of the record. It also has a status reason field, which is a sub-category of the status, and is used to further define the state of the record. When an opportunity is created, the default status is open, and when the opportunity is closed, the status can be set to won or lost. There are various status reasons for each of those status values.

Opportunity products are a way to associate products to an opportunity. They cannot be added unless a price list has been set on the opportunity. An opportunity can be closed when it has been either won or lost. CRM allows an opportunity to be re-opened. An example is if the opportunity was originally lost, but the customer expresses interest again, in which case that same opportunity can be re-opened. As products are added, the estimated revenue field can be re-calculated, providing up-to-date information. The currency field on an opportunity defaults to the base currency, however it can be changed as long as there are no opportunity products, quotes, orders, or invoices associated to it. If an opportunity does not have any of those related records associated to it, then the currency can be changed up until the opportunity is closed. If a currency is changed on the opportunity, then a price list with the same currency must also be set. If the exchange rate is changed for a given currency, this will not affect any existing opportunities. However, any opportunities created after the exchange rate change will have the new exchange rate applied.

One way that CRM helps an organization to monitor sales performance is with the use of goals. In order to properly setup goals, goal metrics must be created first. Once a goal metric is created, rollup fields for the metric must be defined. Next, a rollup query must be created to define search criteria for the records to measure the goals against. Lastly, a goal is created tying the goal metric and rollup query to a specified time period. Goals are one way to analyze sales data, but another method is by using reports and dashboards.

In the next chapter, we'll look more closely at managing products within CRM by using the product catalog and how an organization can manage sales order processing.

5

Managing the Product Catalog and Order Processing

In this chapter you will learn about:

- The product catalog
- Unit groups
- Creating and managing products
- Creating and managing price lists
- Discount lists
- Creating and managing quotes
- Creating and managing orders
- Creating and managing invoices
- Reporting and analysis

An introduction to the product catalog

The product catalog in Microsoft Dynamics CRM consists of products and prices. It provides a central location for managing any goods and services that an organization might sell, along with their respective prices and/or discounts.

Business scenarios

Race2Win Insurance Company has a number of clients that were attained through successful marketing campaigns, which generated a number of leads, which in turn led to a number of opportunities. These opportunities include a range of consulting services to determine the best possible insurance coverage. Consulting services are non-tangible, non-inventory items. Along with these services, Race2Win provides welcome kits which include Race2Win branded souvenirs, safety products, and brochures. These products and services can all be managed via the product catalog.

If you recall from the previous chapter, products can be associated to an opportunity and the estimated revenue can be automatically calculated. When the opportunity is configured in this manner, the system utilizes the product catalog, which uses **products**, **unit groups**, **price lists**, and **discount lists** to calculate a more accurate estimated revenue number.

To enable this business scenario, the organization will have to set up the product catalog. Setting up the product catalog entails creating the following items, in order:

- Unit groups
- Products
- Price list(s)
- Discount list(s) (optional)

Unit groups

A unit group contains the base unit in which a product is available. For example, Race2Win Insurance Company bills out its consultants at a certain rate per hour. The base unit in this case can be 1 hour. The unit group is then comprised of all different increments of the base unit. An example of this is a unit group of one consulting day which is equivalent to 8 hours (8 base units). When a unit group is created, a **primary unit** is needed, which is the core and basic unit from which all other units are created. This may seem a bit confusing at first, but let us try to simplify the definition by providing an example.

Let's take Race2Win Insurance Company's consulting services as an example. They can create a unit group called "One Day" which would contain a quantity of 8 primary units (8 hours). They can also create a unit group called "One Week" which would contain a quantity of 40 primary units (40 hours). To create a unit group, perform the following steps:

1. Start CRM, go to **Settings**, and then under the **Business** section in the left-hand navigation pane, click on **Product Catalog**.
2. On the **Product Catalog** page, click on **Unit Groups**.
3. On the **Unit Groups** ribbon bar in the **Records** group, click on **New**.
4. In the **Create Unit Group** dialog window, enter the following:
    - **Name**: A clear, concise name for the unit group
    - **Primary Unit**: This is the base unit for this unit group

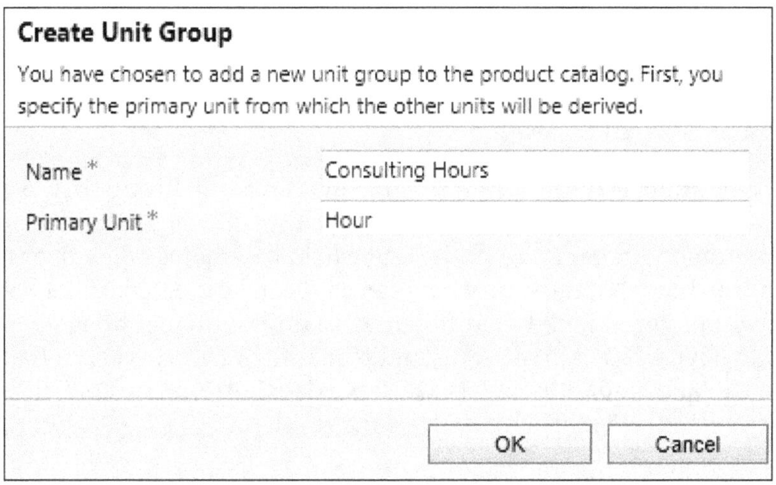

5. Click on **OK**.
6. In the left-hand navigation pane, click on **Units**. You'll see the primary unit entered in step 4 in the list of units.
7. To add more units, go to the **Units** ribbon bar in the **Records** group, and click on **Add New Unit**.

8. Enter the following required information:
    - **Name**: A clear, concise name for the unit.
    - **Quantity**: This is the quantity of the base unit. For example, if the base unit is 1 hour, and you enter the quantity here of `8`, then the total quantity of hours charged will be 1 x 8 = 8 hours.
    - **Base Unit**: Search for the base unit for the unit group.

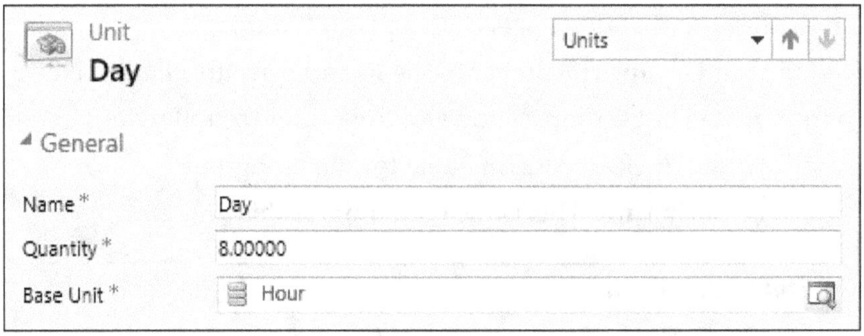

9. Click on **Save and Close**.

There can be multiple ways to configure units within a unit group. In the previous example, we created a unit group called `Consulting Hours`. The unit group contained a primary unit of `Hour`, and a unit called `Day` that is equivalent to eight primary units (8 hours). If necessary, another unit can be created called `Work Week`, which can be configured with two different base units and quantities. The `Work Week` unit can have a base unit of `Hour`, and a quantity of `40` (1 week = 40 hours), or a base unit of `Day` and a quantity of `5` (1 week = 5 days). As you can see, the base unit can be interchanged and still achieve the same results.

Creating and managing products

Products in Microsoft Dynamics CRM 2011 can be defined as any goods or services that an organization might sell. These products can be tangible items, or they can be services that an organization may provide, such as consulting services.

Creating products

To create a product, perform the following steps:

1. Start CRM, go to the **Settings** module, and under the **Business** section click on **Product Catalog**.
2. On the **Product Catalog** page, click on **Products**.

3. On the **Products** ribbon bar in the **Records** group, click on **New**.
4. Enter the following required information:
    - **ID**: Product ID, which can be anything, including numbers and letters.
    - **Name**: A clear, concise name for the product.
    - **Subject**: Subjects can be used to help classify products, which can be helpful when reporting and searching. Subjects are explained in greater detail in *Chapter 7, Managing Service Management Applications*.
    - **Unit Group**
    - **Default Unit**
    - **Decimal Supported**: Number of decimals used in the cost of the product. Usually two decimal places are used, but to avoid any calculation/rounding issues, some organizations opt to use whole numbers for prices; however that is a rare case.

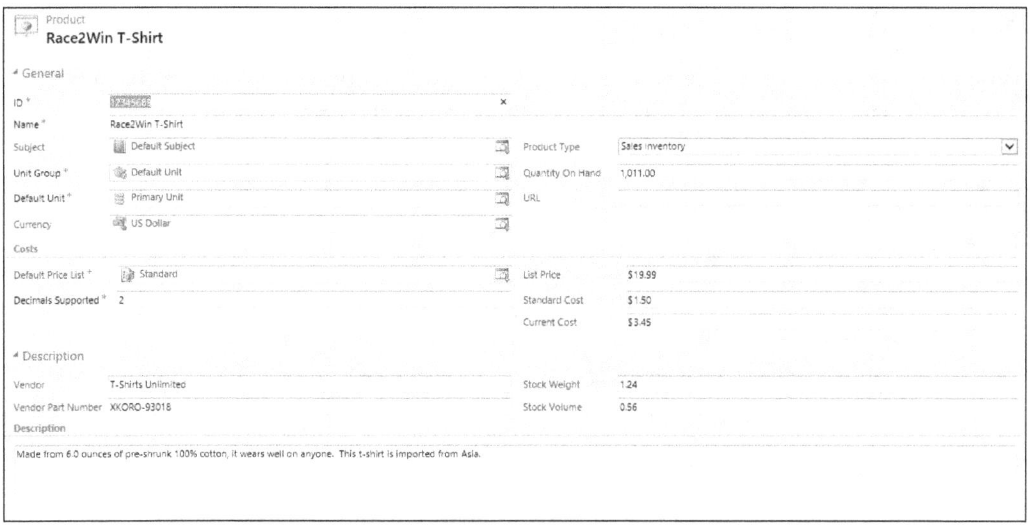

5. The following fields are not required, but are worth noting:
    - **Product Type**: Select the category of the product. The default values are: **Sales Inventory**, **Miscellaneous Charges**, **Services**, and **Flat Fees**.
    - **Quantity On Hand**: Current inventory in stock. Please note that this is a field that the user enters manually. Any integration to a back-end system such as Microsoft Dynamics GP or Microsoft Dynamics AX is *not* out of the box CRM functionality.

  - **Default Price List**: Price lists are discussed more in-depth later in this chapter, but for now, this is a read-only field until the form is saved. A product may be associated to multiple price lists, and although default price list is not required, after you save the product record, it is recommended to set a default price list. Then, if an account or contact record does not contain a price list, the default price list will be used for order processing.
  - **Standard Cost**: This is the standard cost of the item over a period of time.
  - **Current Cost**: The current cost to make or purchase the product.
  - **Vendor**: If the product is manufactured by another vendor and being re-sold by your organization, this field can be used to track who that vendor is.

6. Click on **Save and Close**.

Managing products

When a product is created, it can be classified into categories by using the subject field. CRM provides an easy way to change the subject on one or more products.

Reclassifying products

To reclassify a product, perform the following steps:

1. Start CRM, go to the **Settings** module, and under the **Business** section click on **Product Catalog**.
2. On the **Product Catalog** page, click on **Products**.
3. Select one or more products to change the subject for.
4. On the **Products** ribbon bar in the **Actions** group, click on **Reclassify**.
5. Look up the subject that you wish to change for the product(s).

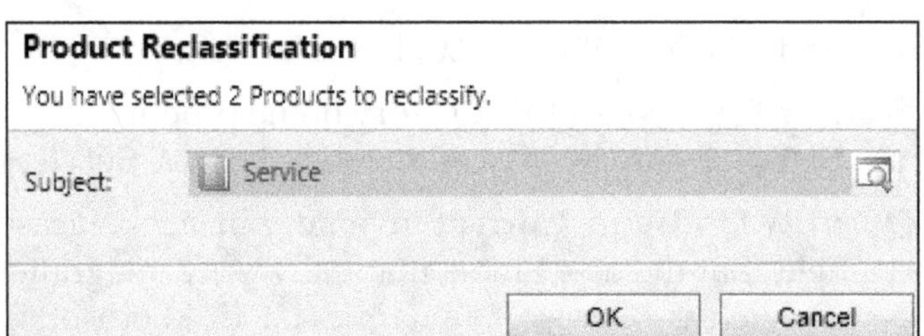

6. Click on **OK**.

As mentioned when creating a product, the default price list is disabled. After the product has been created, the default price list can be set. A product must be associated to a price list before that price list can be set as the default.

Setting the default price list

To set the default price list for a product, perform the following steps:

1. Start CRM, go to the **Settings** module, and under the **Business** section click on **Product Catalog**.
2. On the **Product Catalog** page, click on **Products**.
3. Find and open the product record for which you wish to set the default price.
4. Click on the lookup icon next to the **Default Price List** field.
5. Find and select the price list that you wish to set as the default.
6. Click on **OK**
7. Click on **Save and Close**.

Converting a product to a kit

Products can be bundled into kits. For example, if an organization sells certain products that also come with free items such as a hat or a mug, these can be combined into a kit. Another example is if an organization sells textbooks along with an attached CD. The textbooks and CDs can be separate products in the product catalog, but they can be combined to form a product kit.

To convert a product to a kit, perform the following steps:

1. Start CRM, go to the **Settings** module, and under the **Business** section click on **Product Catalog**.
2. On the **Product Catalog** page, click on **Products**.
3. Find the product that you want to convert to a kit, and open the record.
4. On the **Product** ribbon bar in the **Actions** group, click on the **Convert to Kit** button:

5. In the **Convert to Kit** confirmation dialog box, click on **OK**.

6. Click on **Kit Products** in the left-hand navigation area of the product form.
7. Click on **Add Existing Product**.
8. Add one or more products to this kit.
9. Click on **Save and Close**.

The price of the kit has to be set by using a price list item. No prices from the individual products that comprise the kit will be transferred or summed up.
To convert the kit back to a product, follow the preceding steps, but click on the **Convert to Product** button.

Adding substitute products

CRM allows for products to be associated to other products so they can be used as a substitute. An example of using a substitute product is if one product is discontinued, no longer in stock, or just not available, a substitute product may be used for an opportunity or to process an order. To add a substitute product, perform the following steps:

1. Start CRM, go to the **Settings** module, and under the **Business** section click on **Product Catalog**.
2. On the **Product Catalog** page, click on **Products**.
3. Find the product for which you wish to add substitute products, and open the record.
4. In the left-hand navigation area, click on **Substitute Products**.
5. On the **List Tools** tab, on the **Products** ribbon bar, in the **Records** group, click on **Add Existing Product**.
6. Select one or more products that you wish to add as substitutes.
7. Click on **OK**.
8. Click on the **Products** tab on the ribbon bar.
9. Click on **Save and Close**.

Creating and managing price lists

A price list is basically a collection of price list items. A price list item is a record that sets the price for a particular product. An organization can have multiple price lists with price list items for the same product, in order to price a product differently.

Business scenarios

Race2Win Insurance Company now has an extensive, happy customer base. Some of these customers have done business for quite some time, and have earned preferred customer pricing. Race2Win has also taken on some government clients who have negotiated another set of rates. Microsoft Dynamics CRM 2011 offers the perfect solution by allowing the set up of different price lists that can be associated to different customers.

Creating price lists

To create a price list, perform the following steps:

1. Start CRM, go to the **Settings** module, and under the **Business** section click on **Product Catalog**.
2. On the **Product Catalog** page, click on **Price Lists**.
3. On the **Price Lists** ribbon bar in the **Records** group, click on **New**.
4. Enter the following required information:
    - **Name**: A clear, concise name of price list
    - **Currency**: This is automatically populated to the default currency, but this can be changed

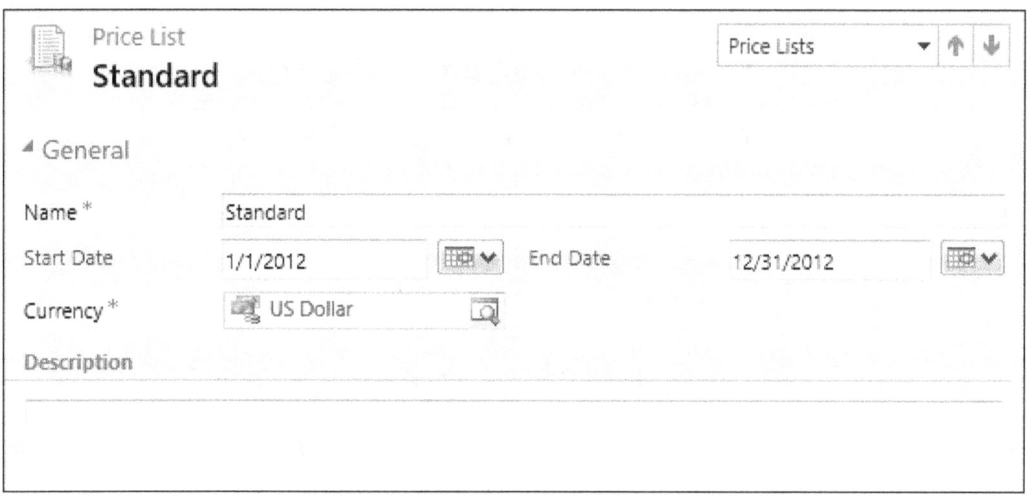

5. Click on **Save and Close**.

The price list itself does not set the price for a product, but rather it is a container for all possible prices for products.

Creating price list items

To set a price for a product, a price list item needs to be created. To create a price list item, perform the following steps:

1. Start CRM, go to the **Settings** module, and under the **Business** section click on **Product Catalog**.
2. On the **Product Catalog** page, click on **Price Lists**.
3. Find and open the price list to which you wish to add price list items.
4. On the left-hand side, click on **Price List Items**.
5. On the **List Tools** tab, on the **Price List Items** ribbon bar, in the **Records** group, click on **Add New Price List Item**.
6. The **Price List** and **Currency** fields will default to the value of the price list from within which the item is being created, and the currency specified on the price list, respectively.
7. Enter the following required information:
    a. **Product**: The product that you want to associate to the price list.
    b. **Unit**: Once a product has been entered, this field becomes enabled. It is filtered on the units associated to the product.
    c. **Quantity Selling Option**: Select from **No Control**, **Whole**, and **Whole and Fractional**. This defines whether whole, fractional, or both types of quantities can be specified in the quantity field of Quote Product, Order Product, and Invoice Product records. For example, mugs cannot be sold in fractional quantities, thus setting this field to whole, will not allow a fractional value to be entered in the quantity field of the aforementioned records.
    d. **Pricing Method**: Select from one of the following options:
        - **Currency Amount**: If this option is selected, the price of the product will be retrieved from the value entered in step 7.f, ahead.
        - **Percent of List**: If selected, the price of the product will be the list price entered on the product multiplied by the percentage entered in step 7.g.

- **Percent Markup - Current Cost**: If this field is selected, then the price of the product will be the percentage entered in step 7.g multiplied by the value of the current cost field on the product, plus the current cost. As a formula, this would be Price of Product = (Current Cost * Percentage in step 7.g) + Current Cost.
- **Percent Margin - Current Cost**: If selected, the margin of the price for the product is a percentage of the current cost of the product (the percentage is entered in step 7.g).
- **Percent Markup - Standard Cost**: If selected, the markup of the price for the product is a percentage of the standard cost of the product (the percentage is entered in step 7.g).
- **Percent Margin - Standard Cost**: If selected, the margin of the price for the product is a percentage of the standard cost of the product (the percentage is entered in step 7.g).

e. **Amount**: This field becomes enabled only if **Currency Amount** is chosen for the **Pricing Method** field.

f. **Percentage**: This field becomes enabled only if any of the percent options are selected in the **Pricing Method** field.

g. **Rounding Policy**: This field is only valid when the pricing method is a percentage. The options are none, round up, round down, or round to the nearest.

h. **Rounding Option**: This field is only valid when the pricing method is a percentage and when the **Rounding Policy** field value is not set to none. The two options are:

- **Ends in**: The price, if rounded, will be rounded up to the next multiple of the amount set in the **Rounding Amount** field.
- **Multiple of**: The price, if rounded, will be rounded to a multiple of the value entered in the **Rounding Amount** field.

i. **Rounding Amount**: Enabled only when the **Rounding Policy** field is enabled and is not set to none.

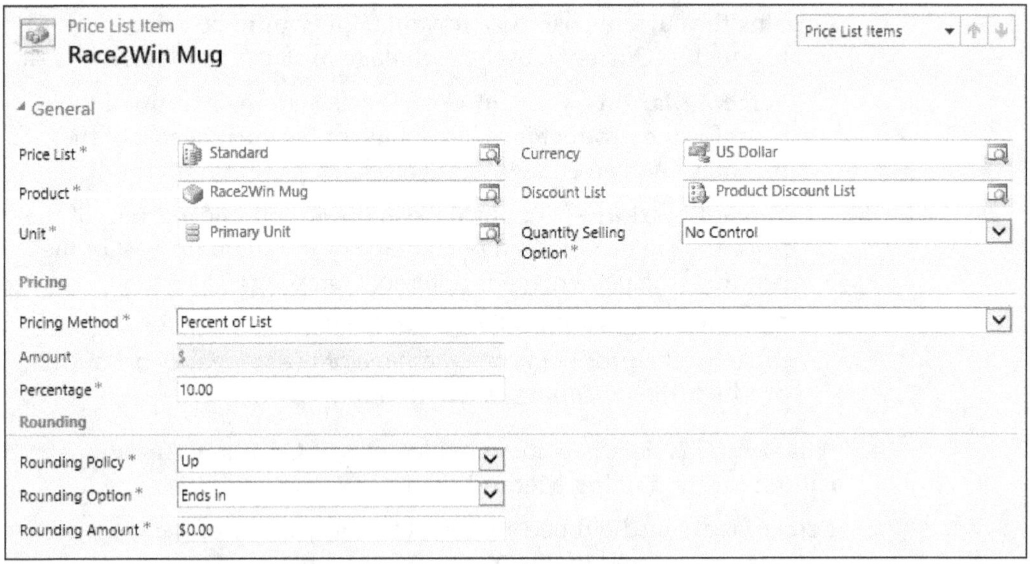

8. Click on **Save and Close**.

The preceding procedure illustrates how to add a price list item from a price list. However, from a product record, a price list item can be created very quickly.

Adding a price list item from a product

To add a price list item directly from the product, perform the following:

1. Start CRM, go to the **Settings** module, and under the **Business** section click on **Product Catalog**.
2. On the **Product Catalog** page, click on **Products**.
3. Find the product to which you wish to add a price list item, and open the record.
4. On the **Product** ribbon bar in the **Actions** group, click on the **Add Price List Item** button.
5. A new price list item form is displayed, with the **Product** and **Unit** fields pre-populated.

Deactivating price lists

When a price list has expired or becomes invalid, it can be deactivated. When a price list is deactivated, any opportunities, quotes, orders, or invoices that are still open will continue to use the price list until they are completed or closed. However, no new records will be able to reference the deactivated price list. As you can see, the pricing options can be as simple or as complex as your organization desires in order to meet the various business scenarios. An optional field in the price list item is the discount list, which can be used to provide discounts on a price for a product.

Discount lists

Discount lists are often referred to as volume discount lists. The key here is the word *discount*. Some organizations have a concept of volume pricing, whereby once a certain quantity of a product has been purchased, a new price will be set. For example, say 1 hour of consulting from Race2Win Insurance Company is USD 100. Now let's say there is a price break for anyone that receives 300 to 500 hours of consulting. Volume pricing dictates the new price to USD 90 per hour (a discount of USD 10).

CRM has a concept of volume discount which is different. Based on the quantity purchased, a discount is given of the price listed on the price list item. Using the previous example, if the rate charged for consulting is USD 100 per hour, and a customer purchases 300 to 500 consulting hours, then volume discount says the customer will get a USD 10 per hour discount.

Creating discount lists

To create a discount list, perform the following steps:

1. Start CRM, go to the **Settings** module, and under the **Business** section click on **Product Catalog**.
2. On the **Product Catalog** page, click on **Discount Lists**.
3. On the **Discount Lists** ribbon bar, in the **Records** group, click on **New**.

4. Enter the following information:
    - **Name**: Enter a clear, concise name for the discount list.
    - **Type**: The discount can be either **Percentage** or **Amount**. Depending on the value selected here, the discount field will be changed.

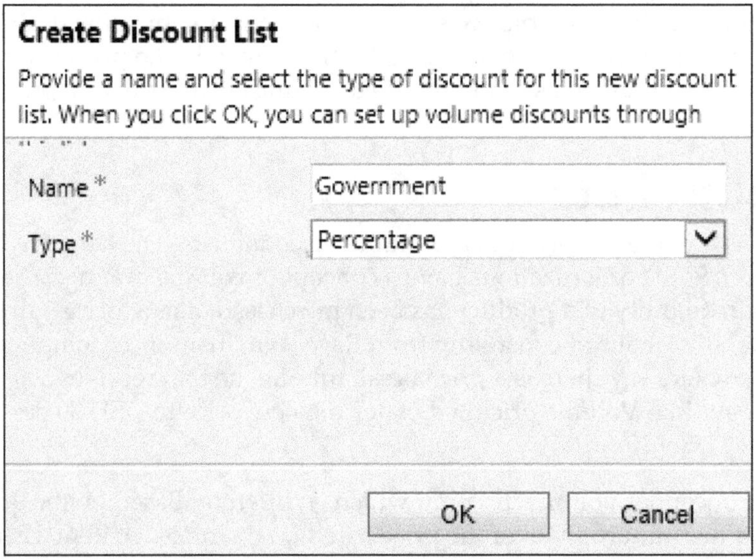

5. Click on **OK**.
6. A new form is displayed, with the name and type entered.
7. In the left-hand navigation area, click on **Discounts**.
8. On the **List Tools** tab, on the **Discounts** ribbon bar, click on **Add New Discount**.
9. Enter the following information:
    - **Begin Quantity**: The minimum quantity needed to obtain this discount. This number must be unique to the discount list, otherwise an error message will appear stating that the quantity is being used in another discount.
    - **End Quantity**: The maximum quantity that must be purchased in order to obtain this discount. This number must be unique to the discount list, otherwise an error message will appear stating that the quantity is being used in another discount.
    - **Amount/Percentage**: Depending on the type of the discount list, this field will either be a discount amount or percentage to be taken off the price.

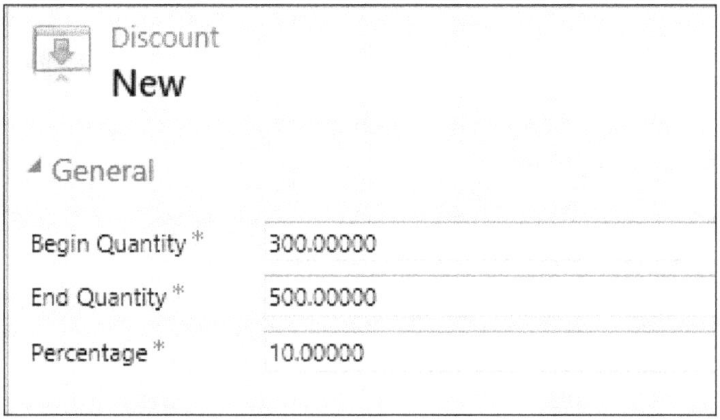

10. Click on **Save and Close** to create the volume discount or **Save and New** to create the volume discount and display a new form to create an additional discount.
11. Repeat steps 8 to 10 to create multiple discounts.
12. Click on **Save and Close** to close the discount list.

A sample discount list, with multiple discounts, is shown as follows:

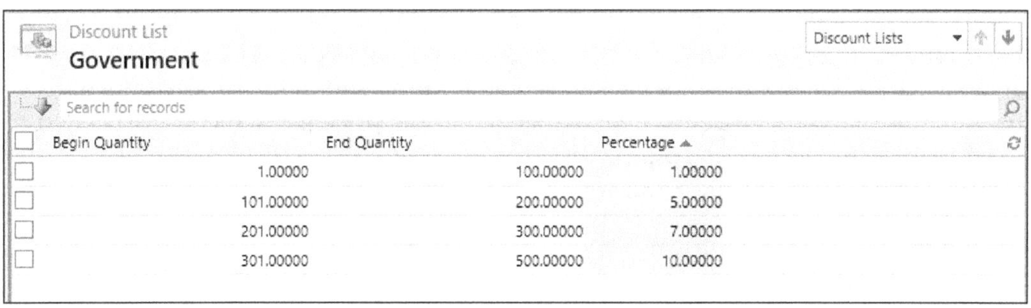

Once a discount list is created, it can be added to a price list. For an example of how the product catalog and pricing flow together, see the following business scenario.

Business scenarios

Race2Win Insurance Company sells individual insurance policies, but it also sells corporate health care packages. Depending on who the customer is and how many employees enroll in the package, various pricing scenarios are available. Race2Win has a sales opportunity with a corporation in the United Sates that has 1,000 employees, but is interested in a life insurance product that it wants to offer to their employees (about 500) that have been there for more than 20 years.

The salesperson in charge of the account creates an opportunity record in CRM to capture information and start tracking the progress of the potential sale. The opportunity is created with a "Standard" price list because the customer has not qualified for any special pricing. The opportunity is also set up to automatically calculate the estimated revenue.

The sales person then creates an opportunity product record from the opportunity. The representative selects an existing product from the product catalog, sets a default unit, and sets the pricing field to **Use Default**, which means that the price of the product will come from the price list. This particular product is associated to the price list via a price list item. That price list item defined the price as a flat amount. The sales person then enters a quantity of 500 on the opportunity product.

After the opportunity product record is saved, the sales person then recalculates the opportunity. CRM will now calculate the estimated revenue of the opportunity. In this scenario, the estimated revenue is equivalent to the quantity entered on the opportunity product, multiplied by the flat amount set on the price list item associated to the price list, which is associated to the opportunity.

Now let's say the sales person informs his contacts at the organization that there is a volume discount for this product of an additional 10 percent if 600 to 700 products are purchased. The corporation is interested in hearing a revised estimate, so the sales person changes the quantity on the opportunity product from 500 to 600. After the opportunity product is saved, the sales person recalculates the opportunity again. In this scenario, the estimated revenue is equivalent to the product price (the flat amount set on the price list item associated to the price list, which is associated to the opportunity) minus the volume discount amount of 10 percent multiplied by the quantity entered on the opportunity product.

The previous scenario describes a few pricing scenarios related to opportunities. This is important to understand because these concepts can be applied when creating and managing quotes, orders, and invoices.

Creating and managing quotes

Quotes can provide customers or potential customers with an estimated amount for all of the products that they wish to purchase. A quote can be created from an existing opportunity or on its own. A quote created automatically from an opportunity will inherit all of the products and pricing specified in the opportunity.

Creating a quote from an opportunity

To create a quote from an opportunity, perform the following steps:

1. Start CRM, go to the **Sales** module, and then click on **Opportunities**.
2. Find and open the opportunity record to which you wish to add a quote.
3. Within the form, locate the **Quotes** sub-grid, and click inside of it.
4. On the **List Tools** tab, on the **Quote** ribbon bar, in the **Records** group, click on **Add New Quote**.
5. The following information will be copied from the opportunity:
    - **Name**: The name of the opportunity
    - **Potential Customer**
    - **Price List**
    - **Detail Amount**: Estimated revenue
    - **Quote Discount (%)**: Discount (%)
    - **Quote Discount**: Copied from the discount
    - **Pre-Freight Amount**
    - **Total Tax**
    - **Total Amount**

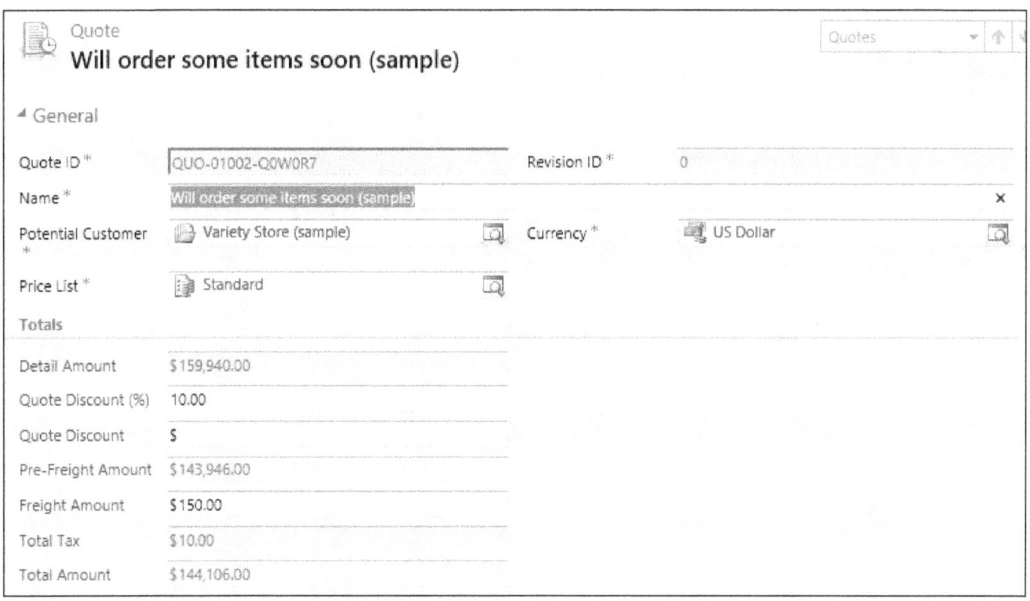

- ◦ **Opportunity**
- ◦ **Source Campaign**

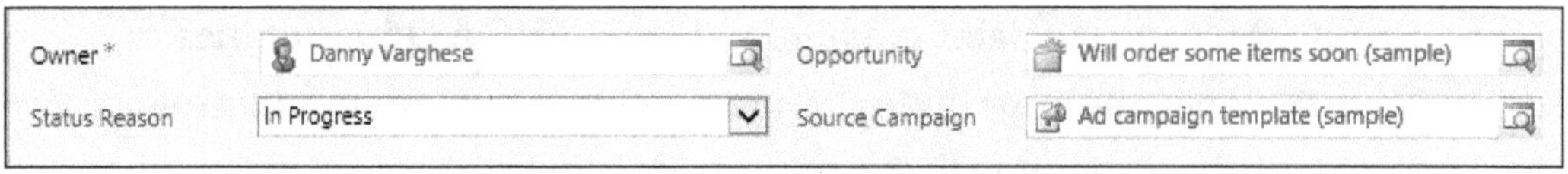

The following screenshot shows the shipping information of the quote:

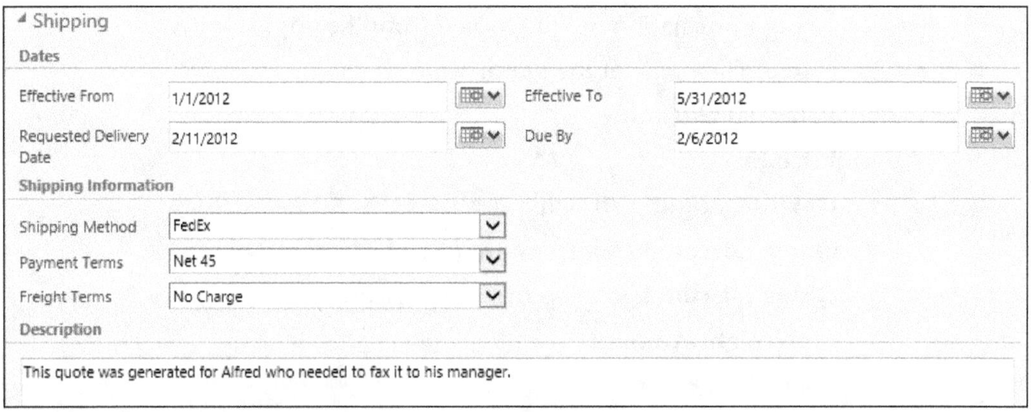

The following screenshot shows the address section of the quote form:

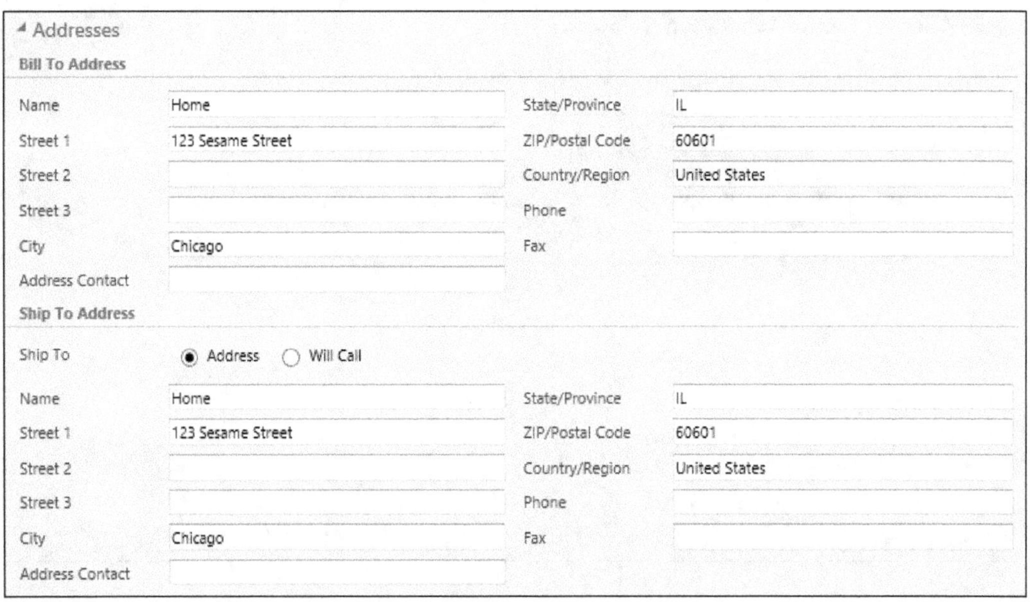

> The address information presented in the previous screenshot can be manually entered or can be pulled from the customer record. The following steps explain how to pull the details from the customer record.

   1. On the **Quote** ribbon bar, in the **Actions** group, click on **Look Up Address**.
   2. Select whether the address you'll be looking up will be applied to the **Bill To Address**, **Ship To Address**, or both.

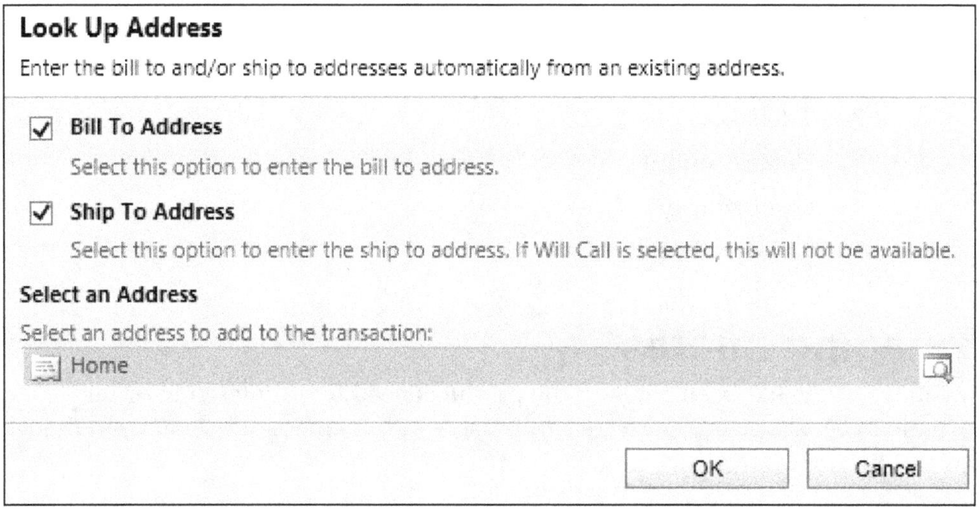

   3. Look up the address to copy to the quote record. This will display all customer address records for the potential customer on the quote.
   4. Click on **OK** to select the address.
   5. Click on **OK** to copy the address to the quote.

6. Click on **Save and Close** to save and close the quote record.

Creating a quote manually

To create the quote separately from the opportunity, you can perform the following steps:

1. Start CRM, go to the **Sales** module, and click on **Quotes**.
2. On the **Orders** ribbon bar, in the **Records** group, click on **New**.

3. Follow the steps performed in the *Creating a quote from an opportunity* section, except for step 5, because these steps will not be automated. The fields from step 5 that will need to be entered manually are:
    - **Name**
    - **Potential Customer**
    - **Price List**
    - **Detail Amount**
    - **Quote Discount (%)**
    - **Quote Discount**
    - **Pre-Freight Amount**
    - **Total Tax**
    - **Total Amount**
    - **Opportunity**
    - **Source Campaign**

Managing quotes

Now that a quote has been entered, the products need to be entered in order for the quote to be complete. There are again two ways to enter a product: from the opportunity and manually.

Adding products by using Get Products

Products are associated to a quote via the **Quote Product** entity. Quote products are automatically created from any existing opportunity products. The **Get Products** feature can be used if you modify the opportunity products after creating the quote, or want to associate products from a different opportunity.

1. Start CRM, go to the **Sales** module, and then click on **Quotes**.
2. Find and open the quote record to which you want to add products.
3. On the **Quote** ribbon bar in the **Actions** group, click on **Get Products**:

4. In the **Get Products** dialog box, select the opportunity from which you wish the retrieve the products.

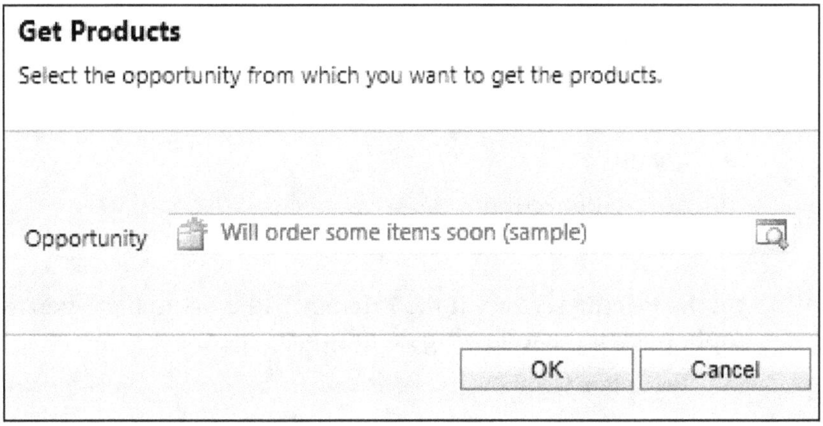

5. Click on **OK**.
6. The products have not been added as quote products.

Adding products directly to a quote

Products are tied to a quote by using the Quote Product entity. To manually associate a product to a quote, perform the following steps:

1. Start CRM, go to **Sales** module, and then click on **Quotes**.
2. Find and open the quote to which you want to add products.
3. In the left-hand navigation area, click on **Quote Products**.
4. On the **List Tools** tab, on the **Quote Product** ribbon, in the **Records** group, click on **Add New Quote Product**.
5. Enter the following required information:
    - **Select Product**: If you choose **Existing**, the **Existing Product** lookup will be enabled allowing you to select a product from the product catalog. If you choose **Write In**, the **Write-In Product** text field will become required, the **Pricing** field will automatically be set to **Override Price**, and the **Price Per Unit** field will become enabled.
    - **Existing Product**: If **Existing** is selected from the **Select Product** field, this field will become enabled and allow you to select a product from the product catalog.

- **Write-In Product**: If **Write In** is selected from the **Select Product** field, this field will become enabled and allow you to create a product with its own name.
- **Unit**: This field is only enabled when an existing product is selected.
- In the **Pricing** section, if the **Pricing** field is set to the **Use Default** pricing option, the following fields are enabled:
  a. **Quantity**
  b. **Manual Discount**
  c. **Tax**
- In the **Pricing** section, if the **Pricing** field is set to the **Override Price** option, then the following fields are enabled:
  a. **Price Per Unit**
  b. **Quantity**
  c. **Manual Discount**
  d. **Tax**

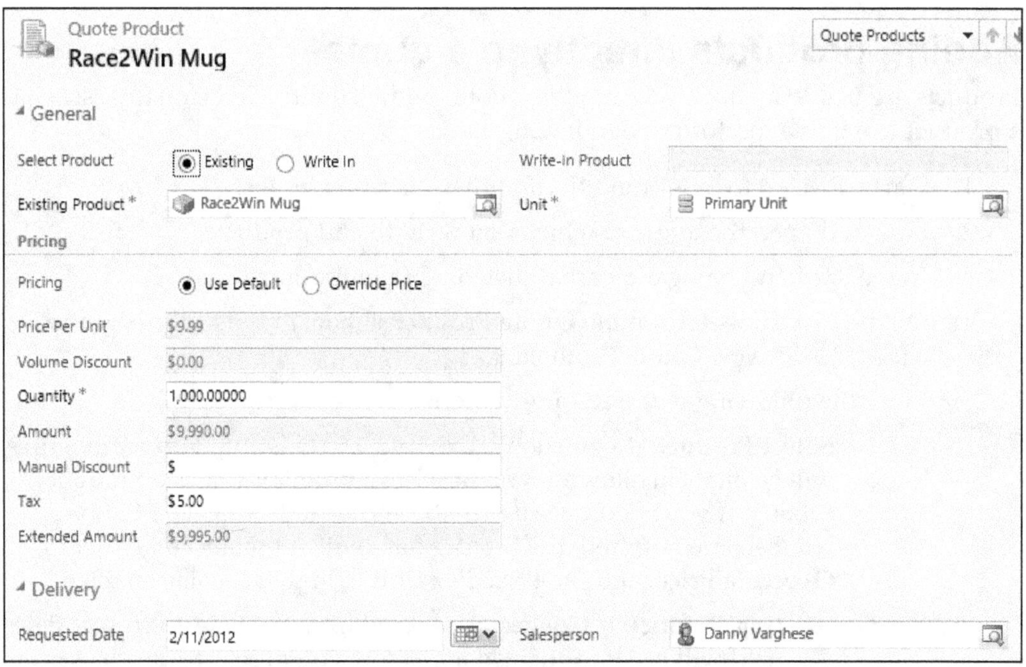

6. Click on **Save and Close**.

Recalculating a quote

Users can add as many products to a quote as they'd like. As products are added or even removed, users can recalculate the quote to update all of the total values on the quote.

Quote statuses

A quote record, like many other records, has various statuses and status reasons that are important to understand. According to MSDN, the status to status reason is as shown in the following table:

Status	Status reason
Draft	In Progress
Active	In Progress, Open
Won	Won
Closed	Lost, Canceled, Revised

When a quote is created, the default status is Draft. Quotes can only be modified while they are in Draft status. When a quote is ready to be sent to a customer, it can be activated by clicking on the **Activate Quote** button. When this happens, the form is saved, the status value gets set to Active, and the form becomes read only. Once this happens, the **Create Order**, **Revise** quote, and **Close Quote** buttons are enabled.

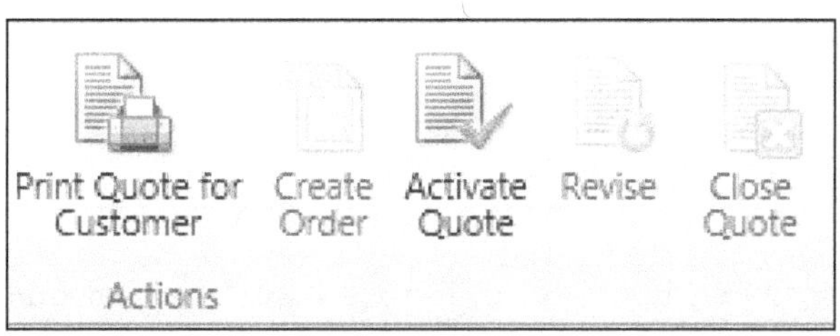

If a quote needs to be revised, users can click on the **Revise** quote button. This will change the status of the quote back to Draft, and the revision number on the quote record will be incremented. This is important because a new quote is not created, but rather the revision ID on the record is updated.

Closing a quote

If users decide to close the quote, the close quote dialog appears:

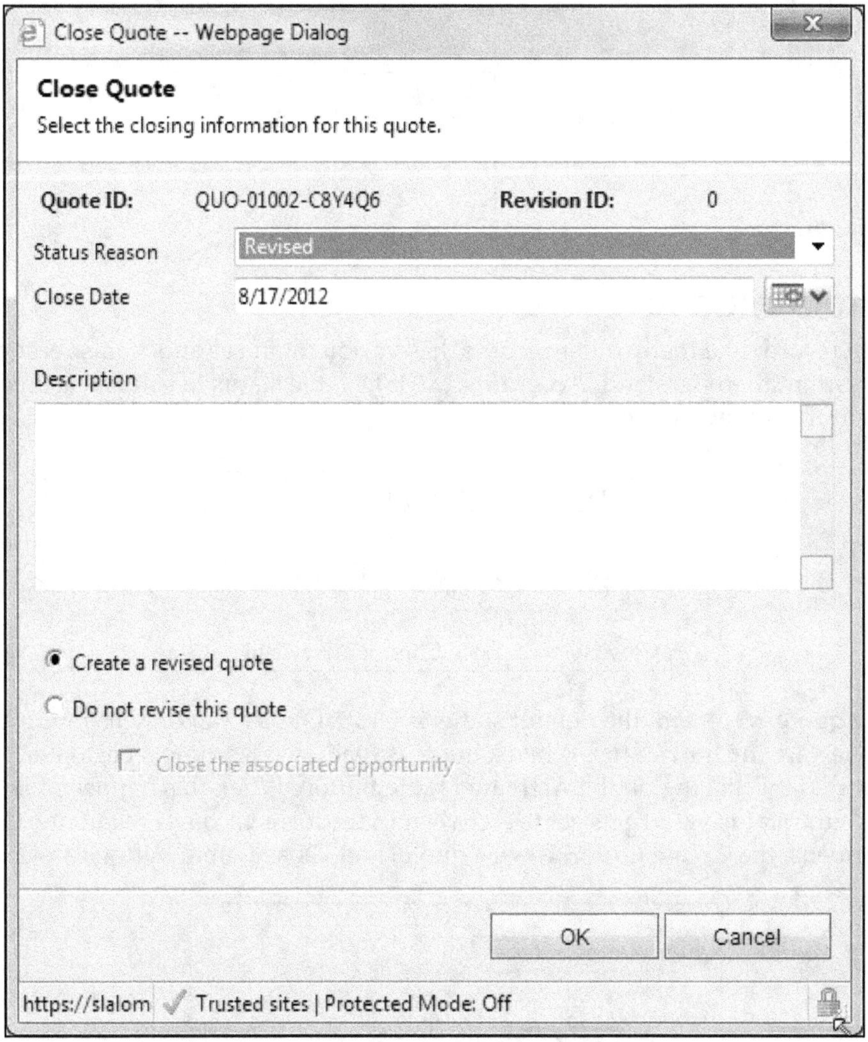

The quote can be closed with a status of **Revised**, **Lost**, or **Canceled**. There is an option to create a revised quote, or not to revise this quote. If the quote is not revised, then the user has the option to close the related opportunity (if one exists). Once a quote is closed, it can always be re-opened by clicking on the **Activate Quote** button.

Business scenarios

Race2Win Insurance Company has sales teams that are creating a number of opportunities. Often, the customer may request a quote. The quote can be generated from the opportunity. This quote, once ready to be sent to the customer, can be activated. Let's now say a customer has decided not to make the purchase; we can close the quote in CRM by clicking on the **Close Quote** button on the **Quote** ribbon, bar in the **Actions** group. If the customer decides to come back to the sales person, expressing interest in the quote again, the quote can reactivated.

Creating and managing orders

Once a customer has accepted the terms of a sale, an order can be created. An order can be created from an opportunity, quote, or manually. Creating an order from an opportunity is similar to the process outlined around creating a quote from an opportunity, which is why we won't discuss that topic any further. Let's take a look at how to create an order from a quote, and how to create one manually.

Creating an order from a quote

In order to create an order from a quote, the quote must be activated. To create an order from a quote, perform the following steps:

1. Start CRM, click on the **Sales** module, and then click on **Quote**.
2. Open the quote from which you wish to create an order.
3. On the **Quote** ribbon bar in the **Actions** group, click on **Create Order**.
4. In the **Create Order** dialog box, enter the following fields:
    - **Status Reason**: This gets set to **Won**.
    - **Date Won**: The date on which the quote was accepted.
    - **Description**
    - **Close Opportunity**: If there is an opportunity associated with the quote, it can be closed.
    - **Actual Revenue is**: Either enter the actual revenue to place on the closed opportunity or grab it from the quote.

  - **Don't update opportunity**: There's also an option not to touch the opportunity. This can be used if there are multiple quotes/orders created from an opportunity.

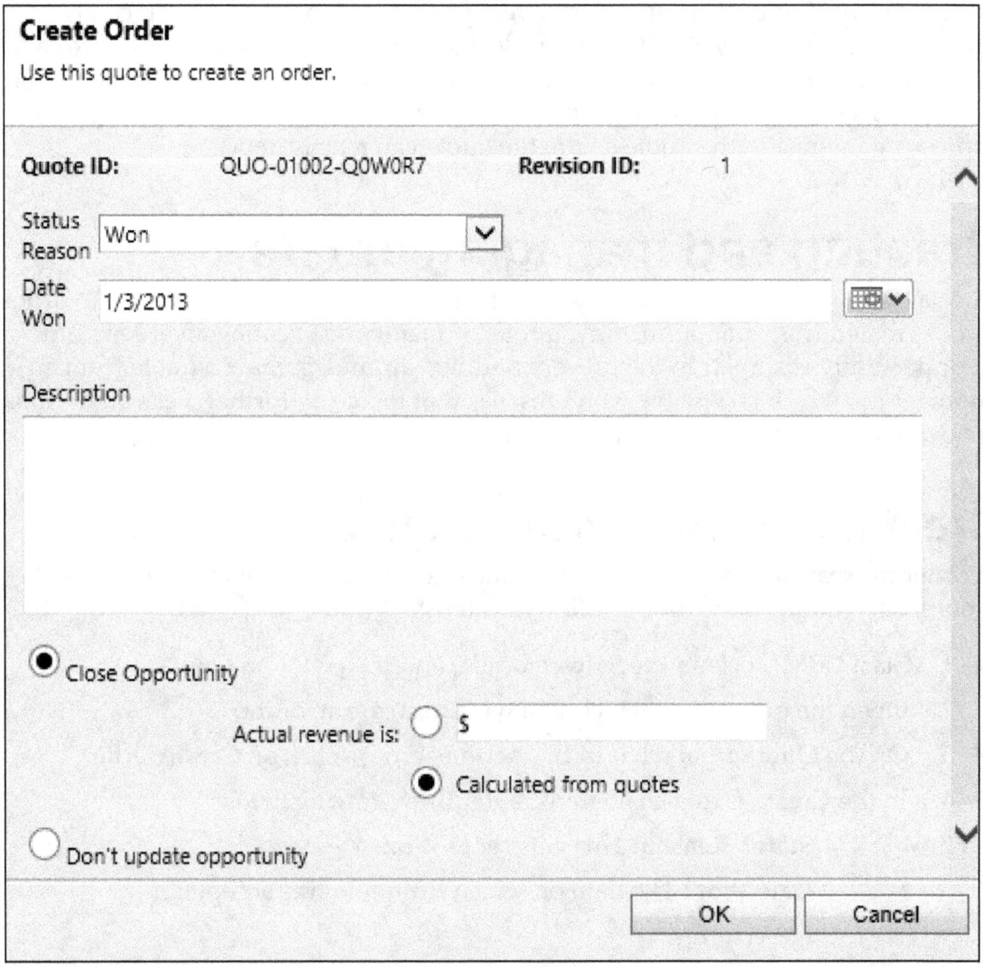

5. Click on **OK**.

   An order form is displayed with information from the quote copied over into the order.

Besides creating an order from a quote, an order can be created manually.

Creating an order manually

To create an order manually, perform the following steps:

1. Start CRM, click on the **Sales** module, and then click on **Orders**.
2. On the **Orders** ribbon bar, in the **Records** group, click on **New**.
3. Enter the following fields:
    - **Name**: Enter a clear, concise name for the order
    - **Customer**: Select either an account or a contact
    - **Price List**
    - **Currency**: This field defaults to the system currency, but can be changed

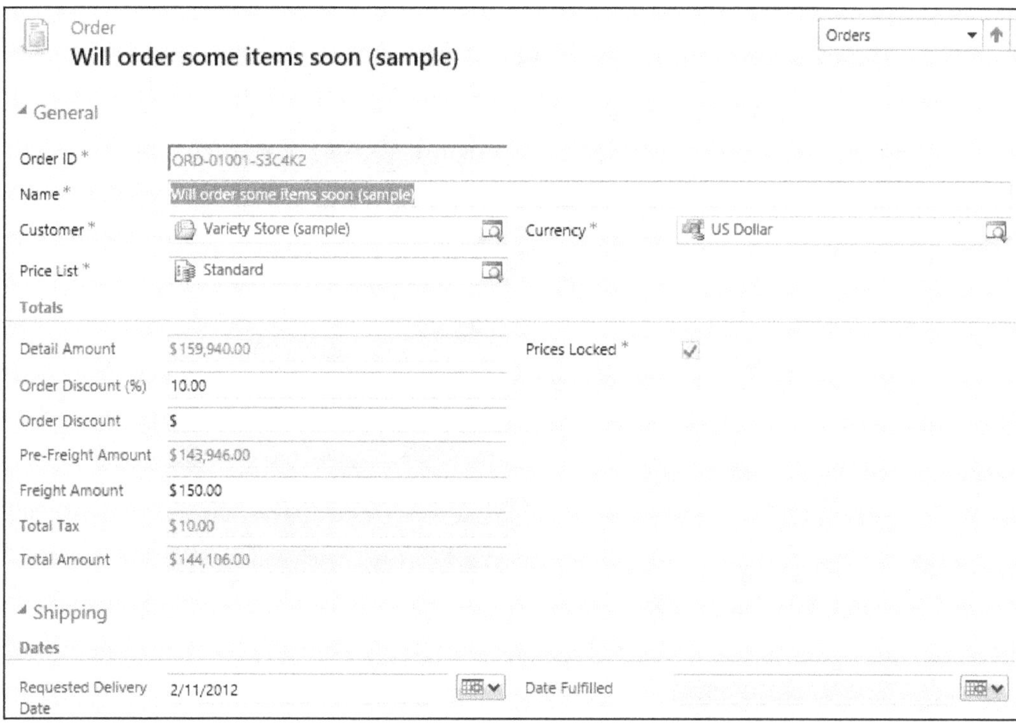

The following screenshot shows the **Shipping Information** section of the order:

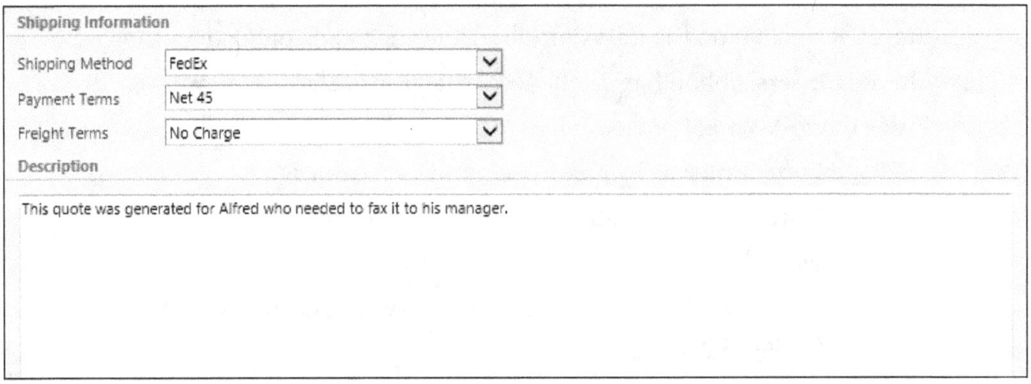

The following screenshot shows the address information section of the quote. The address section is similar to that of the quote and can be manually entered or retrieved from the customer on the order by using the Lookup Address functionality. The Lookup Address process is similar to the one outlined for the quote.

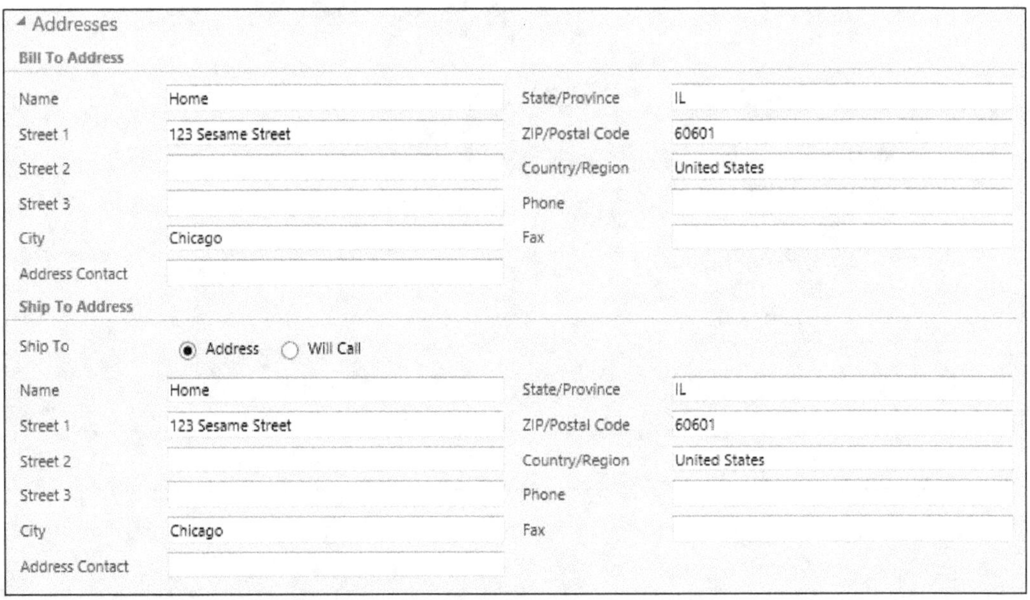

4. Click on **Save and Close**.

Once an order is created, products can be associated to it.

Order products

Products are tied to an order by using the **Order Product** entity. If the order was generated from a quote or opportunity, then the order products will be inherited. The order product form is very similar to the quote product form except for the **Fulfillment** section, which is shown in the following screenshot:

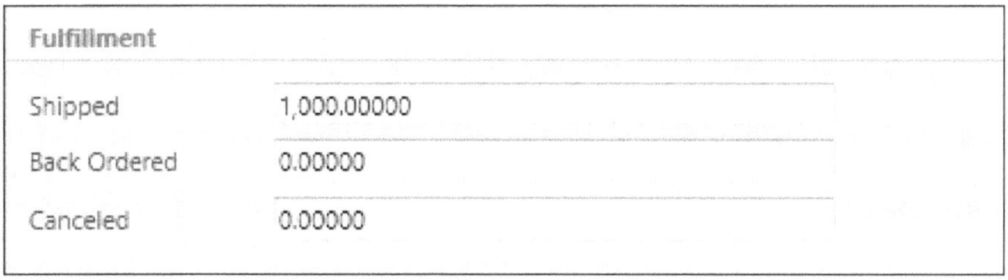

This is because once a customer has accepted the quote, the order can be fulfilled. This means that products can be shipped or back-ordered, or the shipment can be canceled.

Managing orders

Once an order has been created, either by itself or from a quote, users have a few options to manage the order. Like a quote, products can be added by using the Get Products functionality, or can be added manually.

Recalculating orders

As products are added or removed, the totals on the order can be recalculated in a similar way in which a quote can be recalculated—that is, using the **Recalculate** button.

Use current pricing

If an order is created from a quote, all of the pricing is inherited from the quote. By default, when an order is created and products are added, **price locking** takes effect. Price locking prevents changes to the price per unit for products in open orders. Even if the price changes in the product catalog, the original price will remain for any open orders. Let's say now that the order sits in the system for some time and in the meantime prices have changed. The prices will not be updated on the quote because they are locked. To update the price on a quote, perform the following steps:

1. Start CRM, click on the **Sales** module, and then click on **Orders**.
2. Find and open the order record that you wish to update.

3. On the **Order** ribbon bar, in the **Actions** group, click on **Use Current Pricing**:

Once the prices have been updated, the order is not locked. Therefore, if pricing is updated in CRM, the price on this order will be updated. To prevent this, you can click on the **Lock Pricing** button:

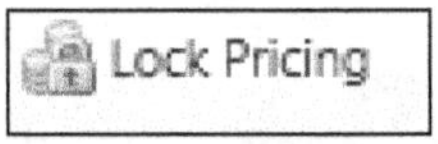

When an order is ready to be shipped, it goes through a fulfillment process.

Fulfilling an order

Microsoft Dynamics CRM will not ship any products, but can be integrated with other systems in order to help in the fulfillment process. The fulfillment process in CRM is merely a way to mark that the order has been fulfilled. To fulfill an order, perform the following steps:

1. Start CRM, click on the **Sales** module, and then click on **Orders**.
2. Find and open the order record that you wish to fulfill.
3. On the **Order** ribbon bar in the **Actions** group, click on **Fulfill Order**:

4. The **Fulfill Order** dialog box is displayed.

5. Enter the following fields:
    - **Status Reason**: Indicates whether it's a full or a partial fulfillment
    - **Date Fulfilled**

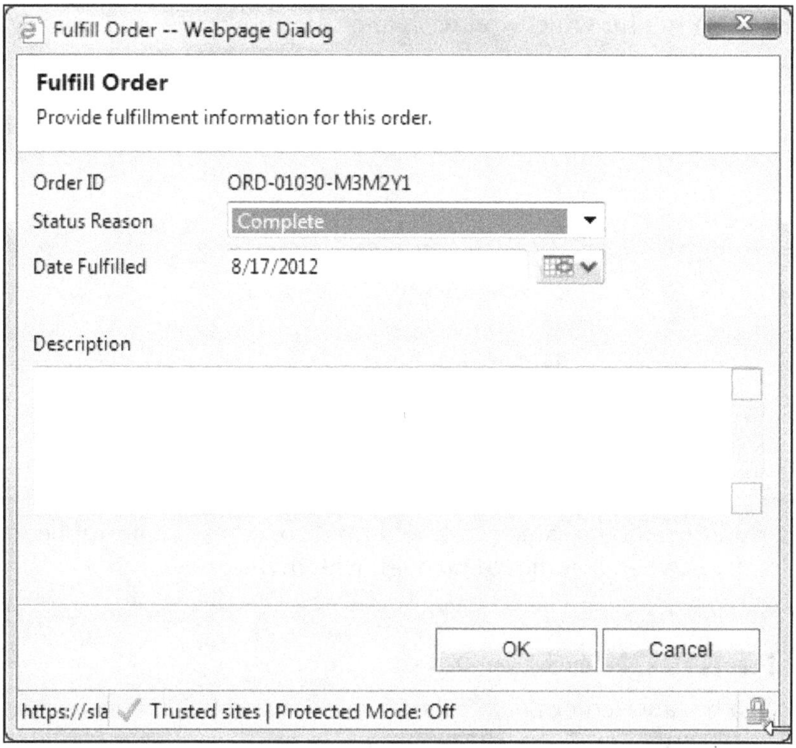

6. Click on **OK**.

Once an order is fulfilled, the order is marked read only and cannot be edited. However the order can be canceled, or an invoice can be generated from the order. Cancelling an order will change the order status to canceled, and will also keep the order as read only.

Creating and managing invoices

One of the last steps for an organization to carry out during sales order processing is to invoice the customer for the products or services sold. An invoice is essentially billing a customer for an order. Invoices can be generated from an opportunity, from an order, or manually. Creating an invoice from an opportunity is similar to the process outlined earlier in the chapter about creating a quote from an opportunity, which is why we won't discuss that topic any further.

Creating an invoice from an order

To create an invoice from an order, perform the following steps:

1. Start CRM, click on the **Sales** module, and then click on **Orders**.
2. Find the order for which you wish to create an invoice, and open it.
3. On the **Order** ribbon bar, in the **Actions** group, click on **Create Invoice**:

4. The invoice form is displayed, with all of the fields copied over from the order.
5. Click on **Save and Close**.

To create an invoice on its own, the same exact steps used to create a quote or order on its own can be used. The same exact fields and concepts can be applied. The only difference really is when it comes to managing an invoice.

Closing invoices

An invoice can be canceled or paid. If the invoice is canceled, the invoice becomes deactivated and read only. To mark the invoice as paid, perform the following steps:

1. Start CRM, click on the **Sales** module, and then click on **Invoices**.
2. Find the invoice that you wish to pay, and open it.
3. On the **Invoice** ribbon bar, in the **Actions** group, click on the **Invoice Paid** button.

4. Select the value for **Status Reason**, indicating how much of the invoice was paid, either **Complete** or **Partial**.

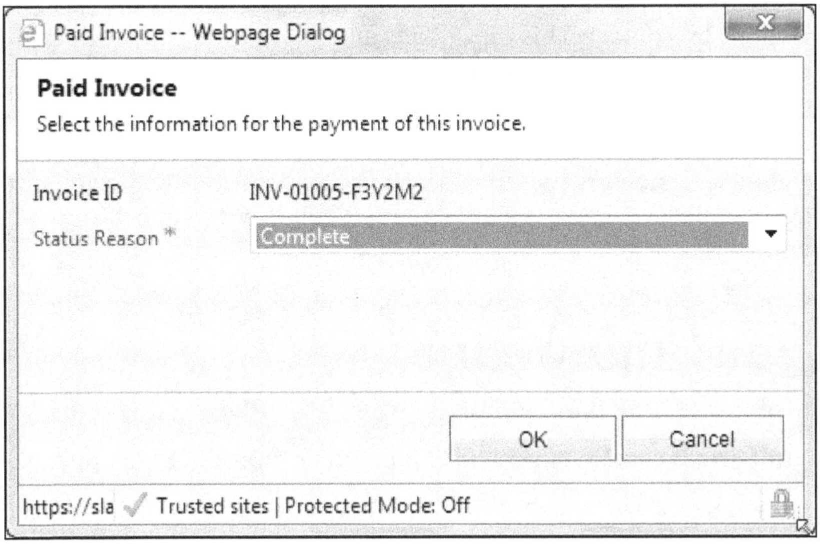

An invoice can also be canceled by clicking on the **Cancel Invoice** button on the **Invoice** ribbon bar, in the **Actions** group.

Invoices are one of the last elements involved in the sales ordering process. There are various reports that can help you to analyze data during sales order processing.

Reporting and analysis

CRM comes with the following out of the box reports:

- **Invoice**: This report enables an organization to print invoices. This report will generate a customer-friendly version of the invoice and will print either all invoices in the system, or a single invoice if you run the report from within the invoice itself.
- **Invoice status**: This report has a chart that displays the number of invoices in the system, grouped by status, with the total amount of invoices in each status.
- **Order**: This report enables an organization to print orders. This report will generate a customer friendly version of the order and will print either all orders in the system, or a single order if you run the report within the order itself.

- **Products by account**: This report lists all accounts and the products they use, taken from orders that aren't canceled, and from opportunities that have been won.
- **Products by contact**: This report lists all contacts and the products they use, taken from orders that aren't canceled, and from opportunities that have been won.
- **Quote**: This report enables an organization to print quotes. This report will generate a customer-friendly version of the quote and will print either all quotes in the system, or a single quote if you run the report from within the quote itself.

Test your knowledge

Q.1. What is true about unit groups? (Choose all that apply.)

1. A unit group contains the base unit in which a product is available.
2. The unit group comprises all different increments of a base unit.
3. When a unit group is created, a primary unit is needed.
4. A primary unit is the core and basic unit to which all other units are created from.
5. All of the above.

Q.2. Why is it important to set the default price list on a product?

1. The default price list is required on the product record.
2. During order processing, if an order or invoice (for example) is generated from an account or contact that doesn't contain a price list, then the default price list will be used.
3. The default price list is recommended on the product record.
4. During order processing, if an opportunity is generated from an account or contact that doesn't contain a price list, then the default price list will be used.

Q.3. What enforces the entry of a whole number for a quantity on a quote product, order product, or invoice product?

1. Quantity option on the price list item.
2. Quantity on the price list item.
3. Selling option on the price list item.
4. Quantity selling option on the price list item.

Q.4. What is true about deactivating a price list?

1. When a price list is deactivated, any opportunities, quotes, orders, or invoices that are still open will continue to use the price list until they are completed or closed.
2. When a price list is deactivated, only quotes, orders, or invoices that are still open will continue to use the price list until they are completed or closed.
3. When a price list is deactivated, any opportunities, quotes, orders, or invoices that reference the price list will have the price list field blanked out.
4. When a price list is deactivated, only opportunities that are still open will continue to use the price list until they are completed or closed.

Q.5. A customer wants to purchase a large quantity of products from your company. What is the best approach to provide the customer with volume discounts?

1. When the order is placed, enter a manual discount.
2. Build the discount into the price by editing the price list item.
3. Set up a discount list and associate it to the price list that is associated to the product.
4. Set up a discount list and associate it to the product itself.

Q.6. What are the different ways in which a quote can be created?
(Choose all that apply.)

1. Manually.
2. From an opportunity.
3. From an order.
4. From an invoice.
5. All of the above.

Q.7. True or False: The **Use Current Pricing** button can be used to update the prices on all orders or invoices that are locked.

Q.8. True or False: When an order is fulfilled, the record is deactivated and no further action can be taken on the record.

Q.9. When an invoice is paid, what are the possible status reason values?

1. Complete.
2. Full.
3. Partial.
4. Incomplete.

Q.10. State true or false: CRM has out of the box reports to print more user-friendly quotes, orders, or invoices.

Summary

Products are goods or services that an organization might sell. A product record contains information such as classification, costs, and vendor-related information. A default price list can be set on the product, so that if an account or contact record does not contain a price list, the default price list will be used for order processing. Let's say there are two products: an insurance brochure and an insurance CD. They may be two separate products in the product catalog, but CRM allows kits to be created which can bundle these two products into a separate product all of its own. Now let's say that a product might become outdated, out of stock, or just not available; other products can be designated as substitute products.

A price list is a collection of price list items, and a price list item sets the price for a particular product. An organization can have multiple price lists with price list items for the same product, in order to price a product differently. The price list item has a number of pricing and rounding (if applicable) options that you need to become familiar with. Price list items can be created from a price list, or even from a product directly. When a price list is deactivated, any opportunities, quotes, orders, or invoices that are still open will continue to use the price list until they are completed or closed.

Quotes are an estimate of the products and services offered to a customer. A quote can be created from an existing opportunity, or can be created manually. Once a quote is created, products can be associated to a quote by using the quote product entity. If you want to retrieve products from an opportunity (this doesn't have to be an opportunity tied to the quote), then the get products functionality is useful. Quotes can be recalculated as long as the quotes status is in draft. The various statuses of a quote are *Draft*, *Active*, *Won*, and *Closed*. Quotes can be closed and reactivated depending on the organizational need.

Once a customer has accepted the terms of a sale, an order can be created. An order can be created from an opportunity, from a quote, or manually. Products are associated to an order via the Order Product entity. Orders can be recalculated, like quotes and opportunities. Price locking prevents changes to the price per unit for products on open orders. Even if a price changes in the product catalog, the original price will remain for any open orders. If the order pricing is locked, the Use Current Pricing feature allows the pricing to be updated.

An invoice can be used in CRM in place of an order. However, typically invoices are viewed as a bill for products or services sold. Invoices are very similar in functionality and form to the order. CRM also provides several out of the box reports related to products and sales order processing. Some of these reports can be used to print more customer-friendly versions of the quote, order, or invoice.

In the next chapter, we'll give an overview of the Microsoft Dynamics CRM Outlook client.

6

Managing CRM 2011 Outlook Client

In this chapter you will learn about:

- The Outlook client
- Tracking and managing e-mails
- Tracking appointments and tasks
- Custom views
- Conditional formatting

An Overview of the Outlook client

Microsoft has made a concerted effort to make sure that its entire product line can be integrated and be familiar to its customer base. That is, a user using Microsoft Office products and Microsoft Dynamics CRM should be able to intuitively navigate through either product. For example, the contextual ribbon in Dynamics CRM should be familiar to those who have used some Microsoft Office 2007, 2010, or 2013 products.

Microsoft Dynamics CRM 2011 integrates with Microsoft Outlook to provide the same functionality as the web client. This integration feature is a key differentiator from other CRM products in the market, and allows users to interact with the CRM system without opening up another application.

Once the Microsoft Office Outlook client has been configured to integrate with CRM, you'll notice that the client look and feel has changed slightly. Namely, a new solution folder has been added to the left-hand pane, along with a new set of buttons on the ribbon, and additional navigation pane items.

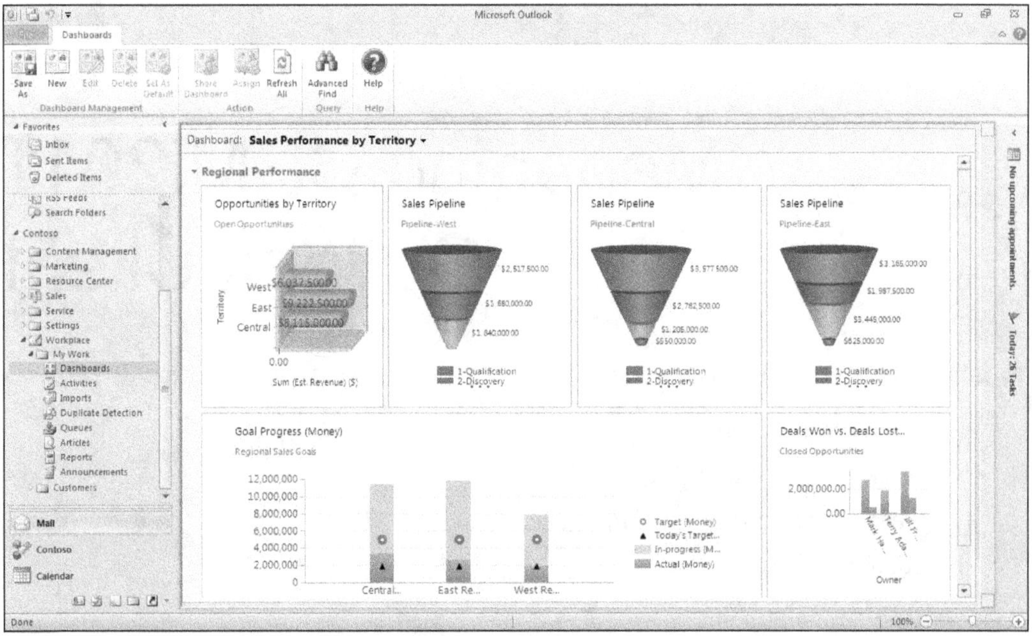

The preceding screenshot illustrates how a user can access their dashboards from within Microsoft Office Outlook.

CRM Outlook client versus web client

Working with the CRM system either via the web client or via Microsoft Office Outlook is fairly seamless, but there are a few key differences:

- **Installation**: The Outlook client needs to be installed and configured on an individual's machine. The web client is accessed through an Internet browser (for now only Internet Explorer is supported).
- **Personalization**: Within Outlook, you can create personalized views, using such things as conditional formatting (this will be discussed later in the chapter).

- **Reminders**: When tasks, appointments, and service activities are created in the web client, they are synchronized down to Outlook. These activities can have reminders tied to them in Outlook, notifying the user when the task is due or the appointment is approaching.
- **Outlook Connector**: Users can click on a contact's name to see e-mail and attachments that they have sent you, meetings you have attended together, and the contact's activities in social networks such as Facebook and LinkedIn.
- **Multiple Organization Access**: Dynamics CRM can have multiple organizations. Using the web client, typically each organization is accessed using a different URL. Within the CRM 2011 Outlook client, multiple organizations can be configured and accessed in one place. However, it is only possible to synchronize data from one organization.
- **Offline access**: The Outlook client allows a user to go offline (more about this later) and make changes to CRM data on their local computer. When the user come back online, the changes can be synchronized.

Offline access

The Microsoft Dynamics CRM Outlook client installs as an add-in to Microsoft Office Outlook and allows the user to interact with Dynamics CRM seamlessly while connected to the Internet. The CRM Outlook client also allows a user to interact with CRM data while offline. The installation of this feature comes with Microsoft SQL Server Express and a database that contains a local copy of the data for CRM. Offline access allows a user to interact with CRM data locally if they lose their Internet connection. When they regain their Internet connection, any changes made can be synchronized with CRM.

Outlook synchronization

Information about outlook synchronization can be found in a whitepaper published by Microsoft at `http://www.microsoft.com/en-us/download/details.aspx?displaylang=en&id=17594`. Outlook synchronization enables users to view CRM data such as accounts, contacts, appointments, e-mails, letters, faxes, phone calls, and tasks. When a record is synchronized, two copies exist: one in the CRM Outlook client, and one in the CRM database. A record is marked for synchronization if:

- The record is marked for synchronization using the **Track in CRM** button.
- A user runs the synchronization process manually.
- A background process runs periodically to synchronize records.

Going *offline* in the CRM Outlook client triggers a process to replicate data from the CRM database to the CRM Outlook client. When a user goes back *online*, changes to the data found in the local database are replicated back to the CRM database. Regardless of whether a user does or does not go offline, a synchronization process still occurs to make sure that records are up-to-date in both Outlook and CRM.

Changes from Outlook synchronized to CRM

When a change is made to a record marked for synchronization, the following process occurs to synchronize the changes:

- Information required to find the changed record in Outlook is added to a local database on the user's machine
- When the synchronization process starts, it looks at the local database and finds information regarding all changed records to be synchronized
- The process then finds the data in Outlook and updates the data in CRM

Changes from CRM synchronized to Outlook

Changes made to records in Dynamics CRM are stored in a database table on the CRM server. Changes are stored on the server for each Dynamics CRM Outlook client, along with the date and time at which the last synchronization occurred. When synchronization starts, the following process takes place:

1. The process calls a service to retrieve a list of changes from the server for a given CRM Outlook client. Only changes made since the last synchronization process are retrieved.
2. These changes are then added to the local database on the user's machine.
3. Changes are applied in Outlook.

Changes made in both CRM and Outlook

Data can be synchronized from both the CRM Outlook client and the CRM database. Whenever synchronization occurs, the latest version of the data is stored in a property called **OriginalXML**, along with the date and time of the synchronization.

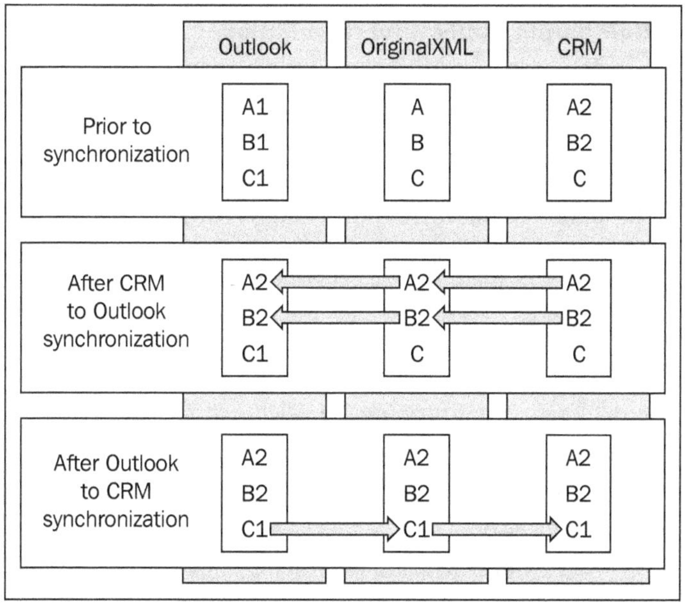

A scenario illustrated in the Microsoft whitepaper is shown in the preceding diagram. Let us say a user makes changes to three fields in Outlook (A1, B1, and C1). At a later time, let us say another user modifies two of the same fields (A2, B2), but in CRM. When the synchronization process begins, the two fields from CRM (A2, B2) are copied down to Outlook because these were the latest changes. Then the one field from Outlook (C1) is copied to CRM because it was changed last in Outlook.

In this scenario, notice the same fields were changed in both Outlook and CRM, but the latest changes were applied in both systems during synchronization. This is an important concept to understand.

Deletion rules

There are various rules applied when certain records are deleted. As mentioned above, one way a record is synchronized is if it's tracked in CRM. A record can be untracked in CRM as well, but still plays a part in the rules as follows:

<table>
<tr><th>Entity</th><th>Rule during Outlook Synchronization</th></tr>
<tr><td>Contact</td><td>A contact deleted in Outlook will not be deleted in CRM.

A contact that is untracked in Outlook will be deleted in CRM.

A contact deleted in CRM will be deleted in Outlook if the Outlook user is not the CRM Owner of the contact. If the user is the owner in CRM, then the Outlook contact will not be linked to the record in CRM.</td></tr>
<tr><td>Appointments</td><td>An appointment deleted or untracked in Outlook will be deleted in CRM only if the following are true:<ul><li>Appointment is open/scheduled</li><li>Appointment Start Time is in the future.</li><li>The user performing the delete action is the Owner or Organizer of the Appointment.</li></ul>An appointment deleted in CRM will be deleted in Outlook if the following is true:<ul><li>Appointment Start Time is in the future.</li></ul></td></tr>
<tr><td>Tasks</td><td>A task deleted in Outlook will be deleted in CRM, and vice versa, if the task is not completed.</td></tr>
<tr><td>E-mails</td><td>An e-mail deleted in Outlook will not be deleted in CRM.

An e-mail untracked in Outlook will be deleted in CRM if the user chooses to have it deleted.

An e-mail deleted in CRM will not be deleted in Outlook.</td></tr>
</table>

Tracking and managing e-mails

An e-mail in Dynamics CRM is considered to be just another activity record. E-mails can automatically be tracked, or when an e-mail is created in Outlook, it can be tracked by clicking on the **Track** button. Let's take a look at the first option.

Automatically tracking e-mail messages

To automatically track e-mail messages, follow these steps:

1. Start CRM.
2. Click on the **File** tab of the ribbon bar.
3. Click on **Options**.

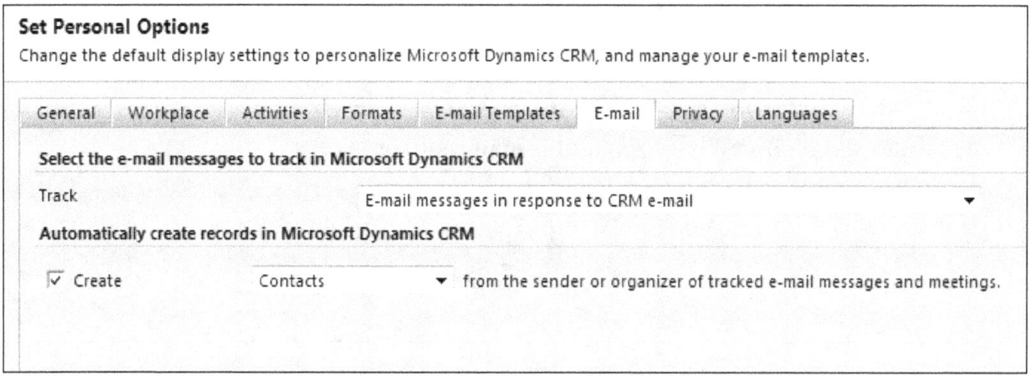

4. Click on the **E-mail** tab.
5. Select a **Track** option (each of the options are described next), and whether or not to automatically create either a contact or a lead when the sender of the e-mail is not already in CRM.
6. Click on **OK**.

E-mails can automatically be tracked in Dynamics CRM in four different ways:

- **All e-mail messages**: This option tracks in Dynamics CRM every e-mail sent and received by the user. This option should be used with caution as there might be sensitive e-mails a user might not want to be tracked in CRM.
- **E-mail messages in response to CRM e-mail**: If a response to an e-mail that is being tracked in CRM is sent, the response itself can be tracked. If the sender of the e-mail is not in CRM, you have the option of automatically creating a record for that sender as a contact or lead.
- **E-mail messages from CRM Leads, Contacts, and Accounts**: If a message is received from a sender that has an e-mail associated to a lead, contact, or account, it will be tracked in CRM.
- **E-mail messages from CRM records that are e-mail enabled**: If the message is sent from a sender that has a record in CRM and has an e-mail address field, it will be tracked in CRM.

Tracking outgoing e-mail messages

Clicking on the **Track** button starts a process where Dynamics CRM is queried for e-mail addresses found in the e-mail. If a match is found, an e-mail activity is created, and then the message is linked to the appropriate records. These records can be system users, accounts, contacts, leads, and queues. All of the aforementioned records have a system e-mail address field which is used for the match.

To track an outgoing e-mail message follow these steps:

1. Open **Microsoft Office Outlook**.
2. Click on the **New** button to create an e-mail message.
3. Enter the recipient, subject, and e-mail message body.

4. On the **Message** ribbon bar, in the **CRM** group, click on the **Track** button.
5. Click on **Send** to send the e-mail.

The second way in which an e-mail can be tracked is by setting the regarding field for the e-mail. As stated earlier, an e-mail in Dynamics CRM is an activity, and like other activity records, the regarding field can be set to associate any record in CRM to the e-mail. To set regarding in the Outlook client, follow these steps:

1. Open **Microsoft Office Outlook**.
2. Click on the **New** button to create an e-mail message.
3. Enter the recipient, subject, and e-mail message body.

4. On the **Message** ribbon bar, in the **CRM** group, click the **Set Regarding** button.

5. Under the **Find** menu option, click on **More**.
6. In the **Look Up Record** dialog box, select the entity type and record that you want to set the e-mail as regarding.
7. Click on **OK**.
8. Click on **Send** to send the e-mail.

Along with tracking outgoing e-mail messages, the Microsoft Dynamics CRM Outlook client can track incoming e-mail messages.

Tracking incoming e-mail messages

Incoming e-mail messages can again be tracked via the two methods described above: either by clicking on the track button or setting the regarding field. This can be done on individual record basis, or can be applied to multiple messages at the same time. Within Outlook, just select multiple e-mails, and then on the ribbon, click on **Track**, **Set Regarding** or both.

Stop tracking e-mail messages

E-mail messages can also be untracked. When an e-mail message is untracked, the e-mail message itself, and all previous e-mail activity records in CRM does not get deleted. However, no new e-mail activity records will be created unless e-mail messages are automatically being tracked (as described above).

Tracking appointments and tasks

Much like tracking and setting regarding for e-mails, similar steps can be taken to track and set regarding for appointments and tasks. The only difference is instead of creating a new e-mail, by clicking on **New E-mail** on the **Home** ribbon bar, click on the next button to the right, **New Items**, and select the activity type to be created.

In any system, the process of entering the data is important, but just as important is how to retrieve and view the data. Like the CRM web client, views can be configured by using the Microsoft Office Outlook CRM client.

Custom views

Custom views, like in the CRM web client, allows users to configure views tailored to their specific needs.

Creating custom views

To create a custom view within the CRM Outlook client, follow these steps:

1. Start the Microsoft Office Outlook CRM Client.
2. Navigate to any of the modules within the CRM section of the Outlook client.
3. Select the entity for which you wish to create a custom view.
4. On the **View** ribbon bar, click on **New Personal View**.

5. An **Advanced Find** dialog box will now appear for you to configure a query to retrieve data.
6. Click on **Results** to view the results of the query.
7. If satisfied, click on **Save As**.
8. Enter the name of the view and a clear, concise description for the view.
9. Click on **OK**.

The newly created view will now show up in the list of possible views for the entity.

Modifying custom views

Similar to the process for creating views, any view can be modified by simply selecting the view and then, on the **View** ribbon bar, clicking on **View Settings**. The **Advanced View Settings** dialog box appears (see the following screenshot):

From this dialog box, various options can be selected in order to modify the view. Let's look at each of these options in more detail.

- **Columns**: Allows the user to specify which columns are displayed in the view. For example, on the opportunity, a user can choose to display the owner as a column.
- **Group By**: Allows the user to group data by like values. This feature allows multiple group-by options. For example, the view can display all opportunities grouped by owner and then status.
- **Sort**: Allows the user to select a sorting order on the columns. A maximum of two columns can be sorted at one time.
- **Filter**: A user can filter the data being presented either by attribute values, SQL, or a more advanced method of using Outlook-specific fields.

- **Other Options**: Lets the user decide the font type, size, color, and reading pane settings.
- **Conditional Formatting**: We will touch more on this shortly.
- **Format Columns**: Lets a user specify the width, label, and orientation of the columns as well as the orientation of the values in a column.

Microsoft Office Outlook provides a rich feature set to allow users to configure custom views and to change the settings on these views in order to provide a more robust user experience. One of these options, conditional formatting, deserves a deeper look as it can be a powerful information management tool.

Conditional formatting

Conditional formatting is a powerful way to draw attention to the data a user most wants to see. When the **Conditional Formatting** option is selected in the **View Settings** dialog (pictured earlier), a dialog box appears as shown in the following screenshot:

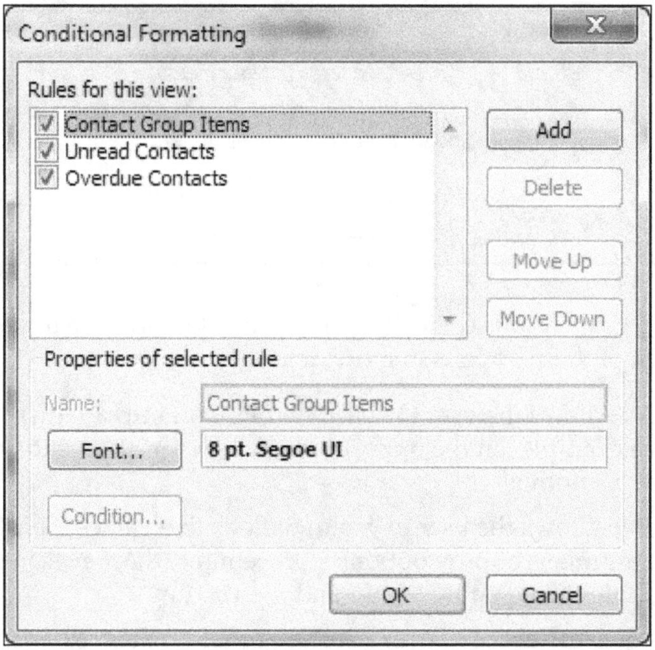

Here, you can add or delete a conditional formatting rule, or give priority to a rule over other rules by moving that rule up in order. After the rule is created, conditional formatting allows you to define the font size, type, and color of the data displayed due to the rule created. Different colors can be used to illustrate different conditional formatting rules.

A user can add their own conditional formatting rule by simply clicking on **Add**. Once a new rule is added, the **Condition** button becomes enabled. By clicking on the **Condition** button, users can define a set of criteria for the rule. These criteria can include filters based on attributes from CRM for a given record. For example, we can create a rule to highlight all of the accounts with an address that has a state of Washington and a country of United States. Then for this rule, we can define a font size, type, and color (say red). Once you click on **OK**, the current view will have rows where, if the conditional formatting rule is met , the row is shown in red.

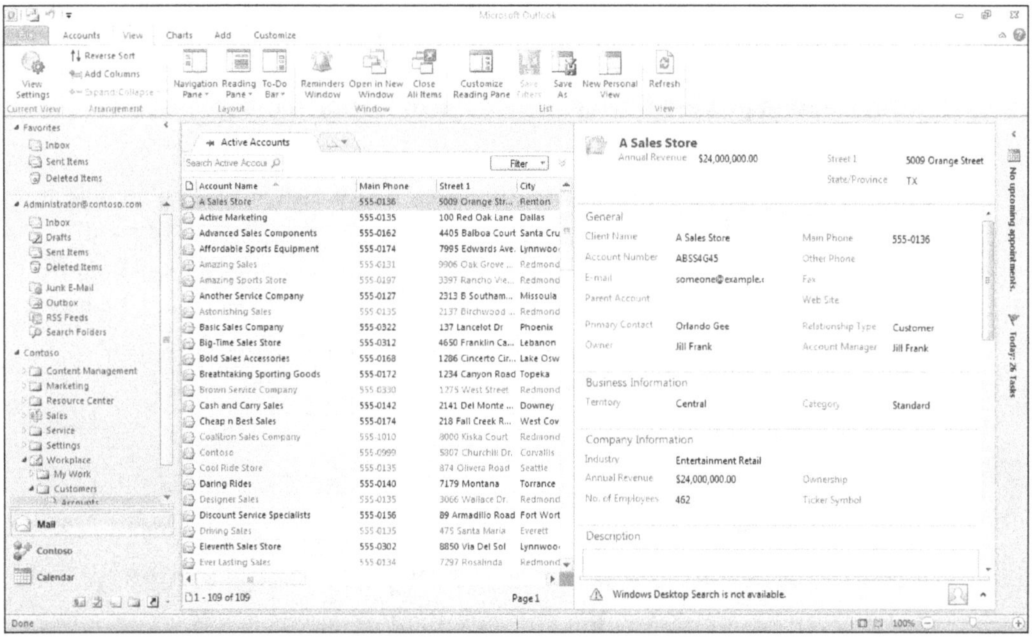

Test your knowledge

Q. 1. Which of the following are key differences between the Microsoft Dynamics CRM Outlook client and the CRM web client? (Choose all that apply.)

1. Using the web client, you can have personalized views by using features like conditional formatting.
2. Using the Outlook client, you can have personalized views by using features like conditional formatting.
3. Using the web client, you can receive reminders for tasks and appointments.
4. The Outlook client can be configured to display and synchronize records from multiple CRM organizations.

Q. 2. What are the following ways in which data can be synchronized between the CRM database and the Microsoft Office Outlook client? (Choose all that apply.)

1. The record is marked for synchronization using the **Track in CRM** button.
2. A user runs the synchronization process manually.
3. A background process runs periodically to synchronize records.
4. Records cannot be synchronized.

Q. 3. Let's say there's an account record in CRM that two users have access to edit. User A edits a field using the web client. An hour later, user B edits the same field in the CRM Outlook client while offline. An hour after that, user B comes back online and a synchronization process runs. Which of the following happens to the field that was edited by both users?

1. After synchronization, the information entered by user A will be the value stored in the field.
2. After synchronization, the information entered by user B will be the value stored in the field.
3. After synchronization, the field will consist of data merged from user A and user B.
4. None of the above.

Q. 4. What happens when a contact record is deleted or untracked in the CRM Outlook client? (Choose all that apply.)

1. A contact deleted in Outlook will not be deleted in CRM.
2. A contact that is untracked in Outlook will be deleted in CRM.
3. A contact deleted in Outlook will be deleted in CRM.
4. A contact that is untracked in Outlook will not be deleted in CRM.

Q. 5. An appointment deleted or untracked in Outlook will be deleted in CRM only if which of the following are true?

1. Appointment is open/scheduled.
2. Appointment **Start Time** is in the future.
3. The user performing the delete action is the Owner or Organizer of the Appointment.
4. All of the above.

Q. 6. State true or false: A task deleted in Outlook will be deleted in CRM, and vice versa, if the task is not completed.

Q. 7 Which of the following are true regarding e-mails that are untracked?

1. An e-mail deleted in Outlook will not be deleted in CRM.
2. An e-mail untracked in Outlook will be deleted in CRM if the user chooses to have it deleted.
3. An e-mail deleted in CRM will not be deleted in Outlook.
4. None of the above.
5. All of the above.

Q. 8. State true or false: Conditional formatting is a setting on a custom view.

Q. 9. State true or false: Conditional formatting can only be done by using CRM-specific fields.

Q. 10. State true or false: Conditional formatting formats the columns a view.

Summary

Microsoft Dynamics CRM 2011 integrates with Microsoft Outlook to provide the same functionality as the web client. There are a few major differences between the CRM web client and the CRM Outlook client. When appointments and tasks are synchronized with CRM, the Outlook client can set up reminders for them. Another difference between the CRM web and Outlook clients is that users can create personalized views and apply conditional formatting rules in Outlook.

The CRM Outlook client also gives users the ability to work with offline. For this functionality, data is stored on a user's local machine in a SQL Server Express database (created during installation of the CRM Outlook client add-in). When a user goes back online, data can be synchronized. Various rules apply when data is synchronized to and from the CRM database. When changes are made both in the CRM Outlook client and in the CRM web client on the same fields in the same record, the changes made last gets applied during synchronization. Besides creating and updating data, synchronization rules around deleting of records also exist.

E-mail messages in Microsoft Office Outlook can be traced in CRM either automatically, or by using the **Track** button. Tracking e-mails automatically is a personal user setting that can be configured in CRM. A user must select one of the following automatic e-mail tracking options: all e-mails, e-mails in response to CRM e-mail, e-mails from CRM Leads, Contacts and Accounts, or e-mail messages from CRM records that are e-mail enabled. Outgoing and incoming e-mail messages can be tracked by using the **Track** button. When an e-mail message is untracked, the e-mail message itself, and all previous e-mail activity records in CRM do not get deleted.

Custom views allows a user to personalize their CRM views within Outlook. Users can configure which columns are displayed, and the data by which to group, sort, and filter. Conditional formatting is another option to help draw attention to various records in Outlook. For example, if we would like to focus on accounts with a business address in the country of the United Kingdom, a rule can be applied to show those records in a different font color. In this way, those records will stand out when looking at them in a larger data set.

In the next chapter, we'll take a look at the service management features of CRM. Specifically we'll walk through managing service cases, knowledge base articles, queues, teams, and contracts. We'll then see how an organization can analyze and report on the service-related data.

7

Managing Service Management Applications

In this chapter you will learn about:

- Managing service cases
- Managing the knowledge base
- Managing queues and teams
- Managing contracts
- Analysis and reporting

Thus far, we have been looking at how Microsoft Dynamics CRM 2011 has the capability to tackle the marketing and sales needs of any organization. The focus up to now has been on how to attract new customers, and how to sell an organization's products and services to these customers. Once a customer base has been established, it's then up to the organization to keep these customers happy by servicing them appropriately.

Introduction

While servicing your customers, regardless of your best efforts, customer questions or issues may arise. When they do, CRM's service module provides an excellent way to manage these cases. Along with managing customer's cases, Dynamics CRM allows an organization to create a knowledge base to track resolutions, and to help resolve future cases efficiently. Cases can be assigned to a queue for users to pick and choose which cases to work on, and in other instances, cases can be assigned to a team of users. All of these assignment functionalities help to drive collaboration and improve the visibility of cases at all levels of an organization. Often, service contracts are created between organizations and its customers. In such cases, CRM provides a way to manage those contracts. Finally, to complete the 360-degree view of the customer, users have the ability to analyze the data via various charts, dashboards, and reports.

Business scenarios

Race2Win Insurance Company has built up a significant customer base by providing valued products to its clients and building a brand that has credibility in the market. No matter how well things may go, there are always issues that may arise. An example is incorrect or late invoices. Race2Win would like to log these cases, have them routed to the appropriate people for resolution, and then create a repository of information to make solving future cases easier.

Furthermore, Race2Win started up a new division called the Race2Win Support Network to help provide customer service and support to all its clients. Race2Win's customers enter into a contractual agreement with the support network. Microsoft Dynamics CRM also provides a way to manage these contracts in order to allow support staff to refer to the conditions of a contract before providing service to a customer.

Lastly, to keep the customer base happy, it's critical that leadership has access to metrics and reports to track case resolution effectiveness. CRM provides charts, dashboards, and reports to help paint a 360-degree view of the customer.

The first step in managing customer service issues revolves around the Microsoft Dynamics CRM service module—namely, cases.

Managing service cases

Service cases can include anything from customer service issues such as late or incorrect invoices, poor quality of products and services, inadequate delivery of products and services, and so on. In this section, we'll explore the case management process, including the following:

- Creating cases
- Assigning cases
- Connecting cases to another record
- Creating a subject tree
- Adding case notes
- Creating a recurring appointment
- Resolving a case
- Using case views
- Searching for case records
- Working with system charts for cases

The first step is for a user to create a case.

Creating cases

To create a case, perform the following steps:

1. Start CRM and go to the **Services** module in the left-hand navigation area.
2. Select **Cases**.
3. On the contextual ribbon, click on **New**.
4. Enter the following required fields:
    - **Title**: A clear, concise description of the case. This field is required.
    - **Customer**: The account or contact record against which the case is being logged.
    - **Owner**: This defaults to the user creating the record, but can be changed. When an owner is assigned, the record also gets assigned to that user's default queue. Case and activity records are the only entity types this happens for.

5. Although they are not required, the following fields are worth mentioning:
    - **Subject**: A lookup to the subject tree. More on the subject tree will be discussed later.
    - **Contract**: This field allows a user to tie a service contract to the case, for reference. A customer must first be selected in order to select a service contact.
    - **Contract Line**: The case can be further tied to a specific contract line item, but a contract must first be selected in order to select this field.
6. Click on **Save and Close**.

Much like opportunities, cases can be created from an e-mail, as well as any activity record. To create a case from an activity record, perform the following steps (for this example, we shall use an e-mail activity record):

1. Start CRM.
2. Navigate to the **Workplace** module and then click on **Activities**, or open the Microsoft Office Outlook client for Dynamics CRM.
3. Open the e-mail that you wish to convert.
4. On the **E-mail** ribbon bar, in the **Convert Activity** group, click on **To Case**:

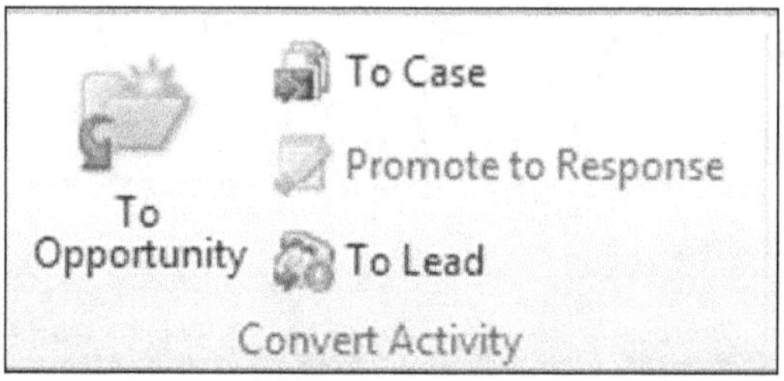

5. In the **Convert E-mail to Case** dialog box, enter the following fields:
    - **Customer**: This field may auto-populate with the customer entered in the **To** line of the e-mail. Otherwise, the user must choose from an account or contact.
    - **Subject**: This is optional and we'll talk more about the subject tree later on in this chapter.
    - **Open the new case**: When this option is selected the newly created case record will be opened when the **OK** button is clicked.

- **Close the e-mail form**: When this option is selected, the e-mail form is closed when the **OK** button is clicked.

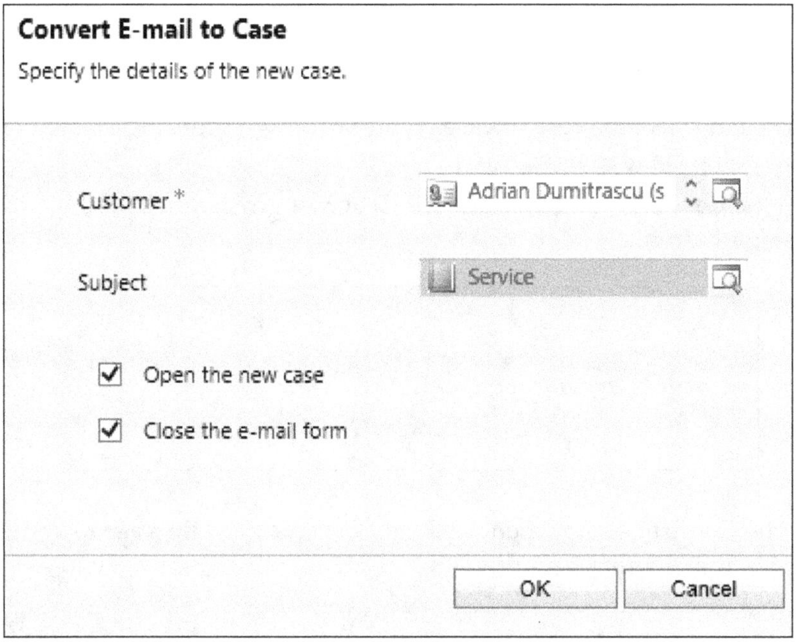

6. Click on **OK**.

Once a case has been created, you'll notice the case number field is populated with an auto-generated case number. This case number is unique and helps an organization to track cases.

Business scenarios

Race2Win Insurance Company uses the case management functionality of Dynamics CRM to manage its cases. The organization's goal is to provide exemplary service and to resolve all cases in an accurate and timely manner. Unfortunately, over the past few months, cases haven't been resolved as quickly as customers would like. To fix this issue, Race2Win has implemented a new process of manager intervention. When a case goes unresolved for more than a certain period of time, an e-mail notification is automatically sent out to the case owner's manager and the case is then assigned to that manager.

As you can see, the assignment of cases can be a powerful tool. Most records in Dynamics CRM can be assigned to other users; however it is often more frequently used in case management.

Assigning cases

To assign a case in Microsoft Dynamics CRM, perform the following steps:

1. Start CRM
2. Navigate to the **Service** module, and then click on **Cases**.
3. Find and select the case or cases (you can assign multiple cases at one time) that you wish to assign.
4. On the **Cases** ribbon bar, in the **Collaborate** group, click on the **Assign** button.

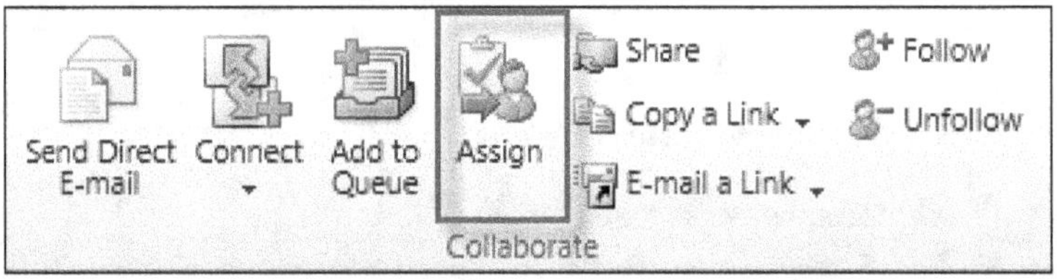

5. In the **Confirm Assignment** dialog, you can assign the case to yourself or assign it to another user or team.

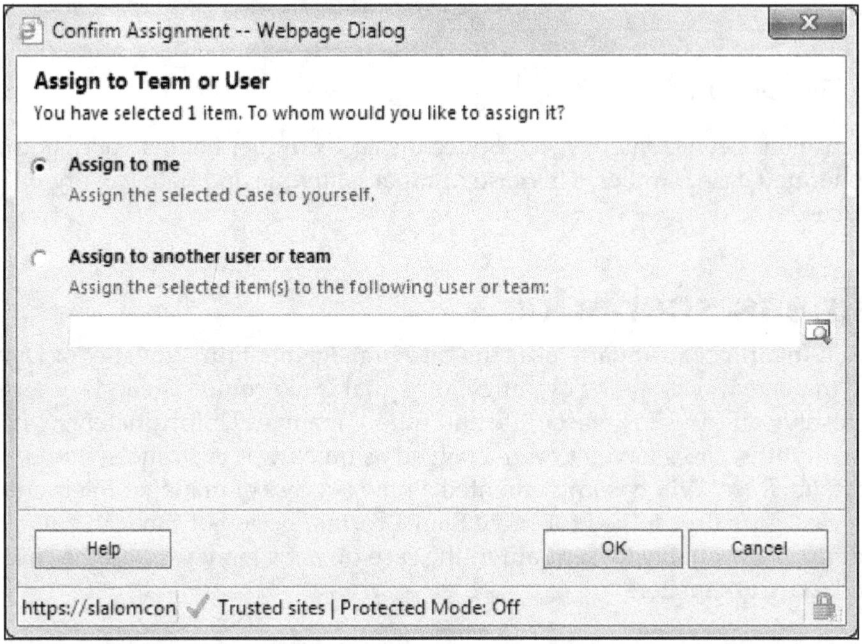

6. Click on **OK**.

Connecting cases

In addition to assigning a case, cases can be connected to other records. Connecting records in Dynamics CRM allows a user to create relationships and apply a meaning to those relationships. For example, out of the box, a case is associated to or "connected" to a customer record (account or contact) via the customer field on the form. Let's say, however, that the case is also connected to another customer, either directly or indirectly. Microsoft Dynamics CRM allows you to connect the case to any other record in the system and to define the meaning of that relationship.

To connect a case to another record, perform the following steps:

1. Start CRM.
2. Navigate to the **Service** module on the left-hand navigation.
3. Find and select the case that you wish to connect. Unlike assigning a case, you can only connect one case at a time.
4. On the **Cases** ribbon bar, in the **Collaborate** group, click on the **Connect** button and choose whether to connect the case to yourself, or to another record.

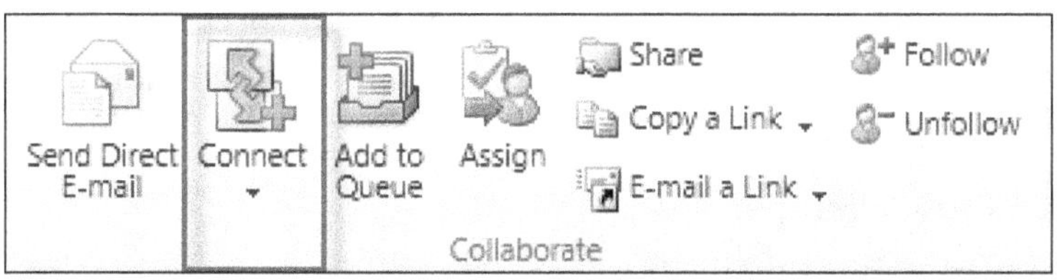

5. Enter the following fields:
   - **Name**: This is a lookup field that allows the selection of any record in your system
   - **As this role**: There are system defined roles that can be selected, but a user can create their own roles

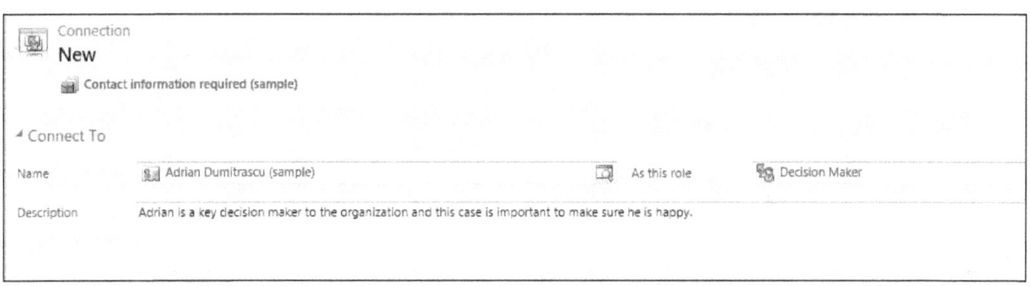

6. Click on **Save and Close**.

Creating a subject tree

During the creation of the cases, a subject can be associated to the case. The **subject tree** is a list of categories that an organization can use to help organize cases or other record types. The key word in the definition is *tree*, because subjects can be defined in a hierarchical manner. An example of a subject tree can be:

- Microsoft
    - Dynamics
        - CRM
        - AX
        - GP
        - NAV

To add a new subject to the subject tree, perform the following steps:

1. Start CRM.
2. Navigate to the **Settings** module in the left-hand navigation area.
3. Under the **Business** section, click on **Business Management**.
4. Click on **Subjects**.
5. Click on **Add a Subject**.
6. In the **Add Subject** dialog box, enter the following information:
    - **Title**: The only required field; enter a clear, concise name for the subject
    - **Parent Subject**: This is optional, but if you enter it here, you can build the hierarchical subject tree, by attaching this new subject below the specified parent subject
    - **Description**

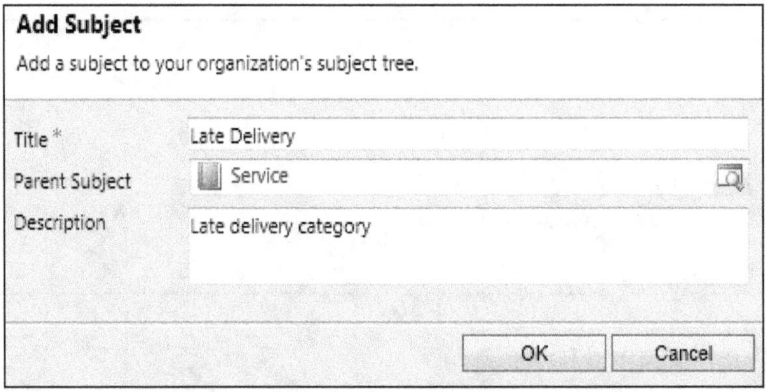

7. Click on **OK**.

To maintain the subject tree, you can go back to the same area in CRM and click on **Edit Subject** tree.

Adding case notes

On the case form, the second tab contains notes. Notes behave the same for cases as in any entity. They may be used more frequently here because multiple users may work on a case, and adding notes is one way to help communicate changes to the next case worker. Notes are date and time stamped, with the latest note appearing on top. Some examples of notes are steps taken to resolve a case, any notes about the customer, or any comments made by management about the case.

In addition to notes, like most other entities in Dynamics CRM, activities can be added to a case. One such activity type that may be used with a case is the recurring appointment.

Creating a recurring appointment

To create a recurring appointment, perform the following steps:

1. Start CRM.
2. Navigate to the **Services** module on the left-hand side and click on **Cases**.
3. Open the case record to which you wish to add the recurring appointment.
4. Click on **Activities** on the left-hand navigation of the case.
5. Click on **New Activity** and select **Recurring Appointment**.

6. Enter the following required field:
   - **Subject**: This is different than the subject tree mentioned earlier in this chapter. This is a clear, concise subject of the appointment being made.

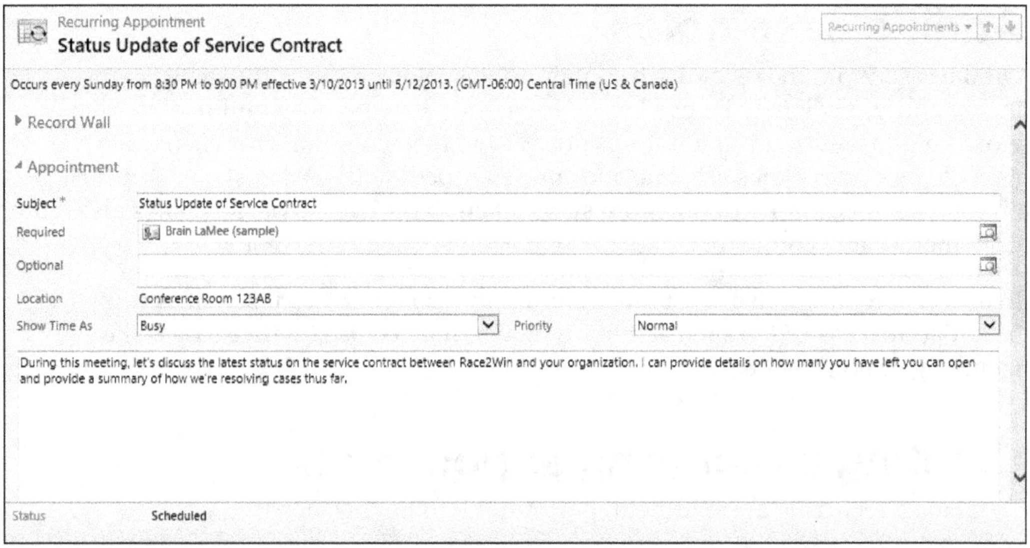

7. On the **Recurring Appointment** ribbon bar, in the **Scheduling** group, click on the **Recurrence** button.

8. Fill out the appropriate timings for the occurrence.

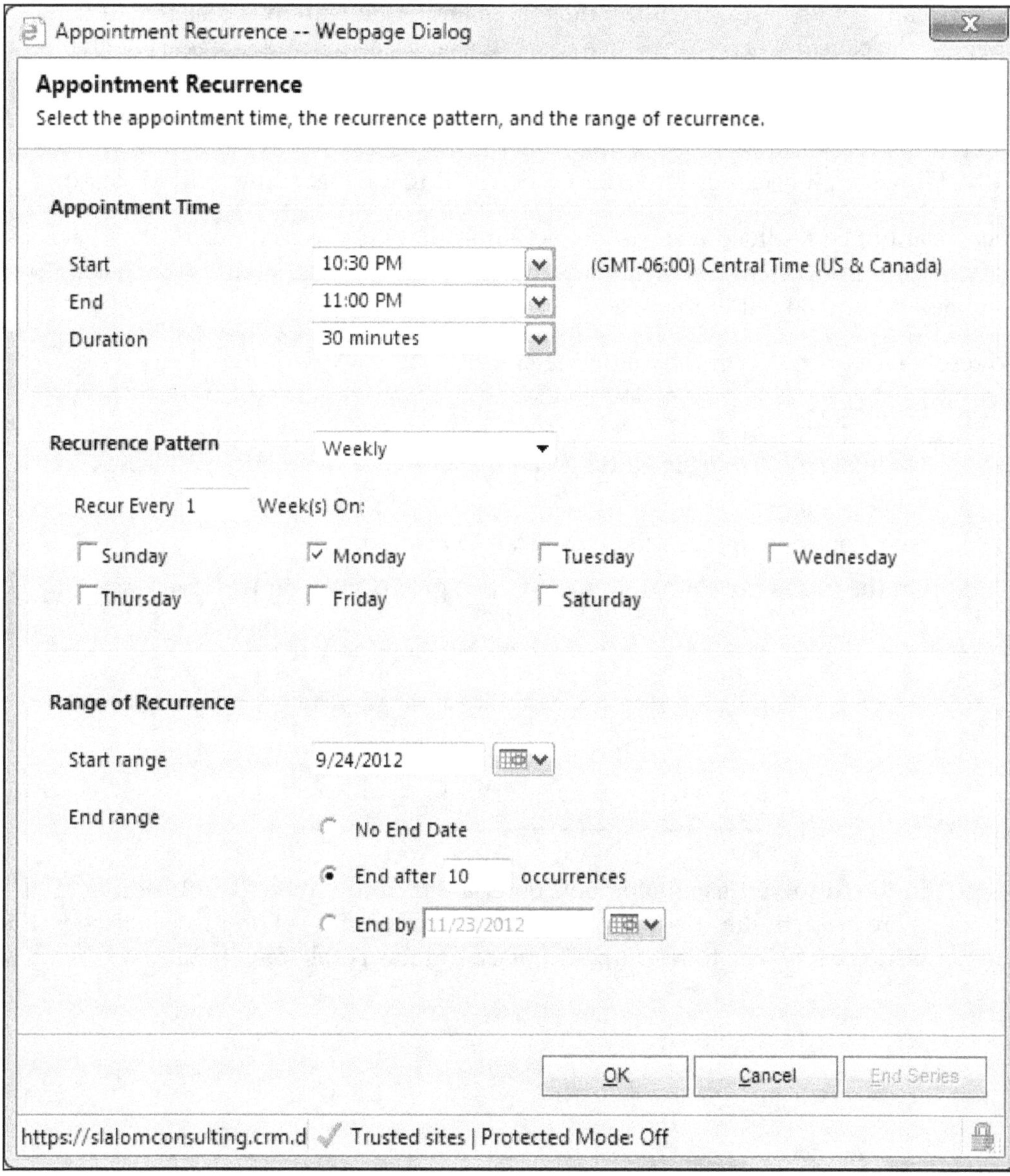

9. Click on **OK**.
10. Click on **Save and Close**.

Resolving a case

When dealing with cases, the ultimate goal of any organization is case resolution. There is one caveat when resolving a case. Activities, as discussed in earlier chapters, can be used to track interactions between an organization and customer. This holds true for cases, but in addition, activities can be used to track time spent on a case. Often times the duration field on an activity is not used when relating it to entities in CRM. However, it becomes important when setting the regarding field to a case.

A case cannot be resolved if it has any activities that are not completed. If all of the activities are completed, then when resolving a case, the time spent on each activity is totaled up and added to the case.

To resolve a case, perform the following steps:

1. Start CRM.
2. Navigate to the **Service** module on the left-hand navigation, and click on **Cases**.
3. Select or open the case that you wish to resolve.
4. On the **Cases** ribbon bar, in the **Actions** group, click on **Resolve Case**.

5. In the **Resolve Case** dialog box, enter a resolution in the **Resolution** field. If there are activities tied to a case and the duration is set on those activities, the durations will be totaled up and placed in the **Total Time** field.

6. Of the total time on activities, a user can say what portion of the time can be billed to the customer.

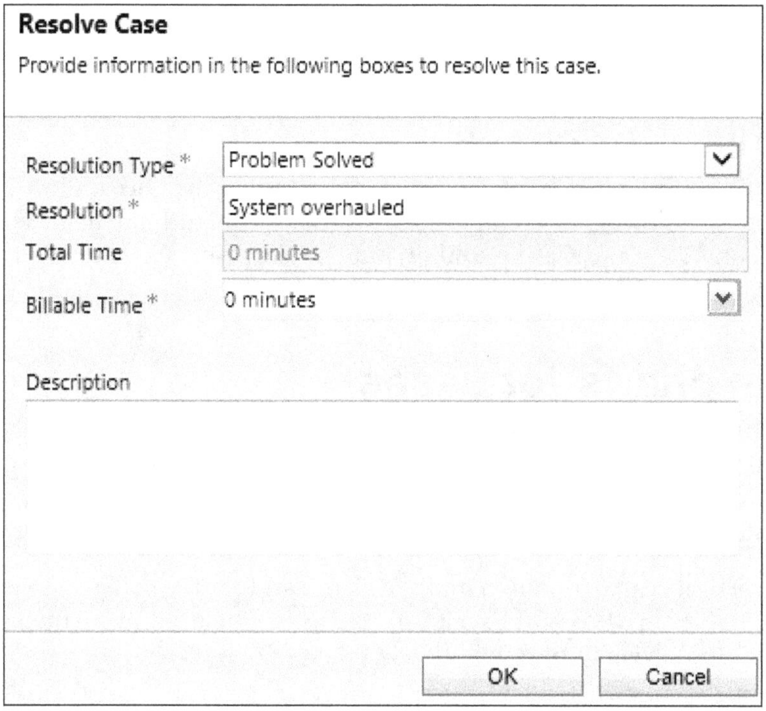

7. Click on **OK**.

Case views

No matter where you are in the process of working a case, it's critical to be able to get to the case records you need. This can be done by using intelligent views, and like many of the other entities in CRM, cases come with their own system views. Some of the system views that are pre-configured are:

- **Active cases**: Cases that are still open and have not been resolved or canceled
- **Active cases opened in the last 7 days**
- **All cases**: All cases, no matter the status
- **Cases opened in the last 7 days**
- **Cases resolved by me in the last 7 days**
- **Cases resolved in the last 7 days**
- **My active cases**: Open cases where the owner is the currently logged in user

- **My active cases opened in the last 7 Days**
- **My resolved cases**: Resolved cases where the owner is the currently logged in user
- **Resolved cases**

Searching for cases

The case entity comes with a pre-configured view called the **Quick Find** view. This view is what is used when searching case records. By default, the fields configured to be searched are: **Title** and **Case Number**, but the view can be customized to include other fields.

System charts for cases

Similar to the other entities in Dynamics CRM, there is a chart pane to the right of many of the views. Users can access these charts and the data within the grid will be displayed. As you use the view filter and change views, or use the quick search to filter the data in the view, the chart will change to reflect the data present in the view.

Furthermore, users can drill down into the charts and perform analysis similar to that of pivot tables in Microsoft Excel. Charts can also be used to create dashboards, providing multiple visual representations of data in one place.

Managing the knowledge base

If an organization undertakes the effort to service their customers by using the case management module, one of its primary goals is to resolve cases quickly and effectively. A tool that can be very helpful is the **knowledge base**. The knowledge base is a location where users can search for articles to help them resolve cases. A unique functionality with knowledge base articles is that this is one of the only places in Dynamics CRM where a full-text search occurs.

In this section, we'll cover the following topics:

- Managing article templates
- Managing knowledge base articles
- Searching for knowledge base articles
- Associating an article with a case

All knowledge base articles must be created by using an article template. Let's look a bit closer into article templates.

Knowledge base article templates

According to MSDN, a knowledge base template allows a user to describe the sections and formatting for the knowledge base article. There are four out-of-the box knowledge base templates that can be used as a baseline for others: Procedure, Question & Answer, Solution to a Problem, and Standard KB Article.

To create a knowledge base article template, perform the following steps:

1. Start CRM.
2. Navigate to the **Settings** module, and under the **Business** section, click on **Templates**, and then click on **Article Templates**.
3. On the **Article Templates** toolbar, click on **New**.
4. In the **Article Template Properties** dialog, enter the following required information:
    - **Title**: A clear, concise name for the article template.

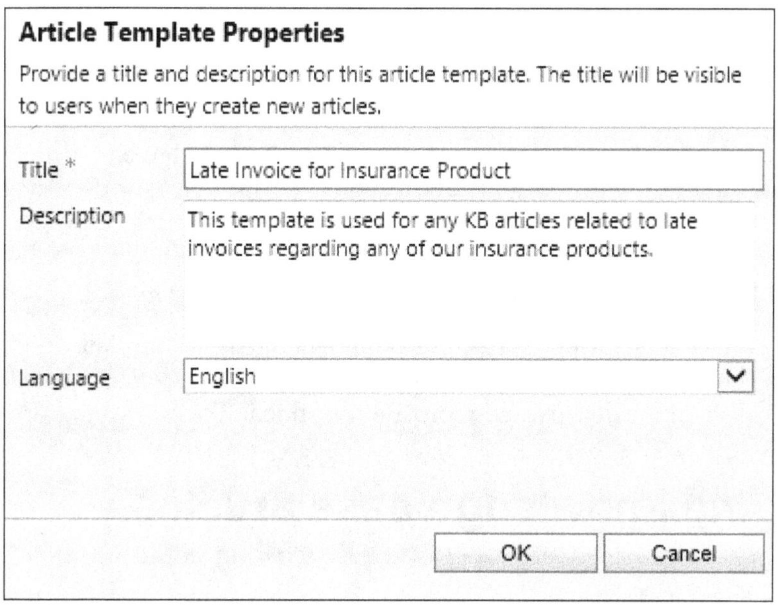

5. Click on **OK**.
6. In the right-hand navigation area, click on **Add a Section**.
7. In the **Add a New Section** dialog box, enter in the title and text for the section.
8. Click on **OK**.

9. Repeat steps 6 to 8 to add more sections.
10. Once completed, click on **Save and Close**.

A sample of a knowledge base article template is shown as follows:

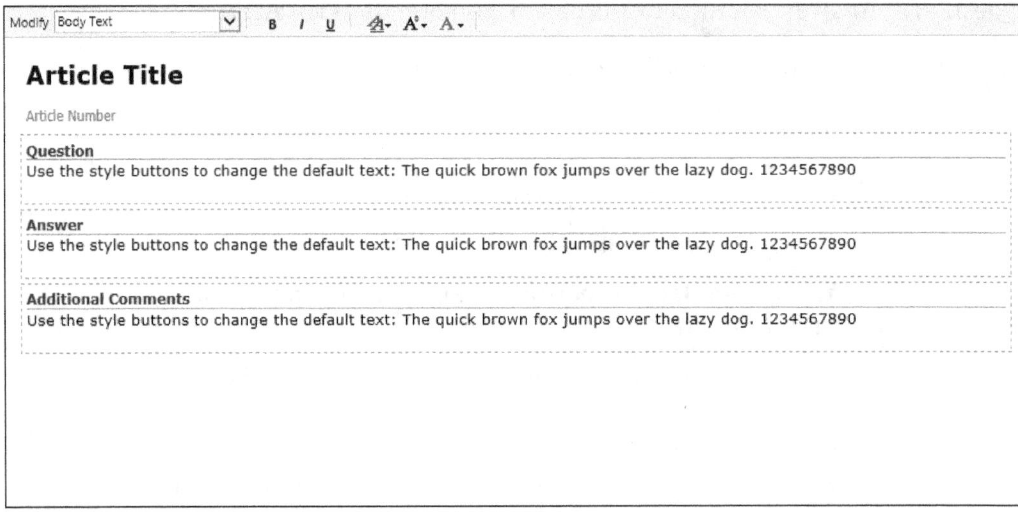

Knowledge base article templates are important, as knowledge base articles can't be created without them. An organization can choose to delete or deactivate article templates. A template can be deactivated even if there are articles created from the template; however no new articles can be created from an inactive template. You can only delete templates if there are no articles tied to that template.

Let's say you have many articles, based on a knowledge base template, in various stages of the publishing process. If you deactivate the knowledge base article template, all articles based on the deactivated template continue in the publishing process.

Managing knowledge base articles

To create knowledge base articles, perform the following steps:

1. Start CRM.
2. Navigate to the **Service** module, and then click on **Articles**.
3. On the **Articles** ribbon bar, in the **Records** group, click on **New**.
4. In the **Article Template** dialog, select a template to use.

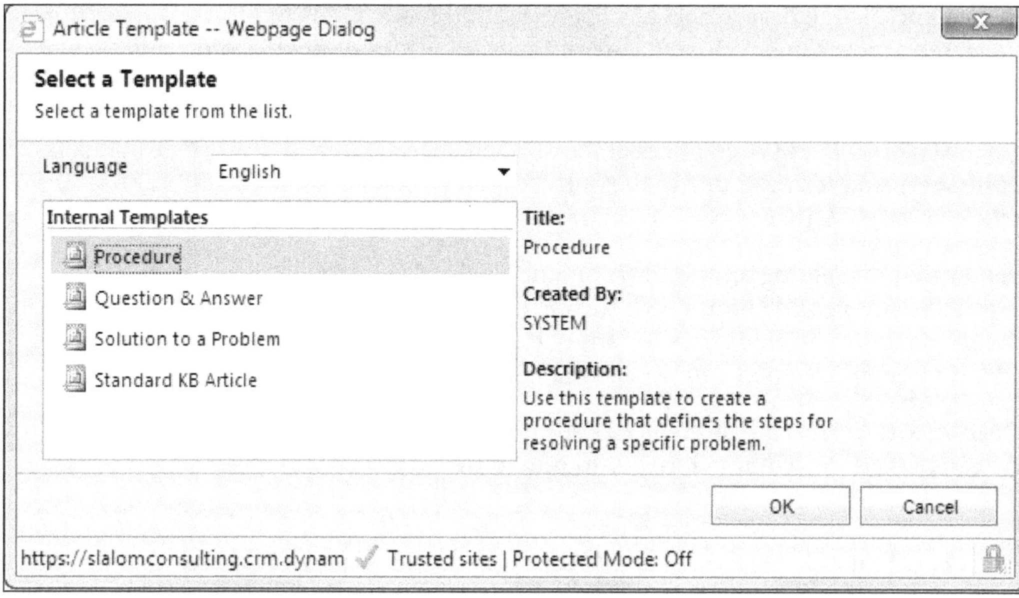

5. Click on **OK**.
6. Enter the following required fields:
    - **Title**: A clear, concise title
    - **Subject**: This is a required field to select the appropriate value from the CRM subject tree

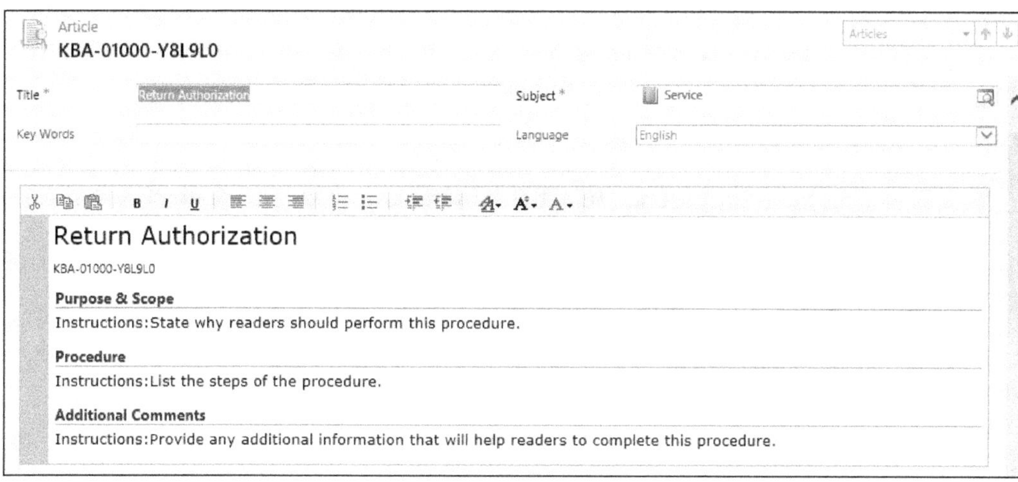

7. Click on **Save**.

Once a knowledge base article has been saved, it has a status of **Draft**. During this stage, the article can be edited as many times as one would like. Doing this also enables a button the ribbon bar called **Submit**. When the article is submitted, the new status of the article is **Unapproved**, which still allows you to edit the article, and the next step is to approve or reject the article. Once approved, the article status is **Published**, and it's available to the entire organization for viewing and for use. If the article is rejected, it goes back into **Draft** status and is available to be edited again.

In addition to creating and publishing knowledge base articles, users in an organization can add comments. Adding comments can help to track any changes to the article, or to provide notes for anyone using the article. Comments can only be added to unapproved or published articles.

Once an article template is created, and then an article created using this template, we can use the search functionality to find knowledge base articles.

Searching for knowledge base articles

The only way knowledge base articles are available for searching is when the article is published. To search for articles in the workplace, perform the following steps:

1. Start CRM.
2. Navigate to the **Workplace** module, and then click on **Articles**.
3. To find an article, enter text in the search box that is typically used for the quick find.
4. When clicking inside the text box, the CRM contextual ribbon changes.
5. Click on **Start Search**, or press the *Enter* key, to search for articles. The search criteria used from the ribbon will be explained next.

The types of searches that can be used are:

- **Full Text Search**: Searches all articles in the knowledge base for the text entered in the search field
- **Keyword Search**: Searches all article keywords for the text entered in the search area
- **Title Search**: Searches all article titles for the text entered in the search area
- **Article Number Search**: Searches articles for the auto number generated by Dynamics CRM

- **Subject Search**: Search by subject tree

When created, found, and used, knowledge base articles provide an organization with a way to quickly search for answers—especially around solving cases. When solving a case, if a knowledge base article is used, it's best to reference it so if future similar cases are created, the same knowledge base article can be used to expedite the resolution process.

Associating knowledge base articles with cases

Associating a knowledge base article with a case begins by first searching for an article within a case. To associate an article with a case, perform the following steps:

1. Start CRM.
2. Navigate to the **Service** module, and then click on **Cases**.
3. Find and open the case to which you want to associate an article.
4. Navigate to the **Notes and Articles** section of the form.
5. Click on the **Article** lookup icon on the form.
6. Use the following search options:
    - **Search type**: This can be **Full Text**, **Keyword**, **Title**, **Article Number**, or **Subject Browse**
    - **Search for**: Enter the text to search for
    - **In subject**: This is optional, and allows you to search by subject
    - **Options**: Either an exact text search or use like words

7. Click on **View Article**.

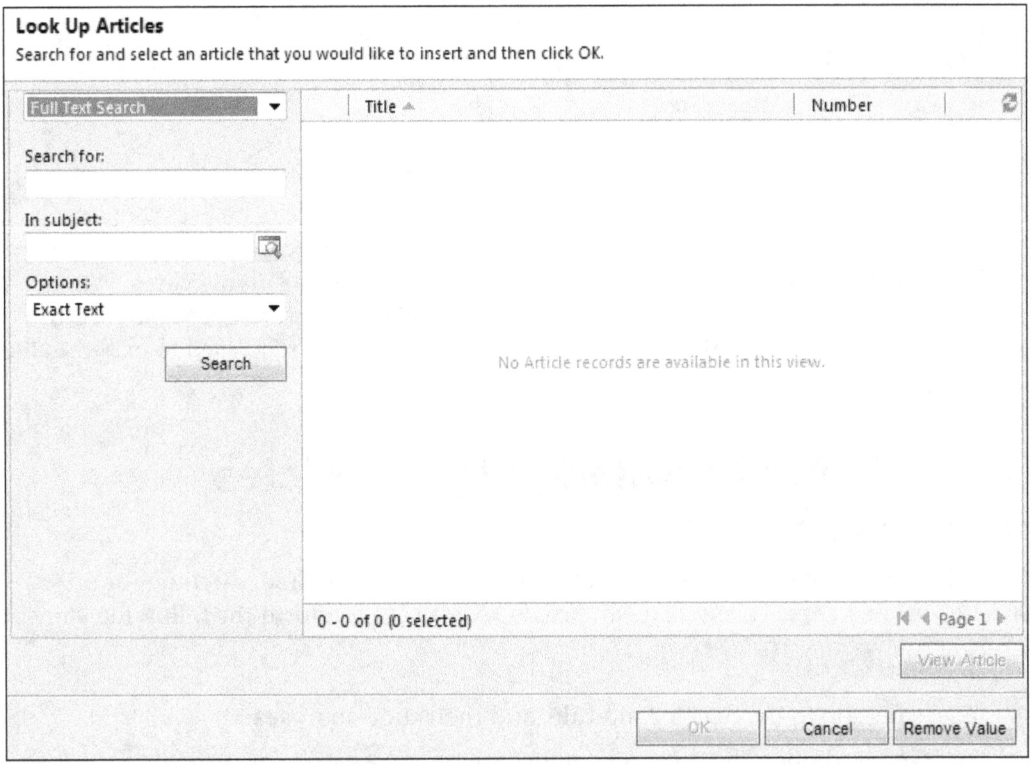

8. Select the article, and then click on **OK**.

The search functionality behaves similar to that of the searching for articles in the workplace. Once the article is associated, it can be e-mailed to the customer quite easily as well. This is an added bonus of associating a knowledge base article to a case.

Managing queues and teams

Queues and teams provide a way of managing work for various individuals across organizations. While they can be used in most places in Dynamics CRM, they're mentioned more often in connection with the service module.

Business scenarios

Race2Win Insurance Company has a business dedicated to the support of its clients. In order to service their clients effectively, Race2Win has employed the use of the Microsoft Dynamics CRM service module. With Dynamics CRM, they can open up cases for any issues a customer may have. To help resolve the case effectively, they have various business rules around routing cases to different departments to be worked on. The organization has various teams to handle a case based on the type of case opened. Let's say a case has been opened because of a billing question. Using the power of Dynamics CRM workflows, as soon as a case is created with a type **Billing**, the case is routed or assigned to the billing queue. From there, folks in the billing department can retrieve cases to be worked on.

Managing queues

When a user or team is created, a default queue is automatically created. A queue can also have an e-mail address. A use case of this would be a queue having an e-mail address that is actually a distribution list of a team. Let's say a case is created and assigned to a queue. Dynamics CRM workflow can automatically send an e-mail to the e-mail address associated with the queue, letting them know that an item has been added to the queue. If this e-mail address is a distribution list for the team, then everyone on the team will get notified.

Also by default, only activities and cases can be assigned to a queue. To enable the use of queues for other entities, you'll need to configure this in the customizations section of an entity.

The following points will be discussed:

- Creating queues
- Deleting and deactivating queues
- Adding cases and activities to queues
- Routing
- Managing queue items

Creating queues

To create a queue, perform the following steps:

1. Start CRM.
2. Navigate to the **Settings** module, and under the **Business** section, click on **Business Management**, and then click on **Queues**.

3. On the **Queues** toolbar, click on **New**.
4. Enter the following required fields:
    - **Queue Name**: A clear, concise name for the queue
    - **Owner**: Defaults to user creating queue
    - **Convert to e-mail activities**: Options are **All e-mail messages, E-mail messages in response to CRM e-mail, E-mail messages from CRM Leads, Contacts and Accounts,** and **E-mail messages from CRM records that are e-mail enabled**
    - **E-mail access type Incoming**: Options are **None, E-mail Router,** and **Forward Mailbox**
    - **E-mail access type Outgoing**: Options are **None, E-mail Router,** and **Forward Mailbox**

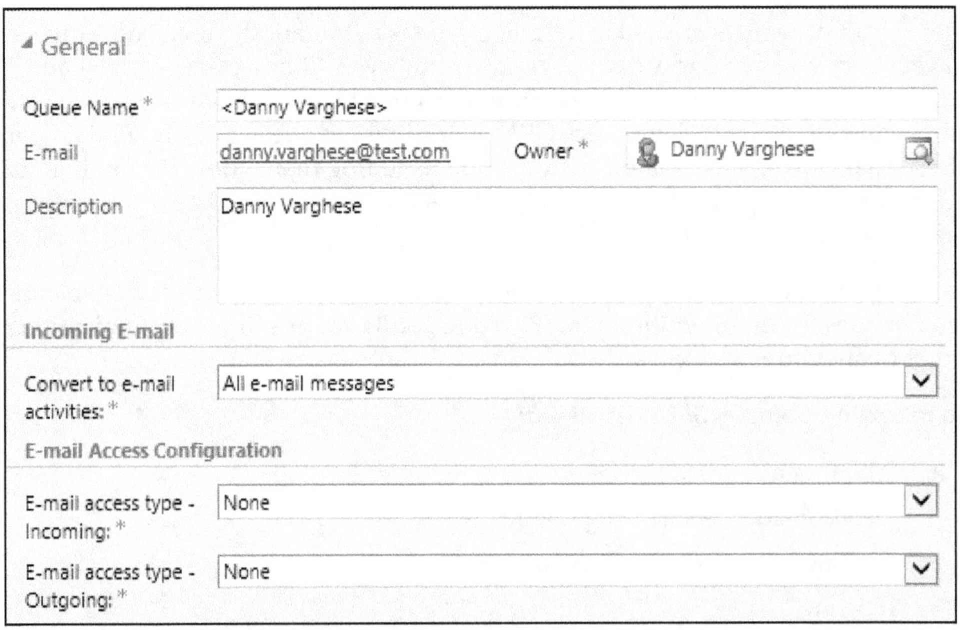

5. Click on **Save and Close**.

Deleting and deactivating queues

There are various rules when deleting or deactivating queues. When a queue is deactivated, all queue items are removed from the queue. A queue cannot be deleted if it contains queue items. In addition to these rules, a queue can be deactivated or deleted at any time. When a queue is active, cases and activities can be assigned to a queue.

Adding activities and cases to queues

To add activities or cases to a queue, perform the following steps:

1. Start CRM.
2. Navigate to the **Workplace** module and then click on **Activities**, or navigate to the **Service** module and then click on **Cases**.
3. Select one or more activities or cases.
4. On the **Activities** or **Cases** ribbon bar, in the **Collaborate** group, click on **Add to Queue**.

5. In the **Add to Queue** dialog box, find the queue to which you wish to add the items.
6. Click on **OK**.

Routing

Routing provides a way for users to route or change the location of a record from one queue to another. As stated earlier, when a case or another record is added to a queue, a queue item is created which is associated to a queue and to the record. To route a queue item from one queue to another, perform the following steps:

1. Start CRM.
2. Navigate to the **Workplace** module, and click on **Queues**.
3. Select one or more queue items. You can use the queue filter to view a single queue that you're interested in.
4. On the **Queue Items** ribbon bar, in the **Actions** group, click on **Routing**.

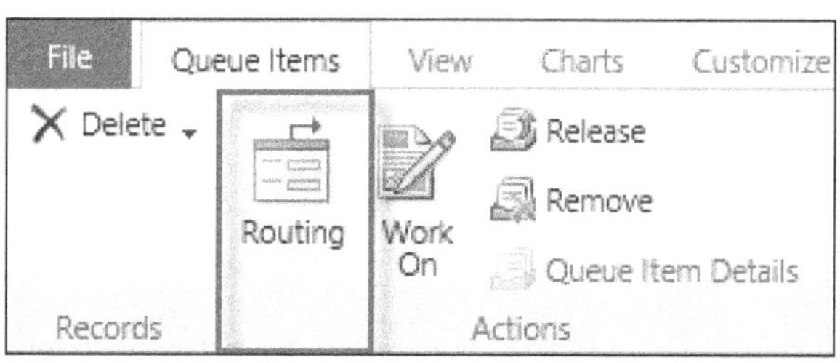

5. Look up a queue to route the items to.
6. Click on **OK**.

Managing queue items

As stated earlier, when a record is assigned to a queue, a queue item is created. The queue item contains a **Worked By** field, which is the user or team that is working on the particular queue item. If a queue item is deleted, the record associated with the queue item is also deleted, so be careful when doing this.

When a user or team wants to work on a particular queue item, they can select the item and click on the **Work On** button. Doing this does not change the ownership of the record, but rather just the **Worked By** field.

Managing teams

Teams are a new concept introduced to Dynamics CRM 2011 that allows an organization to group individuals and assign to those groups records within the system. A couple of interesting notes:

- A team may have a security role assigned to it. Any team member (user) will inherit the team's security. If no security role is assigned to a team, then that team cannot be assigned any records.
- Like other part of Dynamics CRM when it comes to security, the highest privilege wins. That is, if a user has a security role and the team has a security role, when performing an action, the highest privilege wins, regardless of whether that is defined on the user or on the team.
- Teams can be deleted where as users cannot. However, a team can only be deleted if there are no records assigned to it.
- Teams are one way in which users from different business units can interact with a record. For example, let's say you have a user in Business Unit A, and a user in Business Unit B. The user in Business Unit A can read all accounts, while a user in Business Unit B cannot. If both users were assigned the same team with permission to read accounts assigned to them, and an account record was assigned their team, then both users would be able to read the record.

Creating a team

To create a team, perform the following steps:

1. Start CRM.
2. Navigate to the **Settings** module, and under the **System** section click on **Administration**.
3. Click on **Teams**.
4. On the **Teams** ribbon bar, in the **Records** group, click on **New**.
5. Enter the following required fields:
    - **Team Name**: Enter a clear, concise name for the team
    - **Administrator**: User that will be the administrator for the team
    - **Business Unit**

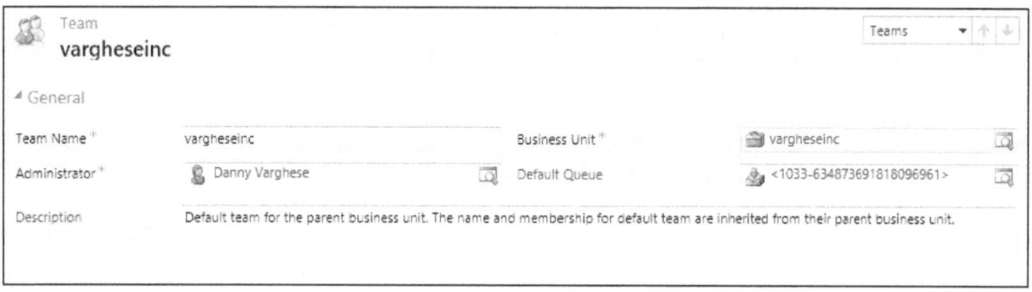

6. Click on **Save**.

Adding team members

To add users or members to a team, perform the following steps:

1. Start CRM.
2. Navigate to the **Settings** module, and under the **System** section, click on **Administration**.
3. Click on **Teams**.
4. Find and open the team to which you wish to add members.
5. Click on **Members** in the left-hand navigation area.

6. On the **List Tools** tab of the **Users** ribbon bar, in the **Records** group, click on the **Add Members** button.

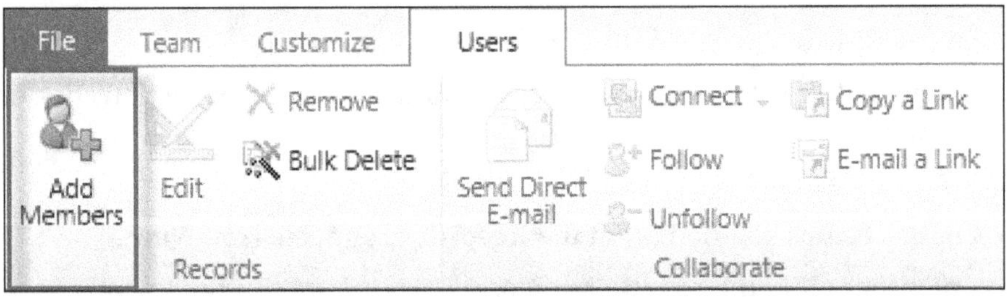

7. In the **User Lookup** dialog box, add one or more users to the team.
8. Click on **OK**.

Adding security roles

To add security roles to a team, perform the following steps:

1. Start CRM.
2. Navigate to the **Settings** module, and under the **System** section, click on **Administration**.
3. Click on **Teams**.
4. Find and open the team to which you wish to add security roles.
5. You can either go to the **Team** ribbon bar, in the **Actions** group, and click on the **Manage Roles** button, or click in the left-hand navigation area on **Security Roles**, and then click on the **Manage Roles** button.

6. Select one or more security roles to add.
7. Click on **OK**.

Managing contracts

Contracts are a way to define the types of service agreement that an organization might enter into with a customer. Contracts, when used with cases, can be referenced in order to see if the service being performed is in line with the agreed upon terms of the contract.

Business scenarios

Race2Win Insurance Company has entered into a service agreement with one of its clients to provide up to 40 hours of support every week for the next month. The terms of the service are that any case created will be worked on within 24 hours and, if it's a high priority item, the case will be worked on within 1 hour. Race2Win can leverage Microsoft Dynamics CRM contract functionality to help track these contract obligations. Race2Win can tie contracts to cases as they work on them, to make sure that the hours are used appropriately.

Contracts in Dynamics CRM consist of contract templates, which are used to create contracts, and then each contact can have one or more contract lines.

Creating a contract template

Much like knowledge base articles, contracts can only be created by using contract templates. To create a contract template, perform the following steps:

1. Start CRM.
2. Navigate to the **Settings** module, and under the **Business** section, click on **Templates**, and then click on **Contract Templates**.
3. Click on **New**.
4. Enter the following required fields:
    - **Name**: Enter a clear, concise name for the template.
    - **Abbreviation**: Enter a short abbreviation of the name.
    - **Billing Frequency**: Choose from **Monthly**, **Bimonthly**, **Quarterly**, **Semi-annually**, or **Annually**.

- **Allotment Type**: Indicates how the contract will be tracked—either by number of cases, time, or coverage dates. For example, if the allotment type is number of cases, then every case opened up referencing this contract will be subtracted from the total cases allotted.
- **Calendar**: Used to indicate the days and times of the week during which the service is available.

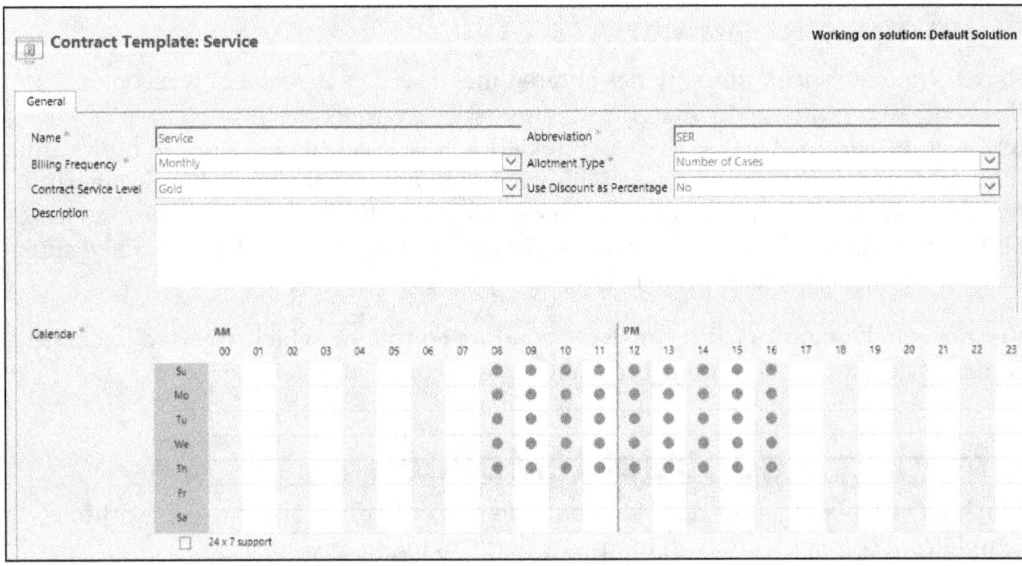

5. Click on **Save and Close**.

Creating a contract

Once a contract template has been created, a contract can be created using that template. To create a contract, perform the following steps:

1. Start CRM.
2. Navigate to the **Service** module, and click on **Contracts**.
3. On the **Contracts** ribbon bar, in the **Records** group, click on **New**.
4. In the **Contract Template** explorer, select the template that you wish to use to create the contract.

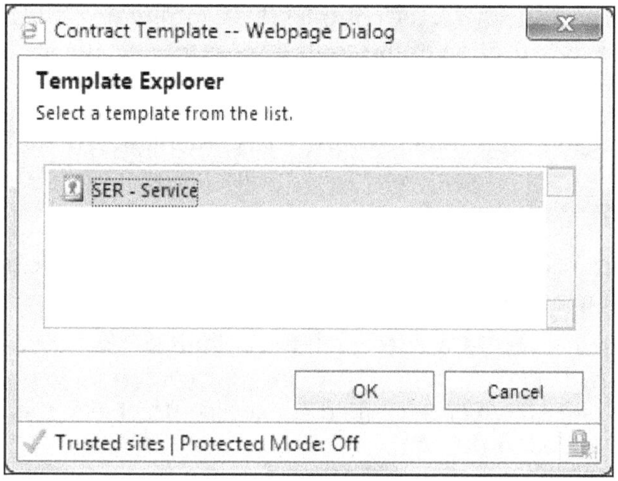

5. Click on **OK**.
6. Enter the following required fields:
    - **Contract Name**: Enter a clear, concise name
    - **Customer**: Look up an account or contact to which you want to associate this contract
    - **Contract Start Date**
    - **Contract End Date**
    - **Bill to Customer**: This will default to the value selected in the customer lookup mentioned in the **Customer** field earlier; however you can potentially bill the contract to another customer

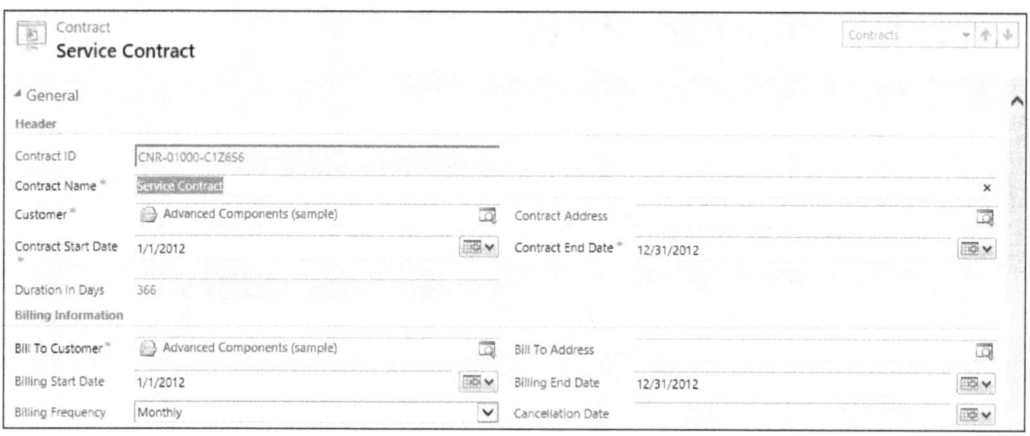

7. Click on **Save**.

Once the record has been saved, the contract ID is automatically generated, the status is set to **Draft**, and the duration of the contract is automatically set as the difference in days between the contract start and end dates.

According to Microsoft Dynamics CRM 2011 documentation (`http://msdn.microsoft.com/en-us/library/bb959312.aspx`), the contract has the following statuses:

- **Draft**: This means that the contract can still be worked on, but it cannot be associated to a case.
- **Invoiced**: Once a contract is saved, the default status is **Draft**. The contextual ribbon now displays a button to invoice the contract. This can only be done if contract lines have been created. Once a contract is in the invoiced state, it cannot be edited or deleted.
- **Active**: The next stage in the contract life cycle is **Active**. A contract will automatically be set to active when the start date of the contract equals today's date. This is the only status that allows a contract to be associated to a case. A contract with this status cannot be edited or deleted.
- **OnHold**: Once a contract has been activated, it can be placed on hold at any time. Once on hold, the contract cannot be edited or deleted.
- **Canceled**
- **Expired**: Once the end date of the contract has been reached, the contract status automatically gets changed to expired.

As mentioned, a contract cannot have its status changed from **Draft** to **Invoiced** until contract lines are created for the contract.

Creating contract lines

To create a contract line, perform the following steps:

1. Start CRM.
2. Navigate to the **Service** module, and then click on **Contracts**.
3. Find and open the contract to which you wish to add lines.
4. On the left-hand navigation of the record, click on **Contract Lines**.
5. On the **List Tools** tab of the **Contract Lines** ribbon bar, in the **Records** group, click on **Add New Contract Line**.
6. Enter the following required fields:
    - **Title**: A clear, concise title for the contract line.
    - **Start Date**: Defaults from the contract, but can be changed.

- **End Date**: Defaults from the contract, but can be changed.
- **Total Case/Minutes**: Enter the total amount of minutes that can be used to solve the cases.
- **Total Price**: Amount of money that is being charged to the customer for the service. This can be zero.

7. Click on **Save and Close**.

Once a contract line item has been added, the contact can be invoiced. Once the contract status has been set to invoiced, the status will change automatically to active once the contract start date has been reached.

Once a contract has been set to active, it can be associated to cases. Contracts can also be placed on hold or canceled.

Contract actions

Once a contract has been set to active, it can be associated to cases. The Dynamics CRM contextual ribbon also changes, enabling actions to taken on the contract.

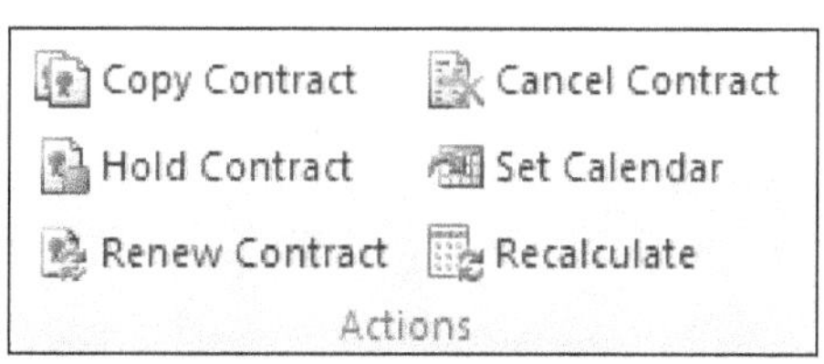

As you can see, a contract can be copied, placed on hold, renewed, or even canceled, once it is active. The **Set Calendar** option allows a user to add the contract dates to be added to the service calendar for viewing. To recalculate the allotment values used, or the total prices, click on the **Recalculate** button.

Analysis and reporting

Microsoft Dynamics CRM 2011 comes with some canned reports specifically related to service management. If a user goes to the reporting area in Dynamics CRM, and filters the list of reports by service reports, the following will be displayed:

- Account overview
- Case summary table
- Neglected cases
- Service activity volume
- Top knowledge base articles

Account overview

This report displays an overview of one or more accounts. It gives a summary of account, primary contact, additional contacts, opportunities, activities, and any cases tied to the account. Specifically around cases, it gives a summary of the level of satisfaction of the cases resolved, and the reasons for the cases.

Case summary

This report displays a report grouped by various factors. The horizontal and vertical groupings can be selected via drop-downs on the report. There's also an option for a second set of groupings. Once displayed, the report displays counts and percentages for the groupings. For example, let's say a user wants to group the case data by owner and priority. This can give someone within an organization a count of all cases by priority or by owner.

Neglected cases

This report displays all cases that have not been updated, or have had no new activities added within a certain period of time (defined in the report). This gives the user running the report possible insights into cases that might be "neglected".

Service activity volume

This report shows a list of all service activities and their durations. The report is grouped by services and time periods.

Top knowledge base articles

This report displays the most commonly-used knowledge base articles, grouped by subject, or grouped by the case, or grouped by the product associated with the case.

Microsoft Dynamics CRM 2011 also provides charts to help visualize this data. Like any other entity in the system, the charts are based on views for each entity. These charts can be used to create dashboards. Dynamics CRM has an out of the box service management dashboard.

Customer service operations dashboard

The customer service operations dashboard gives a visualization of activities by owner, a chart of the leaders when it comes to solving cases, a list of unpublished dashboards, a chart of cases by origin, and a chart of cases by priority.

Customer service performance dashboard

This dashboard displays the leadership board in terms of solving cases, a trending chart of cases resolved by day, a chart on the progress of goals for cases, and a chart of knowledge base articles by status.

Customer service representative dashboard

This last system dashboard displays charts of cases owned by the current user, illustrating cases by origin, cases by priority, a trending chart of cases resolved by day, and the chart of case goals.

Test your knowledge

Q.1 Which of the following fields are required when creating a case? (Choose all that apply.)

1. Title.
2. Case Number.
3. Subject.
4. Customer.

Q.2. What are the required fields when resolving a case? (Choose all that apply.)

1. Resolution.
2. Resolution Type.
3. Total Time.
4. Billable Time.

Q.3. On a quick find search of cases, what are the default search fields? (Choose all that apply.)

1. Title.
2. Customer.
3. Case Number.
4. Priority.
5. None of the above.

Q.4. Let's say you have many articles, based on a knowledge base template, in various stages of the publishing process. If you deactivate the knowledge base article template, what happens to the articles created from the template?

1. All articles based on the deactivated template continue in the publishing process.
2. All articles based on the deactivated template are deactivated.
3. All articles based on the deactivated template are deleted.
4. All articles based on the deactivated template are canceled.

Q.5. What are the search options for a knowledge base article? (Choose all that apply.)

1. Full Text Search.
2. Keyword Search.
3. Title Search.
4. Article Number Search.

Q.6. When a queue is deactivated, what happens to all of the queue items?

1. All queue items are removed from the queue.
2. All queue items are deactivated.
3. All queue items are deleted.
4. You cannot deactivate a queue with queue items.

Q.7. When a queue is deleted, what rules apply?

1. A queue can never be deleted.
2. A queue can only be deleted if it does not contain queue items.
3. A queue can be deleted at any time, no matter what.
4. A queue can only be deleted on Sundays.

Q.8. Where is the **Allotment Type** field found, and what does it do?

1. On the contract template, and it indicates how the contract will be tracked: either by number of cases, by time, or by coverage dates.
2. On the contract, and it indicates how the contract will be tracked: either by number of cases, by time, or by coverage dates.
3. On the contract template, and it indicates how the contract is allotted: either to accounts or to contacts.
4. On the contract, and it indicates how the contract is allotted: either to accounts or to contacts.

Q.9. What status must a contract be in before it's allowed to be associated to a case?

1. OnHold.
2. Canceled.
3. Invoiced.
4. Active.

Q.10. What is the stipulation before a contract can be changed from a status of **Draft** to **Invoiced**?

1. Contract must be active.
2. Contract must have contract lines.
3. Contract must be associated to a case.
4. Contract must be in the OnHold status.

Summary

This chapter provided insight into the service management module in Dynamics CRM 2011. We delved into case management, including creating, assigning, and connecting cases. The subject tree is a list of categories that an organization can use to help organize cases or other record types. A subject can be associated to a case in order to help categorize it for reporting or searching purposes. Adding notes to a case can be important if multiple users work on a case. Some examples of notes are steps taken to resolve a case, any notes about the customer, or any comments made by management about the case.

Resolving cases is the ultimate goal of any organization managing cases. Whatever state a case is in, CRM provides out of the box views to help access case data quickly and efficiently. Charts can visually represent data in a view, and as you filter data in a view, the chart will change to display the filtered data.

To assist users, the knowledge base is a location where users can search for articles to help them resolve cases. Knowledge base articles cannot be created without using a knowledge base article template. CRM provides unique search functionality on knowledge base articles giving users four options: Full Text, Keyword, Title, and Article Number searches.

Queues are a way for users to divide up work within its workforce. Specifically for cases, it provides a place for cases to be routed, and systematically be worked on in a given order. When a case is added to a queue, a queue item is created and associated to the case and the queue. When a queue is deactivated, all queue items are removed from the queue, but this does not mean that the case is deleted. A queue cannot be deleted if it contains queue items. Teams can also be used to help collaborate when it comes to servicing customers.

The service management module also consists of service contracts. Contracts help to track service agreements between an organization and its customers. One example of a service contract is if an organization agrees to service a customer by giving the customer a limited number of cases per year. CRM can be used to track the number of cases created against a service contract. Finally, the service module provides out of the box reports and dashboards to assist an organization in analyzing and visualizing service related data.

In the next chapter, we'll cover service scheduling. Service scheduling enables an organization to manage and schedule resources to help service customers. For example, if a facility, equipment, or even people, are needed to service a customer, CRM can help manage those resources to make sure they're used effectively and efficiently.

8

Managing Service Scheduling Applications

In this chapter you will cover the following topics:

- Introduction to service scheduling
- Setting up service scheduling
- Scheduling service activities
- Report and analyze service activities

Just when you thought Microsoft Dynamics CRM can do everything for your organization from marketing to sales to service, the trend continues. Hopefully by now, you've learned how CRM can help to expand an organization's customer base by using the marketing module, to track opportunities, and sell products and services by using the sales module, and log cases by using the service module. The last piece of out of the box or "vanilla" CRM functionality is in regards to service scheduling.

If cases require resource allocation, CRM's scheduling engine provides a way to manage resources, equipment, and even facilities, in order to help deliver on service requests. Let's look at an introduction into service scheduling.

Introduction to service scheduling

There are a number of key terms important to understand before proceeding:

- **Service** is a type of work that is delivered to a customer and performed by one or more resources. For example, equipment repair, health services, legal services, and accounting services. To define a service, enter general information about that service, identify the resources needed, and then input these requirements into a selection rule.

- **Resources** are people, facilities, and equipment that are used in delivering services. Individual resources have a work schedule that defines when they are available to work.
- **Resource Groups** are pools of similar resources that can carry out a given service. These resources are thought to be interchangeable.
- **Sites** are locations where service operations take place.
- **Capacity Scheduling** is used to consider different sized facilities or users' skill levels when setting up services and resources. An example would be a senior technician that can repair two copy machines in the same time that it takes a junior technician to repair one, or a clinic that has five patient examining rooms where another clinic may have eight.
- **Effort** defined in a selection rule reduces that resources capacity when they are scheduled to deliver that particular service.
- **Selection Rule** is the list of people, facilities, or equipment needed to carry out a service. Each service needs a selection rule.
- **Selection Criteria** helps you determine how resource's should be allocated. An example is if you want to have one technician completely scheduled before another technician is scheduled. Or maybe on the other hand you want all technicians to be scheduled evenly.

Business scenarios

Race2Win Insurance Company has a wide range of insurance products. They insure everything from corporations to homes and automobiles. In situations such as a natural disaster, Race2Win has a division that handles the processing of claims by their customers. They have a whole customer service division dedicated to this effort. Coordinating claims processing, especially during times of natural disasters, can be challenging as multiple people, with different skills sets, and who work different shifts, may be needed along with the use of various equipment, all at different customer sites. There are numerous service scheduling scenarios that can make servicing a customer challenging for Race2Win.

Service scheduling scenarios

There are four service scheduling scenarios that can be applied in CRM:

- Individual scenario
- Different skills and shifts
- Different skills, shifts, equipment, and sites
- Different skills, equipment, and sites

Individual scenario

This is the most simple/basic example of service scheduling. In this scenario, Dynamics CRM can schedule one individual to meet with a customer. For example, let's say a client of Race2Win Insurance Company raised an issue with a duplicate bill being sent. Race2Win can offer someone from the billing department to go to the client site, meet with the person that raised the issue, and resolve it.

Different skills and shifts

The next scenario is where you might have individuals with different skill sets that work different shifts. For example, Race2Win Insurance Company has a disaster relief insurance claims team made up of adjustors, building architects, corporate policy specialists, and auto claims adjustors. They all work with another division of Race2Win to provide customer support. The adjustors, architects, auto, and corporate policy specialists have different skill sets. Also, these resources may work during various shifts throughout the day to support Race2Win's customers.

Different skills, equipment, and sites

This scenario entails individuals with different skill sets, needing to use different equipment, at different sites. For example, Race2Win Insurance Company needs to service a customer that has multiple locations. They might schedule a team to go out to these sites, and at each of these sites, the use of specialized computers, hardware, or software might be necessary.

Different skills, shifts, equipment, and sites

This final scenario is where you might have people with different skills, working in different shifts that may need to use different equipments at different sites. Using the example from above, Race2Win has a disaster relief insurance team that goes to areas hard hit by natural disasters to assess damages and provide support in processing insurance claims. These teams may be made up of architects, auto and building policy specialists, as well as people entrenched in the disaster recovery efforts. These people may work on various teams during various shifts, as well as utilize different equipment such as computers and heavy machinery. Since natural disasters may occur all over the world, these support teams may need to be deployed to different sites.

Selection rules

As stated earlier, every service requires a selection rule, which is a way to define how a resource, facility and/or equipment can be used to perform the service. The selection rule comprises of the following components:

- **Resource**: Which and how many resources are required to complete the service.
- **Selection Criteria**: The resource can be scheduled as least busy, most busy, or randomly. A least busy criteria means that the resource with the most availability will be scheduled first; most busy will mean that an individual that has the least availability (until they are no longer available) will be scheduled first; and randomly will schedule the resources on a random basis.
- **Selection Site**: Whether the resource should be scheduled at the same site or another location.

Given the scheduling scenarios and selection rules, one other major component of service scheduling is service activities.

Service activities

A service activity is like any other activity in Dynamics CRM; however it's specifically related to service scheduling. Think of it as an appointment activity, but it's related to a service. It can be associated to one or more customers, and resources (user, equipment, and facility).

Another interesting aspect of the service activity is when the service activity is scheduled; the Microsoft Dynamics CRM scheduling engine can automatically assign the best resource based on the selection rules setup.

Now that you're familiar with some key terms and concepts regarding service scheduling, the next step is to look at how to set it all up.

Setting up service scheduling

When setting up a service and scheduling it, the following steps may be involved:

- Setting up work hours
- Setting up business closures
- Setting up time off
- Setting up capacity scheduling
- Creating facilities and equipment

- Creating a site
- Creating a service
- Creating resource groups
- Configuring customer service preferences

The first task to complete before setting up any service, is to make sure that every resource's (user, facility/equipment) work hours are set up. If this is not set up, an error will appear when scheduling the service. Note that all of the setup instructions shown in this section assume service scheduling is being set up for a resource that is a user. The same steps can be applied to facilities or equipment.

Setting up work hours

To set up work hours, follow these steps:

1. Start CRM.
2. Navigate to the **Settings** module, and under the **System** section, click on **Administration**, then on **Users**.
3. Open the user record that you wish to configure working hours for.
4. On the left-hand navigation, under the **Common** section, click on **Work Hours**.

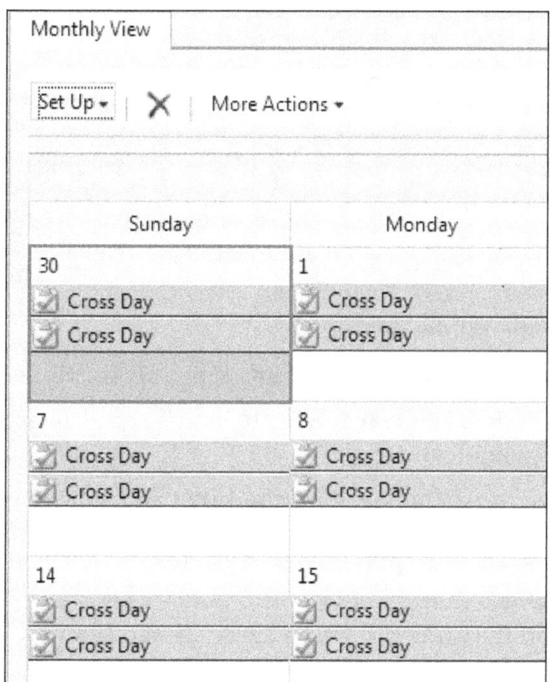

5. In the calendar view, if you click once on a day, it will highlight the day in red (as shown above). To edit the schedule for the day, double-click on the entry shown in the day (in the case above, double-click on **Cross Day**).

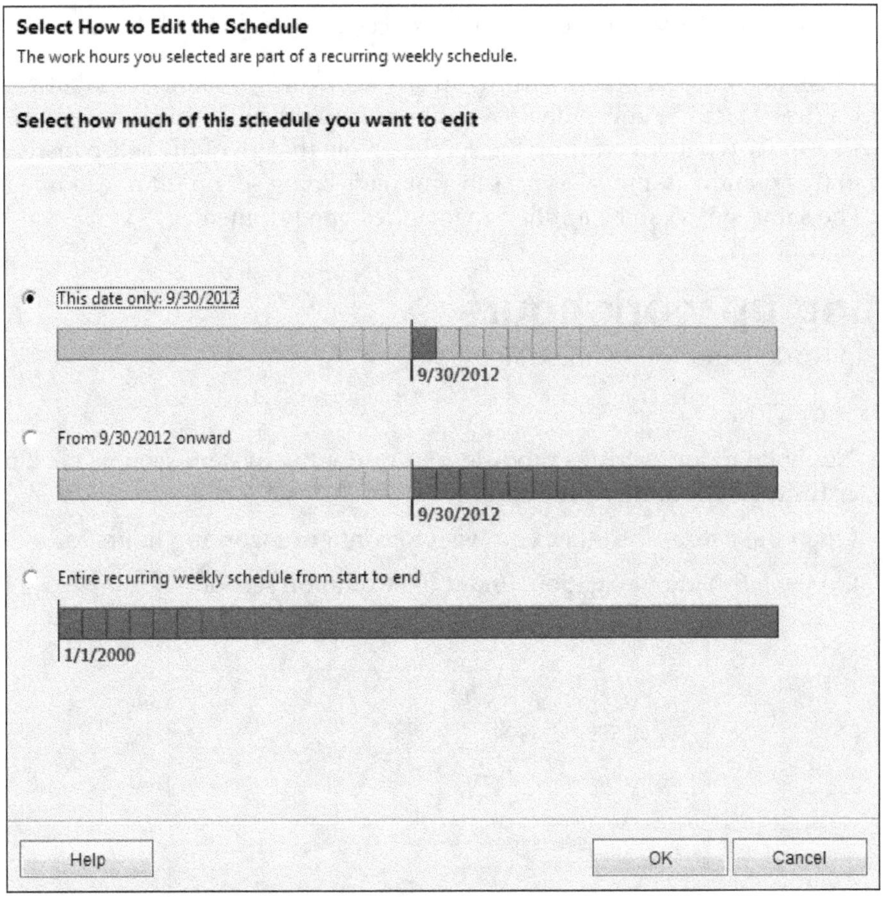

6. Select one of the following options:
   i. **This date only**: Edit the user's schedule for the current day.
   ii. **From <date> onward**: Edit the user's schedule from the current date going forward.
   iii. **Entire recurring weekly schedule from start to end**: Start from 1/1/2000 going forward.
7. Click on **OK**.
8. Depending on the option that you chose in step 6, a new window will appear that allows you to set up work hours for the given day or time period.

9. The next screenshot illustrates setting up work hours for a single day. You can add your work schedule here, along with any planned breaks, such as for lunch.
10. Enter the following fields:
    i. **Work Hours**
    ii. **Add Break**: Add a break if necessary, for example, add a one hour break for lunch.
    iii. **Time Zone**

> The time zone here is important here as it affects service activity scheduling. Imagine a resource in one time zone needing to service a customer in another. In order for the schedule to accurately reflect the times at which a resource is available for service, the time zone needs to be correctly set.

    iv. **Service Restrictions**: The service restrictions tab allows a user to enter a time period during which a particular service for a given day(s) is restricted.

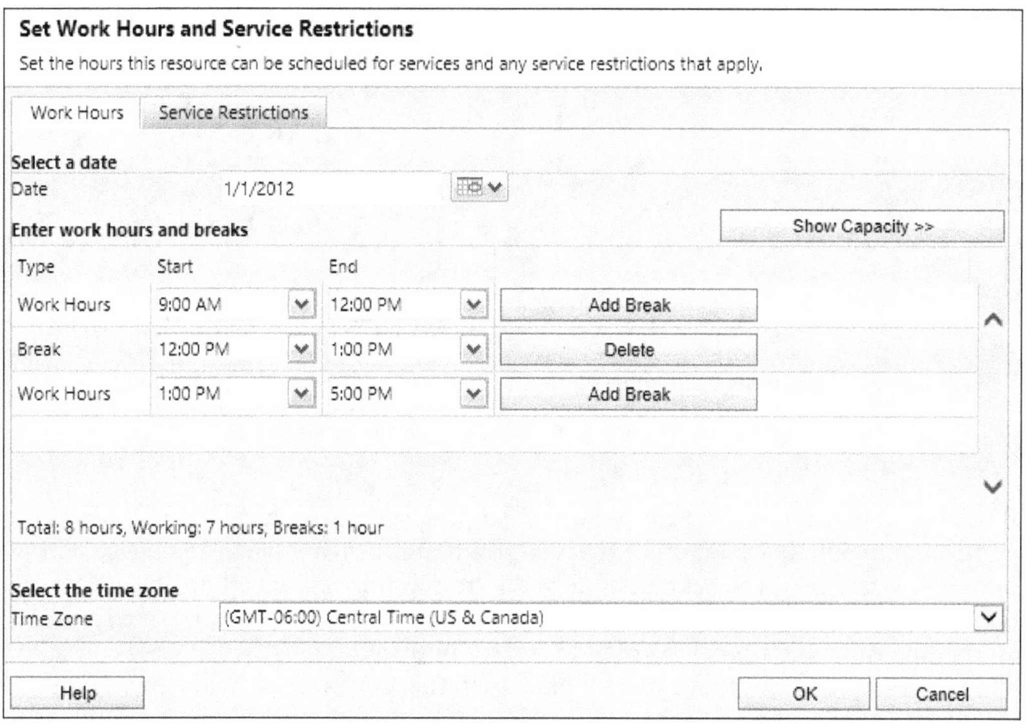

11. The next screenshot illustrates setting up work hours for more than one day. Enter the following fields:
    i. **Work Hours**: Set to be either the same for each day of the week, to vary by day, which will show values for each day where you can configure different times for each day, or none to indicate the user/resource is not working.
    ii. **Work Days**: Which days of the week the resource is considered working. If "None" is selected in work hours, this option becomes disabled.
    iii. **Business Closures**: If you wish the user to be off during business closures, click observe.
    iv. **Time Zone**: You can set a time zone for the working hours of the resource.

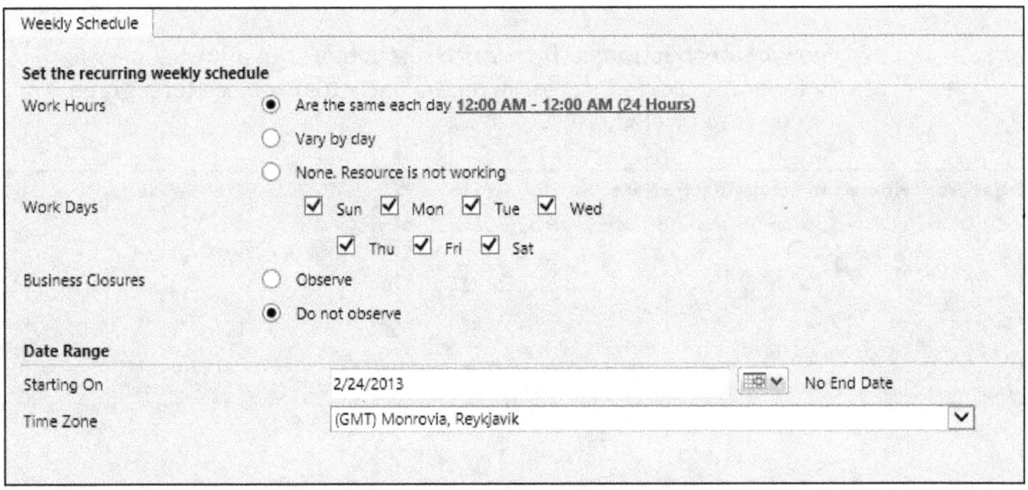

12. Click on **Save and Close** to close the schedule.
13. On the **User** ribbon, in the **Save** group, click on **Save and Close** to close the user record.

Work hours play an integral role when scheduling service for a customer. These hours help to define availability for a resource to perform a scheduled service. For example, a person can be scheduled to work from 9 a.m. to 5 p.m. one day and then the next day they can be scheduled to work from 11 p.m. to 7 a.m.. If a service appointment for a customer is going to last for two days, and the customer can only allow access to a site from 9 a.m. to 5 p.m., then this person may not be the right resource to service the customer.

Setting up business closures

To set up a business closure (a date and time the business may be closed, for example, a business holiday), follow these steps:

1. Start CRM.
2. Navigate to the **Settings** module, in the **Business** section, click **Business Management**.
3. Click on **Business Closures**.
4. On the **Business Closures** toolbar, click on **New**.

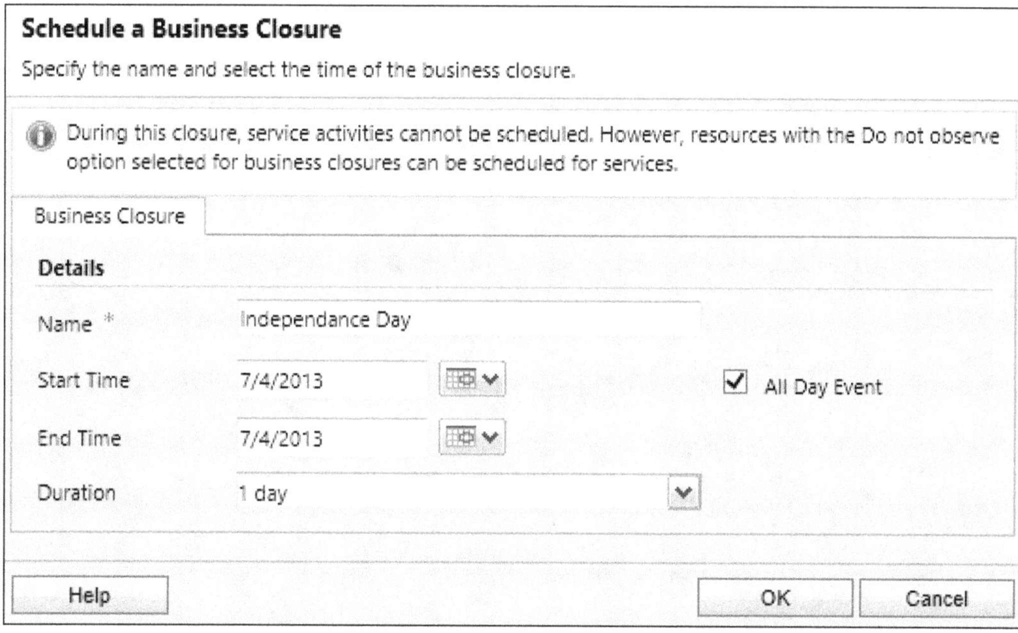

5. Enter the name of the business closure, **Start Time**, and **End Time**.
6. Click on **OK**.

If appointments or service activities have already been scheduled, they will not be changed. However, you can use the **Show Conflicts** button on the Service Calendar to highlight appointments and service activities that have scheduling conflicts (this will be discussed in more detail later in this chapter). During this time, no new service activities can be scheduled unless resources have the **Do not observe** option selected in their **Work Hours** configuration.

Setting up time off

You can schedule a period of time during a schedule when a resource is not available to be scheduled for a service activity. An example is if a user is on vacation, or a facility or equipment had a failure. To set up time off, follow these steps:

1. Start CRM.
2. Navigate to the **Settings** module, and under the **System** section, click on **Administration**, then **Users**.
3. Open the user record for which you wish to configure the working hours.
4. On the left-hand navigation, under the **Common** section, click on **Work Hours**.
5. Select a date on the calendar.
6. On the **Work Hours** toolbar, click on **Set Up** and then select **Time Off**.

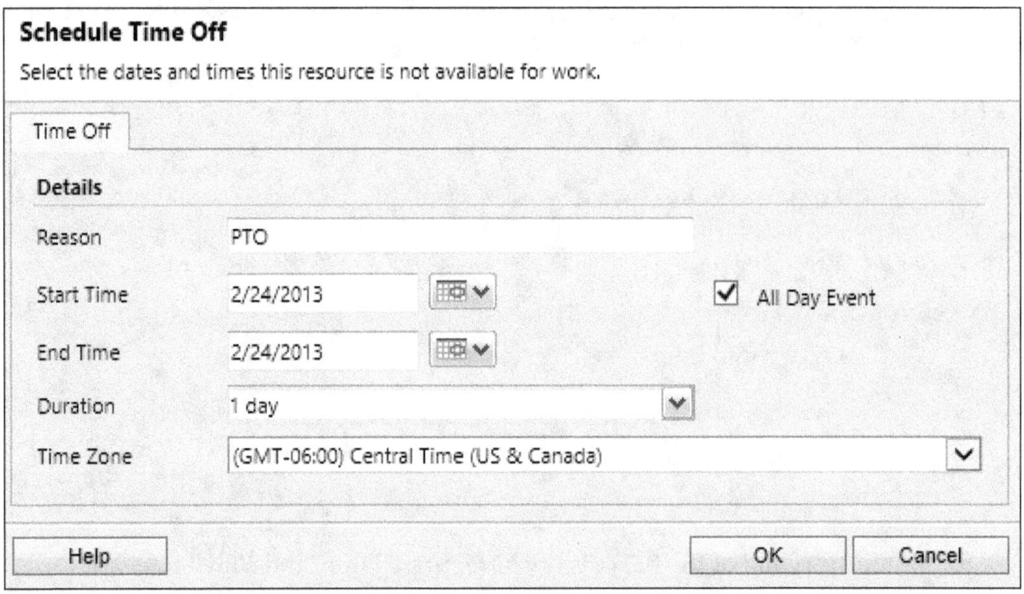

7. In the **Schedule Time Off** dialog, enter the following:
    i. **Reason**: This is a free text field where you can enter text such as `PTO` or `Sick`.
    ii. **Start Time**
    iii. **End Time**
    iv. **All Day Event**: If this is unchecked, users are given the option to enter a time.

   v. **Duration**
   vi. **Time Zone**

8. Click on **OK**.

After this is set, the working hours calendar shows the time off as a red block, and the service calendar displays the time as a white block. Setting up time off prevents any service activities from being scheduled for the resource during that time period.

Setting up capacity scheduling

Capacity is used to determine how many services a resource can perform at one time. For example, if an insurance agent of Race2Win is working with an adjustor to process a claim for a customer the agent may only be able to do one claim at a time. In that case the capacity would be one. Now let's say Race2Win Insurance Company has a fleet of cars that it provides to its sales people. It may have a facility to help service these vehicles. In this case, the facility might have a much larger capacity.

In order to use capacity scheduling, the resource must have a capacity defined, and the selection rule for a service must define a minimum capacity level.

Defining resource capacity

To set the capacity for a resource, follow the steps outlined below:

1. Start CRM.
2. Navigate to the **Settings** module, and under the **System** section, click on **Administration**, then **Users**.
3. Open the user record for which you wish to configure capacity scheduling.
4. In the left-hand navigation pane, under the **Common** section, click on **Work Hours**.
5. In the **Edit Weekly Schedule** dialog box, select the appropriate option.
6. Click on **OK**.

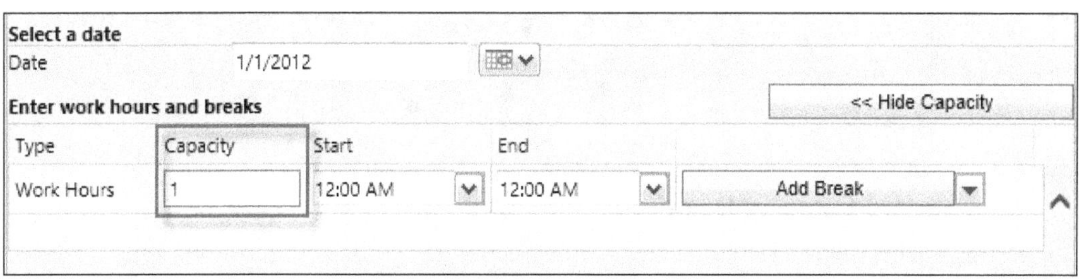

7. In the **Work Day** dialog box, click on **Show Capacity**, and then in the **Capacity** column, enter the capacity.
8. Click on **OK**.
9. Click on **Save and Close**.

Defining service capacity

To set up a service capacity, follow these steps:

1. Start CRM.
2. Navigate to the **Service** module, and click on **Services**.
3. Select and open the service record that you wish to modify.
4. Navigate to the **Required Resources** part of the form.
5. Double-click on the **Selection Rule** to modify it.
6. In the **Edit a Selection Rule** dialog box, expand the **Scheduling Details** section.

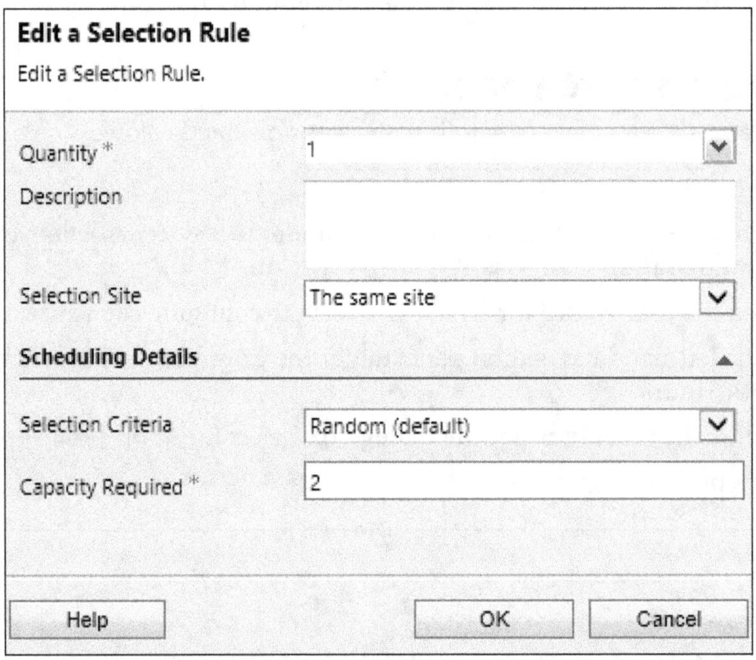

7. Enter the **Capacity Required**.
8. Click on **OK**.
9. Click on **Save and Close**.

Creating facilities and equipment

To create a facility/equipment record, follow these steps:

1. Start CRM.
2. Navigate to the **Settings** module, and then in the **Business** section, click on **Business Management**.
3. Click on **Facilities/Equipment**.
4. On the **Facilities/Equipment** toolbar, click on **New**.

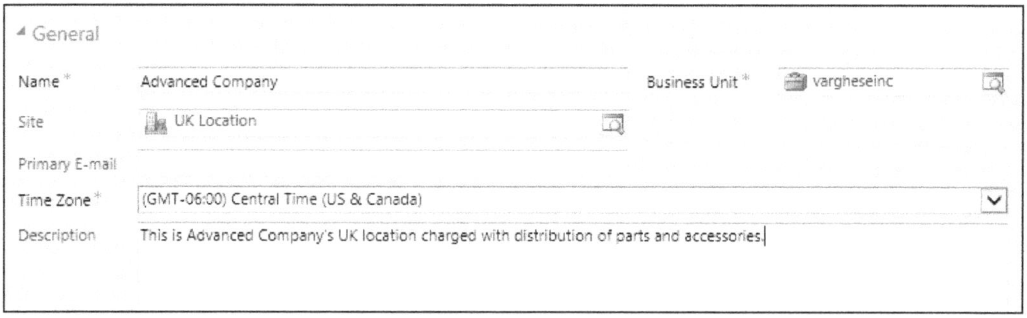

5. Enter the following required fields:
    i. **Name**: A clear, concise name for the facility or equipment.
    ii. **Business Unit**: This will default to the primary business unit.
    iii. **Time Zone**: Enter the time zone that the facility is in or equipment is being stored in or used at.
6. Click on **Save and Close**.

The site field is a lookup on the facility/equipment record, but is worth mentioning, as a facility or equipment can be associated to a site (as stated earlier, a site is the physical location at which the service can be stored or performed).

Creating a site

To create a site, follow these steps:

1. Start CRM.
2. Navigate to the **Settings** module, and then in the **Business** section, click on **Business Management**.

3. Click on **Sites**.
4. Click on **New**.

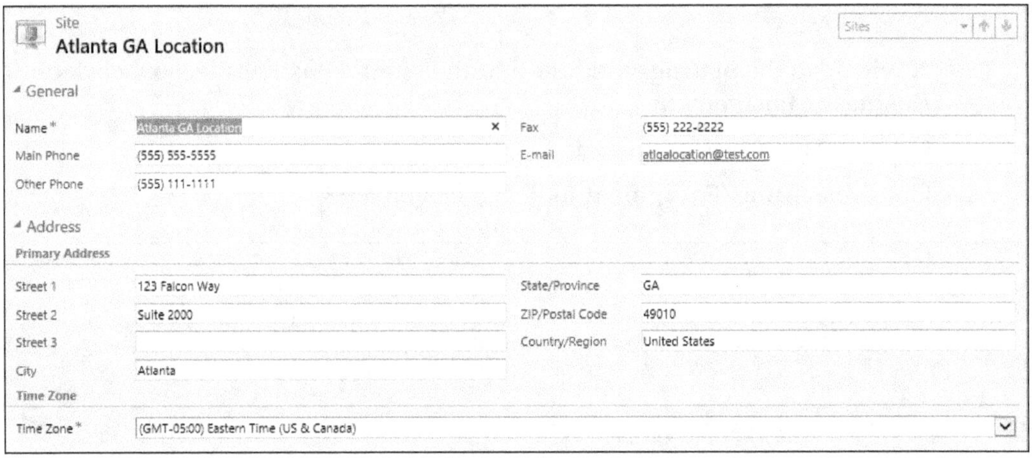

5. Enter the following required fields:
   i. **Name**: A clear, concise name for the site.
   ii. **Time Zone**
6. Click on **Save**.
7. In the left-hand navigation pane, you can associate various users to a site. For example, if you have a warehouse site, you can associate a number of users, teams, facilities/equipment, or resource groups to this site. This is optional, however, it's required when your resource selection rules are site-specific.
8. Click on **Save and Close**.

Creating a service

A service in CRM is a type of work that is delivered to a customer and performed by one or more resources. To create a service record, follow these steps:

1. Start CRM.
2. Navigate to the **Service** module, and then click on **Services**.

3. On the **Services** ribbon bar, in the **Records** group, click on **New**.

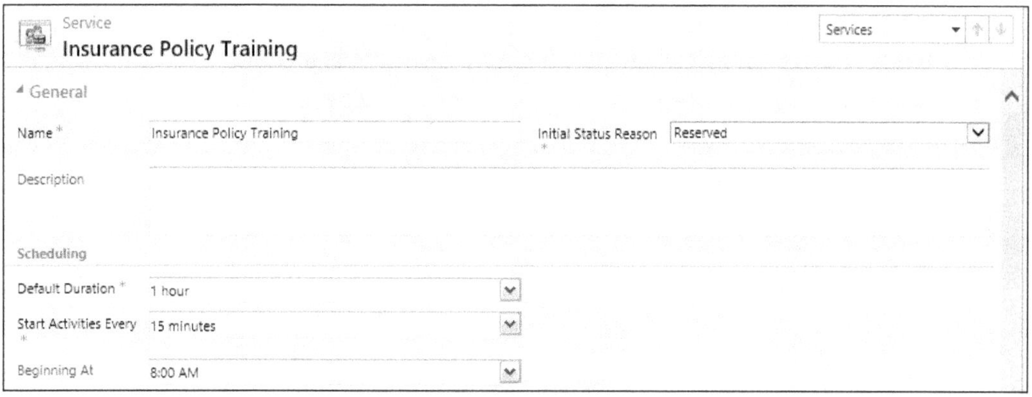

4. Enter in the following required information:
   i. **Name**: A clear, concise description of the service.
   ii. **Initial Status Reason**: This is the status of the service when initially booked.
   iii. **Default Duration**: This determines how long the service will last by default.
   iv. **Start Activities**: The frequency with which new activities can be started.

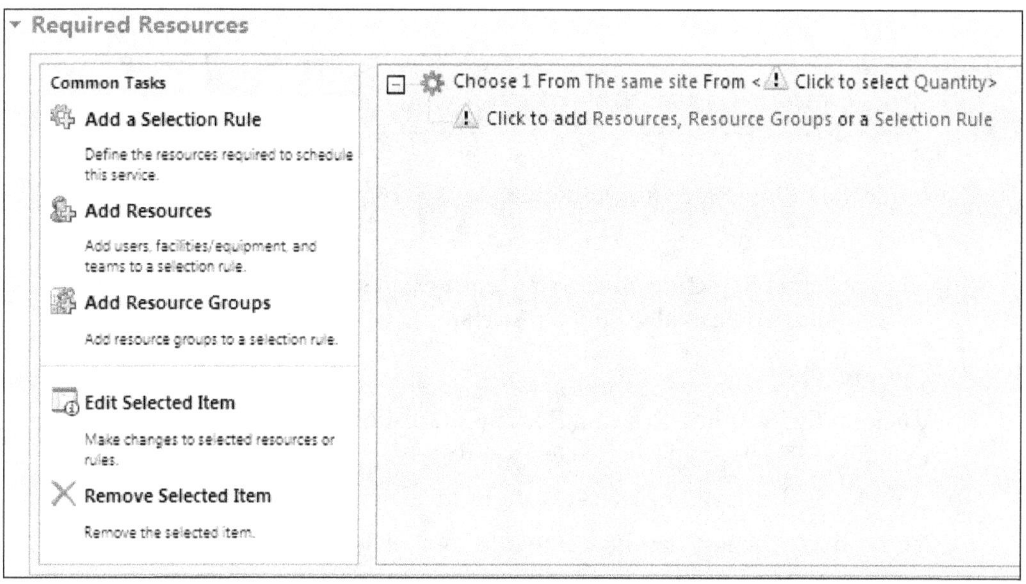

5. For each service, the selection rule (the rule that defines how the resource is used to perform the service) must be defined. By default, the selection rule is set to **The same site**, which means that the resource will be used to perform the service at the same site at which the resource is located.
6. Select the **Quantity** link.

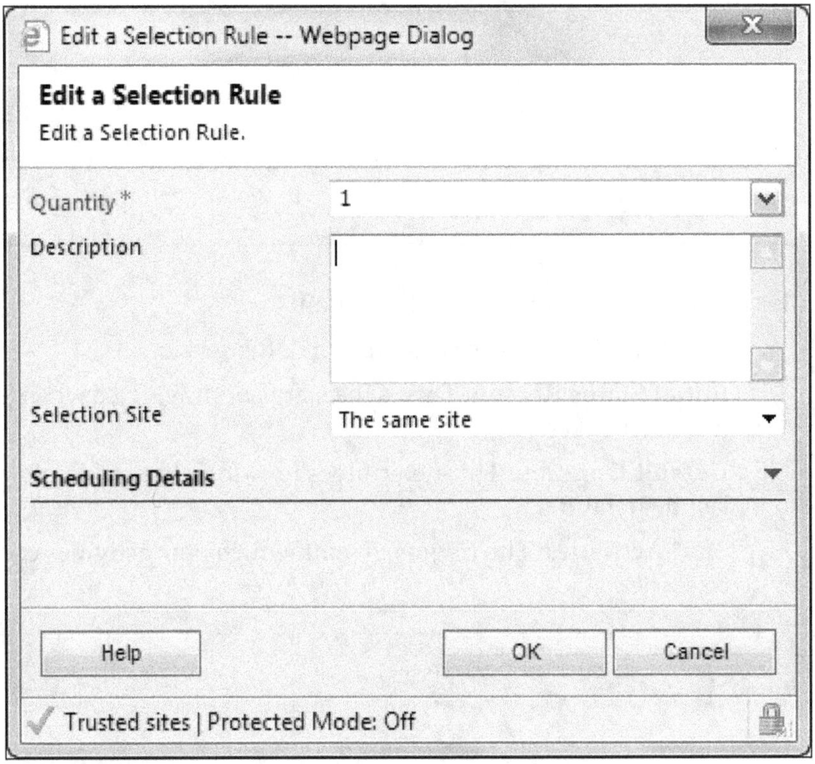

7. Enter the following required fields:
    i. Quantity
    ii. While **Selection Site** is not required, it's defaulted to **The same site**. You can also choose **Any site**.
8. Click on **OK**.
9. Click on the next line to add a **Resource**, **Resource Group** (this will be explained later), or another **Selection Rule**.
10. A dialog is displayed to select one or more users, facilities, or equipment.
11. You can use the left-hand pane to add more selection rules or resources.
12. Click on **Save and Close**.

Creating resource groups

While creating a site, you might have noticed an option when creating the service to create a resource group. A resource group is a way to group resources by a set of criteria; for example, skill sets.

To create a resource group, follow these steps:

1. Start CRM.
2. Navigate to the **Settings** module, and under the **Business** section, click on **Business Management**.
3. Click on **Resource Groups**.
4. On the **Resource Groups** toolbar, click on **New**.
5. Enter the following required fields:
    i. **Name**: A name for the resource group.
    ii. **Business Unit**: This will be pre-populated with the default business unit.
6. Click on **Save**.
7. On the left-hand navigation, click on **Resources**.
8. Click on **Add Resources**, and add one or more users, teams, facilities, equipment, or even other resource group records.
9. Click on **Save and Close**.

Configuring customer service preferences

Customer service preferences are configured on a customer record (an account or contact). To configure a customer's service preferences, follow these steps:

1. Start CRM.
2. Navigate to the **Workplace** module, and then under **Customers**, click either on **Accounts** or **Contacts**.
3. In the view, select and open either an account or contact record.

4. Navigate to the **Preferences** tab of the form.

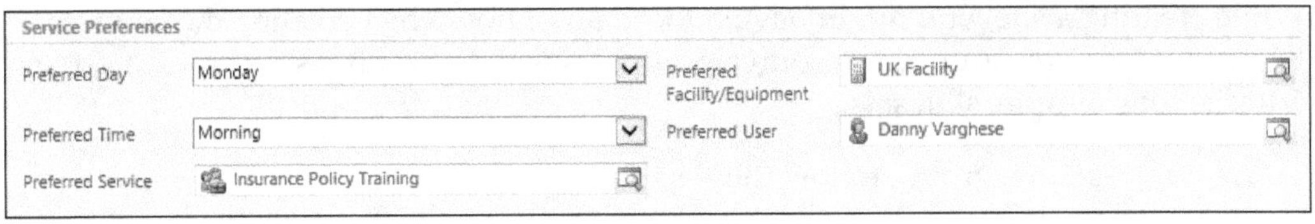

5. Under the **Service Preferences** section, you can set the following fields:
   i. **Preferred Day**: Choose the day of the week on which the customer prefers servicing.
   ii. **Preferred Time**: Choose from **Morning, Afternoon**, or **Evening.**
   iii. **Preferred Service**: Select the preferred service activity that the customer usually wants to schedule.
   iv. **Preferred Facility/Equipment**: Select the preferred facility or equipment.
   v. **Preferred User**: A lookup to select the preferred CRM user to service the customer.
6. Click on **Save and Close.**

When creating a service activity from a customer record, these preferences will be copied to the service activity, to make creating activities easier. Also, when services are scheduled by using the Dynamics CRM scheduling engine, these preferences are taken into account.

Scheduling service activities

Service activities are scheduled for a specific time, can include a site, can be tied to one or more customers, and can include one or more resources. Once the activity is created, a user can trigger what is called the **service scheduling engine**. The scheduling engine gives the user the best option of resources to complete the given service. The scheduling engine looks at the service preferences of the customer, the schedules defined for the resources, and the selection rule for the service.

The first step to schedule service activities is to create service activities.

Creating service activities

To create service activities, follow these steps:

1. Start CRM.
2. Navigate to **Workplace** module, and then under the **Customers** section, click on **Accounts** or **Contacts**.
3. Select and open either an account or a contact record.
4. On the **Add** ribbon bar, in the **Activity** group, click on **Service Activity**.

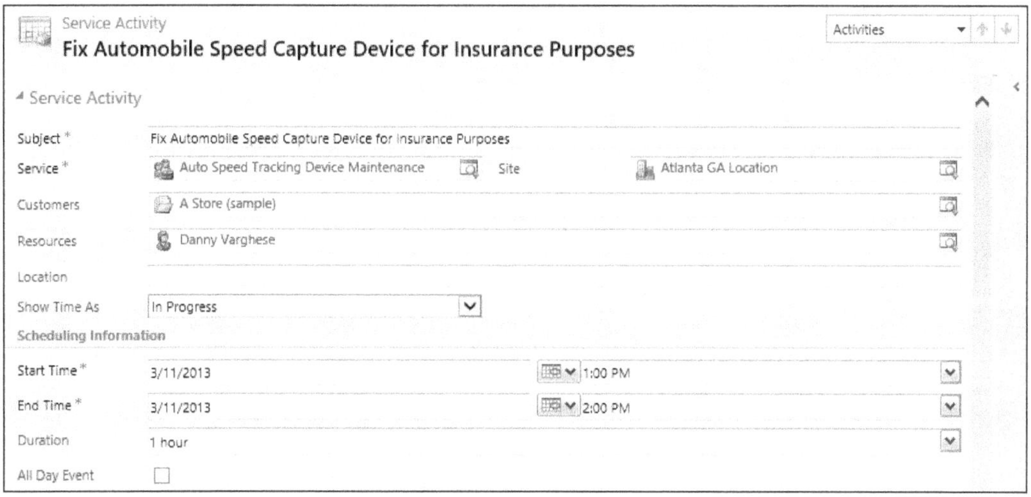

5. Enter the following required fields:
    i. **Subject**: Give a clear, concise name for the service activity.
    ii. **Service**: Select an existing service.
    iii. **Start Time**
    iv. **End Time**
6. Click on **Save and Close**.

If the **Resource** field is not set, and you try to save the record, a warning message will appear. You have the opportunity to add the resource yourself, or use the CRM scheduling engine. Furthermore, if the resource selected is not available, or the resource doesn't meet the selection rule criteria, an error message will appear.

Using the scheduling engine

As discussed earlier, the scheduling engine can help to schedule resources, taking into account customer service preferences, resource schedules and service selection criteria. To launch the scheduling engine from within a service activity record, follow these steps:

1. On the **Service Activity** ribbon, in the **Actions** group, click on **Schedule**.

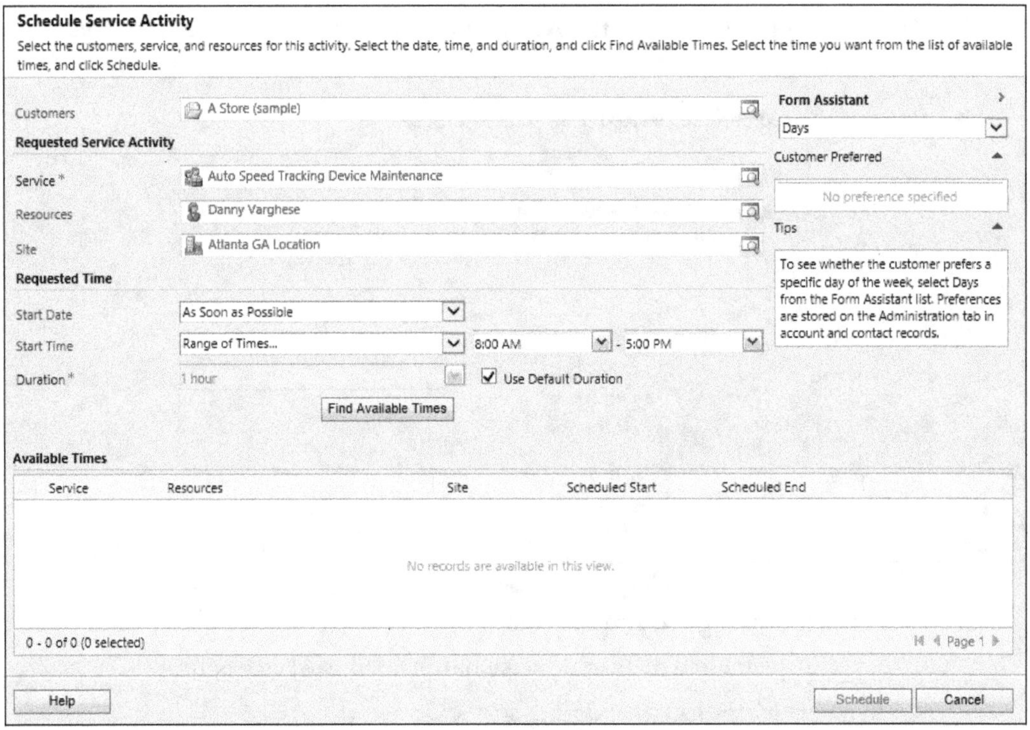

2. Enter the following information:
    i. **Customers**: This should be pre-populated from the service activity record.
    ii. **Service**: This should be pre-populated with the service activity record.
    iii. **Resources**
    iv. **Sites**
    v. **Start Date**: This is the option to choose as soon as possible, for a specific date, or by date range.

vi. **Start Time**: This is the option to choose any time, a specific time, or a range of times.

vii. **Duration**

viii. **Use Default Duration**: This will use the default duration of the service.

3. Click on **Find Available Times**.
4. A list of available times will be displayed, given the service and resource. You can select one or more resources, and then click on **Schedule**.

Managing service activities

Using the CRM service calendar can aid in displaying scheduling conflicts, rescheduling service activities, changing statuses, and making general modifications.

Service calendar

The service calendar allows an organization to view a high-level view of service activities by day, week, or month. It's also another place to create new appointments and to manage service activities. Lastly, it's the ideal place to look for conflicts in a service schedule.

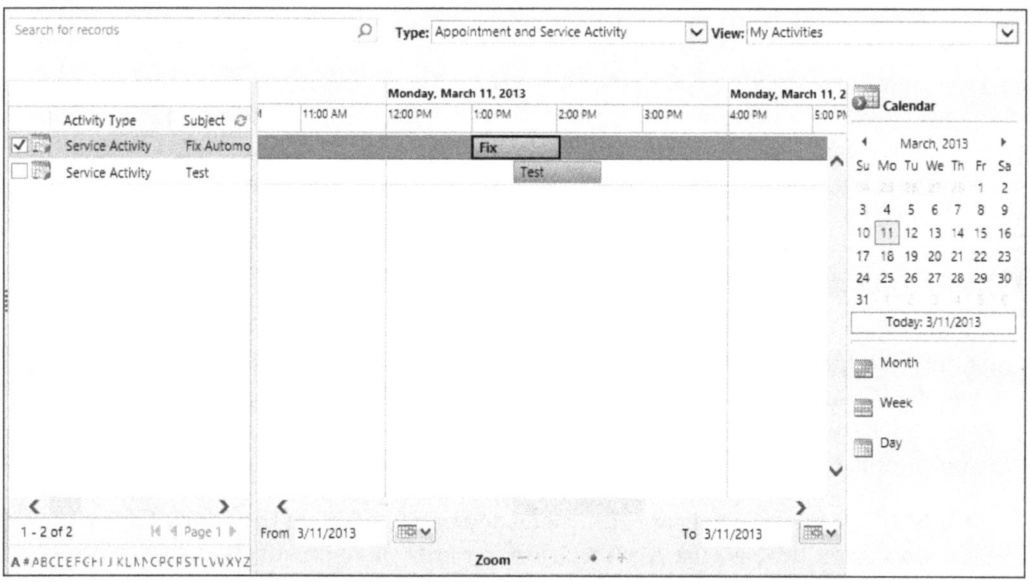

The service calendar has various search and filtering options. You can search for a specific record in the calendar, filter by record type (appointment and service activity, service activity, appointment, resource, user, or facility/equipment). When the type filter is set, the view filter will automatically change.

Using the calendar, new service activities can be created by going to the **Service Calendar** ribbon, and clicking on **Service Activity** in the **New** group, or by clicking on the **Schedule** button in the **Actions** group. The difference is that if a user clicks on the **Schedule** button, the user will be directed to the CRM scheduling engine. Other actions can be taken to manage the service activities as well.

Displaying scheduling conflicts

When a service activity is scheduled, an alert will indicate a potential conflict. Users can choose to select another time, or to save the service activity anyway. At any time, users can identify service activities or appointments with conflicts by clicking the **Conflicts** on the **Actions** toolbar on the **Service Calendar** ribbon. The conflicts will be highlighted in red.

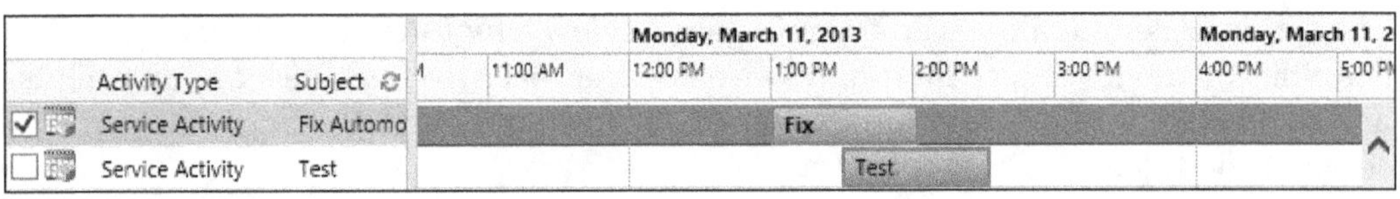

Rescheduling activities

From the service calendar, a user can open the service activity and reschedule it by changing the date and time of the service activity. The other option is selecting the service activity on the calendar itself, going to the **Service Calendar** ribbon, and then in the **Actions** group clicking on the **Reschedule** button. Doing this will direct the user to the CRM scheduling engine to assist with rescheduling the activity.

Changing activity status

To change the status of an activity, a user can select the service activity in the calendar, and then go to the **Service Calendar** ribbon, and then in the **Actions** group click on the **Change Status** button. An example use case is if users wanted to cancel or mark the service activity as completed, then they can do so from the calendar. The other option is to open the activity itself and to do one of the following:

- Mark the service activity complete: a user can click on **the Mark Complete** button on the **Service Activity** ribbon in the **Save Group**.
- Change the status of the service activity: a user can click on the **Close Service Activity** button on the **Service Activity** ribbon, in the **Actions** group. This gives the user the option to set the status to **Completed**, **Canceled**, or **No Show**.

Reporting on service activities

Out of the box, Dynamics CRM provides a service activity volume report. The service activity volume report can be run from the view of reports, or from the view of cases, on the **Cases** ribbon bar in the **Data** group, by clicking on the **Run Report** button, and then selecting the report. It's important to note that no out of the box charts are available. However charts and other reports can be created, as noted in *Chapter 3, Managing Marketing Automation Applications - Marketing Lists and Campaigns*.

Service activity volume report

The following screenshot illustrates the service activity volume report. This report displays **Subject**, **Scheduled Start**, **Scheduled End**, **Duration**, **Service Name**, and **Status Reason** of the service activities in a table format for the last twelve months. The filter criteria for this report can be changed. For example, if you want to display service activities for the last six months instead of twelve.

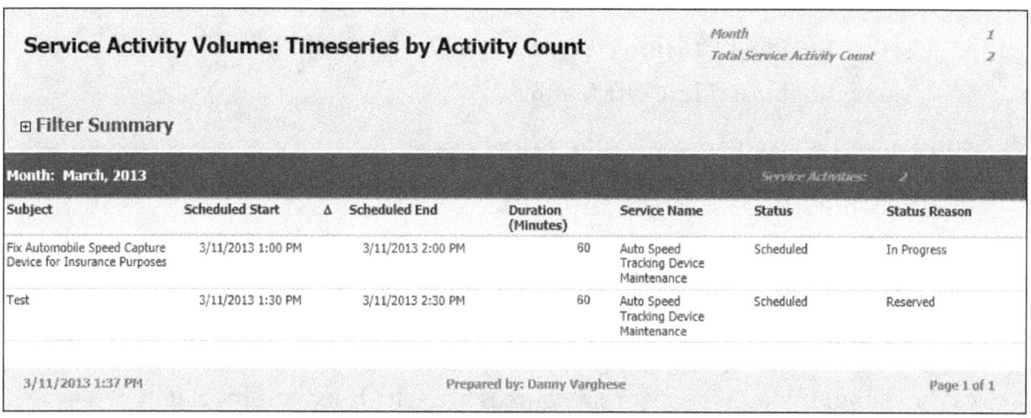
Service Activity Volume: Timeseries by Activity Count

Month 1
Total Service Activity Count 2

⊞ Filter Summary

Month: March, 2013 *Service Activities:* 2

Subject	Scheduled Start	Scheduled End	Duration (Minutes)	Service Name	Status	Status Reason
Fix Automobile Speed Capture Device for Insurance Purposes	3/11/2013 1:00 PM	3/11/2013 2:00 PM	60	Auto Speed Tracking Device Maintenance	Scheduled	In Progress
Test	3/11/2013 1:30 PM	3/11/2013 2:30 PM	60	Auto Speed Tracking Device Maintenance	Scheduled	Reserved

3/11/2013 1:37 PM Prepared by: Danny Varghese Page 1 of 1

The other option is for the report to display a bar chart of the total number of activities by month. The report can also be grouped by user, facility or equipment, service, site, customer, and status reason. The service activity volume report is a great way to get a high-level picture of the volume of service requests being created, scheduled, and completed. This can help an organization to determine if the proper resources are being allocated to service their customers.

Test your knowledge

Q. 1. When scheduling services, where do you define the resources required to perform a service?

1. On the user record.
2. In the resource group.
3. In the service activities.
4. In the resource selection rules.

Q. 2. Your organization needs an easy way to ensure that no service appointments are scheduled during a national holiday. What is the best method to ensure this?

1. Set up a reminder in Outlook to alert the user when he/she gets in to not schedule service appointments on the specific day.
2. Use the **Time Off** feature in CRM to set up vacation days for every service individual.
3. Use the **Business Closures** feature.
4. Use the **Business Time Off** feature.

Q. 3. Where do you configure a facility's time zone?

1. The work hours for the facility.
2. The facility's settings.
3. The service appointment's settings.
4. The calendar settings.

Q. 4. What should you do to ensure resources are scheduled appropriately when dealing with a service at a facility? (Choose all that apply.)

1. Edit the work hours for the facility.
2. Edit the service selection rule.
3. Edit the service activity.
4. Edit the work hours for the users.

Q. 5. What are the required fields on a service activity?

1. **Subject**.
2. **Service**.
3. **Start Time**.
4. **End Time**.
5. All of the above.
6. None of the above.

Q. 6. What are the various statuses of a service activity? (Choose all that apply.)

1. **Completed**.
2. **Canceled**.
3. **No Show**.
4. **On Hold**.

Q. 7. When scheduling services, how would an organization ensure an employee is fully utilized before scheduling services for another employee?

1. On the service activity record, set the selection criteria to "least busy".
2. On the service activity record, set the selection criteria to "most busy".
3. On the service activity record, set the selection criteria to "random".
4. On the service activity record, set the selection criteria to "least happy".

Q. 8. How are conflicts shown for a service activity? (Choose all that apply.)

1. Using the service calendar, click on the **Conflicts** button.
2. Using the service calendar, click on the **Show Conflicts** button.
3. Open the activity that caused the conflict when it was created.
4. Open the activity that didn't cause the conflict.

Q. 9. How can you reschedule an activity? (Choose all that apply.)

1. Open the activity record and change the date and time.
2. Use the **Reschedule Activity** button on the Calendar.
3. Use the **Reschedule button** on the Calendar.
4. Click on the service activity on the calendar, and drag-and-drop it to another date and time.

Q. 10. From where can the service activity volume report be run?
(Choose all that apply.)

1. From the view of all reports.
2. From the view of all service activities.
3. From the **Run Report** menu on the view of cases.
4. From the **Run Report** menu on the view of all activities.

Summary

Service scheduling allows an organization to allocate the proper resources to help service their customers. Service is a type of work that is delivered to a customer and performed by one or more resources. For example, equipment repair, health services, legal, or accounting services. It's important to understand service scheduling terminology, such as resources, resource groups, sites, capacity scheduling, selection rules, and selection criteria. All of the aforementioned components may be needed when scheduling services for a customer. CRM helps to tackle four major scheduling scenarios:

- Individual scenario
- Different skills and shifts
- Different skills, shifts, equipment, and sites
- Different skills, equipment, and sites

A service activity is like any other activity, but it is related to a service. It can be associated to one or more customers, and resources (user, equipment, and facility). Setting up service scheduling entails the following potential tasks:

- Setting up work hours, business closures, time off, and capacity scheduling
- Creating facilities and/or equipment
- Creating a site and/or service
- Creating resource groups
- Configuring customer service preferences

Work hours are configured per resource and indicates the times at which a resource is available to work. Configuring business closures for the organization and time off for users helps an organization to understand for which hours or days a resource may be unavailable for service. Capacity is used to determine how many services a resource can perform at one time. Configured capacity is two fold: one on the resource to define how many service activities the resource can perform during work hours, and one, on the service to define how many resources can perform the service at one time. A resource group is a way to group resources by a set of criteria—for example, skill sets. Lastly, as part of the setup involved in service scheduling, customer service preferences can play a role, especially when the scheduling engine is involved.

Service activities are scheduled for a specific time, can include a site, can be tied to one or more customers, and can include one or more resources. To assist with the scheduling of service activities, the scheduling engine takes into account customer service preferences, resource schedules, and service selection criteria to display a list of potential resources. Using the CRM service calendar can help users to schedule appointments, display scheduling conflicts, reschedule activities, and change the status of service activities.

Reporting is a tool to help an organization analyze their service scheduling landscape. The service activity volume report displays either a bar graph of the number of service activities by month, or a table listing each service activity for the past twelve months. The report can also be grouped by user, facility/equipment, service, site, customer, and status reason.

A
Sample Certification Exam Questions

This appendix will assess your understanding of applications within Microsoft Dynamics CRM 2011 and your readiness for the certification exam by presenting 75 questions similar to those found in the MB2-868 exam.

Sample exam questions

Q. 1. The required fields when creating a marketing list are which of the following? (Choose all that apply.)

1. **Member Type**.
2. **Campaign Type**.
3. **List Name**.
4. **Type**.
5. **Owner**.

Q. 2. Which of the following entities can you select as the member type when creating dynamic marketing lists? (Choose all that apply.)

1. Lead.
2. Opportunity.
3. Contact.
4. Account.
5. Campaign.

Q. 3. Which of the following entities can a marketing list be associated to? (Choose all that apply.)

1. Campaigns.
2. Sales Literature.
3. Products.
4. Quick Campaigns.
5. Activities.

Q. 4. When creating a static marketing list, what answer describes all the ways a member can be initially added or removed from a marketing list?

1. Use lookup and advanced find to add and remove members.
2. Use lookup and advanced find to add members, but remove members manually.
3. Use lookup to add members and use advanced find to remove members.
4. Use advanced find to add members and lookup to remove members.
5. None of the above.

Q. 5. State true or false: When a static marketing list is created, the only way to add or remove members is to do it manually.

Q. 6. When updating a static marketing list, what are the ways in which members can be managed?

1. Using the **Manage Members** button on the ribbon.
2. Inside a lead, account, or contact, click on the **Add to Marketing List** button.
3. If you're on a view for the accounts, contacts or leads, click on **Add to Marketing List** button.
4. From the advanced find view for accounts, contacts, or leads, click on **Add to Marketing List** button.
5. All of the above.

Q. 7. Which of the following statements about marketing lists are true? (Choose all that apply.)

1. You can copy a dynamic marketing list to a static marketing list.
2. A marketing list can contain account and contact members.

3. You can add members to a static marketing list by using an Advanced Find query.
4. You can remove members from a dynamic marketing list by using an Advanced Find query.

Q. 8. State true or false: Products can be associated to a campaign and campaign activities.

Q. 9. Which of the following fields are automatically calculated on a campaign? (Choose all that apply.)

1. Total Cost of Campaign Activities.
2. Miscellaneous Costs.
3. Total Cost of Campaign.
4. Expected ROI.
5. Actual ROI.

Q. 10. Which of the following can be done with a quick campaign?

1. Create an appointment activity.
2. Associate sales literature.
3. Associate products.
4. Create planning activities.
5. Distribute activities of multiple types.

Q. 11. When distributing campaign activities, what are the possible options for assigning an owner to the activity? (Choose all that apply.)

1. You cannot assign the owner of the activity during distribution.
2. The person distributing the activities can own them.
3. Assign to another user or team.
4. Assign to the owner of the campaign.
5. Assign to the owner of the targeted marketing list.

Q. 12. What are the ways in which a campaign response be created automatically? (Choose all that apply.)

1. Campaign responses cannot be created automatically.
2. Importing using Data Import Wizard.

3. If e-mail tracking is enabled, and an e-mail from a campaign is responded to, the response can be created automatically.
4. By converting an activity to a campaign response.
5. Manually creating a response.

Q. 13. State true or false: A campaign response can be converted into an account.

Q. 14. What entities can be created from a campaign response?

1. Lead, Account, Contact.
2. Lead, Account, Contact, Quote, Order, Opportunity.
3. Lead, Quote, Order, Opportunity.
4. Account, Contact, Quote, Order, Opportunity.
5. Quote, Order, Opportunity.

Q. 15. What are the options available to a user when exporting data to a spreadsheet?

1. Static Worksheet.
2. Dynamic PivotTable.
3. Dynamic Worksheet.
4. All of the above.
5. None of the above.

Q. 16. Which of the following types of personal charts can you create? (Choose all that apply.)

1. Funnel charts.
2. Pie charts.
3. Line charts with multiple series.
4. Line charts with single series.
5. All of the above.

Q. 17. When analyzing data in Dynamics CRM 2011, which of the following can you use? (Choose all that apply.)

1. SSRS reports.
2. SSIS reports.
3. Charts.
4. Auditing.
5. Advanced Find.

Q. 18. What are the required fields needed to setup a goal metric? (Choose all that apply.)

1. Metric Type.
2. Entity Type.
3. Track Stretch Target.
4. Description.

Q. 19. What is the first step in defining a goal?

1. Creating a rollup field.
2. Selecting a goal metric, and if no goal metric exists, one needs to be created first.
3. Assigning an owner.
4. Defining a child goal.
5. Defining a goal period.

Q. 20. Which of the following statements describes the difference between a goal metric and a goal target?

1. Goal target is a way to measure a goal, and a goal metric is a way to measure value over a given period of time.
2. Goal target is a way to measure your expectations, and a goal metric is a way to capture data around ROI.
3. Goal target is a way to capture an expected value or dollars, and goal metric is a way to measure the dollars.
4. Goal target is a way to measure a goal metric, and a goal metric is a way to track actual revenue.
5. Goal target is a way to measure a goal metric, and a goal metric is a way to measure a goal.

Q. 21. What is the primary difference between a custom activity and custom entity? (Choose the best one that applies.)

1. Custom activities can be customized.
2. Custom activities can be added to a queue.
3. Custom activities can be used to track text messages.
4. Custom activities inherit all the properties of the base activities.
5. Custom activities inherit all the properties of a custom entity.

Q. 22. Which of the following are required fields when creating a lead?

1. Topic.
2. Topic, Last Name.
3. Topic, Last Name, Company Name.
4. Topic, Last Name, Company Name, Lead Source.
5. None of the above.

Q. 23. State true or false: An e-mail activity can be converted into a lead.

Q. 24. How can an opportunity be created from a lead? (Choose all that apply.)

1. Qualify the lead and convert it to an account or contact; create the opportunity with the values of the lead, and then attach it to the account.
2. Qualify the lead and convert it to an opportunity.
3. Qualify the lead and convert it to an account, contact and opportunity.
4. Create the opportunity with the values of the lead, and then attach the opportunity to the account or contact.
5. None of the above.

Q. 25. How can you send a customer or even an internal user a piece of sales literature from within Dynamics CRM? (Choose all that apply.)

1. Create an e-mail message, add the sales literature attachment, and send the e-mail message.
2. Open the sales literature and send it as an e-mail message.
3. Open the attachment tied to the sales literature and send it to the customer as an e-mail message.
4. Create an e-mail message, add the sales literature record, and send the e-mail message to the customer.

Q. 26. What records can a competitor be attached to? (Choose all that apply.)

1. Accounts.
2. Products.
3. Sales Literature.
4. Opportunities.
5. Contacts.

Q. 27. State true or false: An e-mail can be converted into an opportunity.

Q. 28. Your company's default CRM currency is set to U.S. Dollar, but you created an opportunity for a customer that deals in British Pounds. After the opportunity was created, you realized you forgot to change the currency to British Pounds for this customer. What is the easiest way to change the currency?

1. Open the opportunity, and then change the currency.
2. Create a new opportunity that has the correct currency, and then delete the original opportunity.
3. Create a copy of the opportunity, change the currency on the copy, and then delete the original opportunity.
4. Change the default currency for your user account, and then open the opportunity and run the Recalculate Opportunity command.

Q. 29. What are the required fields when creating an opportunity? (Choose all that apply.)

1. Topic.
2. Potential Customer.
3. Est. Revenue.
4. Sales Stage.
5. Rating.

Q. 30. Which of the following is required to be set/done when closing an opportunity as won?

1. Close all open activities on the opportunity.
2. Actual Revenue.
3. Estimated close date.
4. Must have at least one opportunity product.

Q. 31. What are the various statuses of an opportunity?

1. Open, Won, Lost.
2. Won, Lost.
3. Won, Canceled, Lost.
4. Open, Canceled, Closed.
5. Open, Won, Canceled, Lost.

Q. 32. What is a unit group?

1. A way to group two products together based on a common theme.
2. A single value for a group of measurements of a product.
3. A compilation of the different measurements that a product is available in.
4. A way to track costs of products for price lists.

Q. 33. What in Dynamics CRM must be created first before you can create a product?

1. Currency.
2. Price list.
3. Discount list.
4. Unit group.

Q. 34. What entities can a product be associated to?

1. Sales Literature.
2. Accounts.
3. Competitors.
4. Contacts.
5. Contract Line.

Q. 35. How would you set up different prices for products in Dynamics CRM 2011?

1. Create product and then add that product to different price lists.
2. Create product and then add that product to different price list items.
3. Create a product for every price list.
4. Create a product, create a price list, create a price list item and add the product to the price list item.
5. None of the above.

Q. 36. All of an organization's customers want a discounted price as they purchase more units of a product. What is the best way to achieve this?

1. Apply a manual discount to the product when they are purchased.
2. Set up a discount list with an amount or percentage off the list price for ranges of quantities purchased.
3. Set up a discount list with the discounted price for ranges of quantities purchased.
4. Override the price of the product.

5. All of the above.

Q. 37. When setting the rounding option for a price list item, what is the field dependant on?

1. Quantity Selling Option.
2. Pricing Method.
3. Amount.
4. Rounding Amount.
5. Rounding Policy.

Q. 38. What is the best option for creating a quote for a customer that has an existing opportunity and have that opportunity related to the quote?

1. Create the new quote and relate the existing opportunity.
2. Create the new quote and get the products from the existing opportunity.
3. Create the new quote directly from the existing opportunity.
4. Create the new quote and re-associate the products from the opportunity to the quote.

Q. 39. What are the various statuses of a quote?

1. In Progress, Open, Won, Revised, Lost or Canceled.
2. Open, Won, Lost.
3. Lost, Won, Canceled.
4. Open, Closed, Canceled.
5. Open, Closed, Revised.

Q. 40. When an order is created from a quote and the pricing changes, how can the order reflect the updated prices?

1. It can't; the order will need to be canceled or deleted, and then re-created with the new price list.
2. Create a new order with the same products and change the price list.
3. Click on the **Use Current Pricing** button.
4. Change the price list on the order.

Q. 41. How can an invoice be created? (Choose all that apply)

1. Manually.
2. From a quote.
3. From an order.
4. From another invoice.
5. From an opportunity.

Q. 42. If you're on an invoice product, how can you get to the invoice?

1. Click on the invoice lookup field.
2. Open a new window, copy the invoice detail URL, and then change the entity name from invoice detail to invoice.
3. Click on the left hand navigation and click on invoices.
4. From an invoice detail record, you cannot get to the invoice record.

Q. 43. What can a user do with the Microsoft Dynamics CRM 2011 Outlook client? (Choose all that apply)

1. Synchronize activity records that the employee owns.
2. Synchronize activity records assigned to a team that the user is a part of.
3. Automatically create contact or lead records from tracked e-mail messages while online.
4. Automatically create contact or lead records from tracked e-mail messages while offline.

Q. 44. Which statement is true about the use of Microsoft Dynamics CRM 2011 Outlook client?

1. Deleting a contact record in Microsoft Dynamics CRM for which you are the owner will delete the contact from Outlook.
2. Deleting a completed task that is tracked in Outlook will delete the task activity record from Microsoft Dynamics CRM.
3. Deleting an e-mail message in Microsoft Dynamics CRM will delete the tracked e-mail message from Outlook.
4. Deleting a tracked e-mail message in Outlook will delete the e-mail message from Microsoft Dynamics CRM.

Q. 45. How can a case be resolved when it has open activities?

1. Close the open activities, and then close the case.
2. You can close the case even if there are open activities.
3. Close the case, and then close the open activities.
4. Close the case and leave the activities open.

Q. 46. Which of the following statements about cases in Microsoft Dynamics CRM 2011 are true? (Choose all that apply.)

1. Cases can be assigned to teams.
2. A case must be assigned a subject.
3. Custom activity types can be converted into cases.
4. Only out of the box activities can be converted to a case.

Q. 47. Which of the following actions can be taken on a resolved case? (Choose all that apply.)

1. Creating notes.
2. Adding activities.
3. Assigning a new owner.
4. Modifying the case fields.

Q. 48. How can a case be tied to a specific queue? (Choose all that apply.)

1. Add the case to the queue directly.
2. Assign the case to the queue.
3. From any view, select the case and assign the case to the queue.
4. From any view, select the case and route the case to a queue.

Q. 49. What is required when creating a knowledge base article? (Choose all that apply.)

1. Knowledge base article template.
2. Title.
3. Subject.
4. Key Words.
5. Language.

Q. 50. If you deactivate a Knowledge Base article template, what happens to the knowledge base articles created from that template that are in various stages of the publishing process?

1. All articles based on the deactivated template are disabled.
2. Nothing happens to draft articles, but published articles get deactivated.
3. All articles based on the deactivated template are still active.
4. Unapproved and Draft articles using the article template are deactivated.

Q. 51. What are the different options for searches that can be performed on a knowledge base article?

1. Full Text, Keyword, Title, Subject, Article Number.
2. Article Number, Exact Word Search, Use Like Words Search.
3. Exact Word Search, Similar Word Search, Full Text.
4. Full Text, Keyword, Exact Word, Article Number.
5. Full Text, Keyword, Exact Word, Use Like Word.

Q. 52. Which of the following actions can you perform with knowledge base articles? (Choose all that apply.)

1. Attach an article to a case.
2. Attach an article to a product.
3. Attach an article to a campaign.
4. E-mail an article to a contact.
5. Attach an article to a marketing list.

Q. 53. Which of the following is true about deactivating and deleting queues? (Choose all that apply.)

1. When a queue is deactivated, all queue items are removed from the queue.
2. A queue cannot be deleted if it contains queue items.
3. Besides 1 and 2, a queue can be deactivated or deleted anytime.
4. All of the above.
5. None of the above.

Q. 54. What happens when something is added to a queue?

1. A queue item is created associated to the queue and to the record being associated.
2. The record is directly added to the queue.
3. A queue item is created and associated to the record added and associated to nothing else.
4. The record becomes deactivated until someone chooses to work on the item.
5. The worked on field automatically gets set to the name of the user adding the record to the queue.

Q. 55. When users are added to a team, how is the security role on the team applied?

1. The security role on the team supersedes that of the users.
2. The security role of the user supersedes that of the team.
3. The role of the user with the highest privilege is applied to all the users.
4. The privileges are additive between the team and user.

Q. 56. State true or false: A team can be deleted; a user cannot.

Q. 57. What are the advantages of a team? (Choose all that apply.)

1. It allows users to work collaboratively across an organization.
2. It is one way in which users from different business units can work on a record when individual security roles might not allow that.
3. It lets multiple users create a record at the same time.
4. It allows multiple users to own a record at the same time.

Q. 58. What are the required fields when creating a contract template? (Choose all that apply.)

1. Name.
2. Abbreviation.
3. Billing Frequency.
4. Allotment Type.
5. Calendar.

Q. 59. What are the different contract allotment options?

1. Number of cases, time, and coverage dates.
2. Numbers of cases, time for each case, begin and end dates.
3. Time, Coverage Dates, and length of each case.
4. Number of Active Cases, time, and coverage dates.

Q. 60. What statuses of a contract make it ineligible to delete?

1. Draft, Invoiced.
2. Invoiced, Active.
3. Draft, Active.
4. Canceled, Expired.
5. Draft, Canceled, Expired.

Q. 61. If a contract is in the active status, what can you do with the contract?

1. Delete the contract.
2. Edit the contract.
3. Add contract lines.
4. Add it to an opportunity.

Q. 62. When a contract is on hold, what can you do?

1. Add contract lines.
2. Edit the contract.
3. Copy contract.
4. Add the contract to a case.

Q. 63. What resource allocation should be used if you want to distribute work evenly across all resources?

1. Even.
2. Least Busy.
3. Distributed.
4. Shared.

Q. 64. Where is the configuration for the resources required to perform a service?

1. In the resource selection rules section.
2. In a resource group.
3. On the user record.
4. On the resource record.

Q. 65. How can the capacity of a facility be set? (Choose all that apply.)

1. Edit the resource selection rule.
2. Edit the equipment's work schedule.
3. Edit the service selection rule.
4. Edit each facility's work schedule.

Q. 66. What fields are required to create a service activity? (Choose all that apply.)

1. Account.
2. Contact.
3. Service.
4. Start Time.
5. Subject.

Q. 67. What is the scheduling scenario that defines one customer working with one service person?

1. Individual scenario.
2. Individual contributor scenario.
3. Singular scenario.
4. One person scenario.

Q. 68. When setting up a user's work schedule, how can it be configured to observe holidays the business observes?

1. Don't schedule the user on holidays.
2. Click on exclude holidays in the user's record.
3. When setting up a user's weekly schedule, click on **Observe**, under the business closures option.
4. When setting up a user's weekly schedule, click on **Acknowledge**, under the business closures option.
5. When setting up a user's weekly schedule, click on **Off**, under the business closures option.

Q. 69. Where are customer service preferences configured?

1. On the service activity record.
2. On the account or contact record.
3. On the account, contact, or lead record.
4. On the user's record.

Q. 70. State true or false: When setting up customer service preferences, the preferences are copied to the service activities.

Q. 71. What does the service scheduling engine do?

1. Gives users the best option for the resource to use to complete the given service.
2. Automatically schedules resources and resolves any conflicts.
3. Uses the selection rule for the service as the primary factor.
4. Starts up, schedules all services, and then goes back to sleep.

Q. 72. What are the different ways in which a service activity can be rescheduled? (Choose all that apply.)

1. Open the activity and change the dates.
2. Open the activity and click on schedule.
3. Close the original service activity and create a new one with the new date.
4. Clone the service activity and reset the date of the cloned activity.

Q. 73. What are the different status reasons of a service activity?

1. Open, Won, Lost.
2. Completed, Canceled, No Show.
3. Completed, Canceled, Lost.
4. Completed, Canceled, Did Not Show.
5. Completed, Canceled, No Appointment.

Q. 74. What are some advantages of the service calendar? (Choose all that apply.)

1. Helps resolve scheduling conflicts.
2. Helps search for service activities.
3. Shows a list of all appointments, including service activities, for a user.
4. Automatically adjusts for daylight savings.

Q. 75. What does the service activity volume report display? (Choose all that apply.)

1. Total duration of all tasks.
2. Total number of activities.
3. Total count of service activities.
4. Total duration of all service activities.
5. Total sum of hours worked on service activities.

Bonus question

State true or false: Microsoft Dynamics CRM 2011 is awesome.

B
Answers to Sample Certification Exam Questions

In this appendix we shall review the answers and explanations for the sample questions from *Appendix A, Sample Certification Exam Questions*.

Q. 1. The required fields when creating a marketing list are which of the following? (Choose all that apply.)

1. **Member Type**.
2. **Campaign Type**.
3. **List Name**.
4. **Type**.
5. **Owner**.

Answer: 1, 3, 4, and 5

> The required fields when creating a marketing list are **List Name**, **Type**, **Member Type**, and **Owner**. This is a bit of a trick question because although the **Owner** field is always pre-populated with the name of the user creating the record, it is still a required field.

Q. 2. Which of the following entities can you select as the member type when creating dynamic marketing lists? (Choose all that apply.)

1. Lead.
2. Opportunity.
3. Contact.
4. Account.
5. Campaign.

Answer: 1, 3, and 4

> When creating marketing lists (dynamic or static), we can define leads, accounts, or contacts as a **Member Type**, and only one of those record types can be added as members. An opportunity is not tied to a marketing list at all, and a campaign can have related marketing lists, but cannot be a **Member Type** option.

Q. 3. Which of the following entities can a marketing list be associated to? (Choose all that apply.)

1. Campaigns.
2. Sales Literature.
3. Products.
4. Quick Campaigns.
5. Activities.

Answer: 1 and 4

> Unlike Q. 2., this question is asking for the types of entities to which a marketing list can be associated. A marketing list can be associated to campaigns and quick campaigns from the choices above. Sales Literature and products can be associated to a campaign. Activities can be added to almost every other entity in CRM, but not to marketing lists.

Q. 4. When creating a static marketing list, what answer describes all the ways a member can be initially added or removed from a marketing list?

1. Use lookup and advanced find to add and remove members.
2. Use lookup and advanced find to add members, but remove members manually.

3. Use lookup to add members and use advanced find to remove members.
4. Use advanced find to add members and lookup to remove members.
5. None of the above.

Answer: 5

> When creating a static marketing list, a member can be added by using a lookup, or by using the advanced find. To remove members, we can use advanced find. There is another option, which is to use advanced find to **Evaluate** members, but that is not what the question asked.

Q. 5. State true or false: When a static marketing list is created, the only way to add or remove members is to do it manually.

Answer: False

> When creating a static marketing list, a member can be added using a lookup, or advanced find. To remove members, we can use advanced find. There is another option which is to use advanced find to "evaluate" members, which allows us to evaluate which members to keep on the marketing list.

Q. 6. When updating a static marketing list, what are the ways in which members can be managed?

1. Using the **Manage Members** button on the ribbon.
2. Inside a lead, account, or contact, click on the **Add to Marketing List** button.
3. If you're on a view for the accounts, contacts or leads, click on **Add to Marketing List** button.
4. From the advanced find view for accounts, contacts or leads, click on **Add to Marketing List** button.
5. All of the above.

Answer: 5

> To update a static marketing list, the way members can be managed is by using the manage members button on the ribbon, on the actual record form or in a view for a particular record type, or within advanced find we can click on the **Add to Marketing List** button.

Q. 7. Which of the following statements about marketing lists are true? (Choose all that apply):

1. You can copy a dynamic marketing list to a static marketing list.
2. A marketing list can contain account and contact members.
3. You can add members to a static marketing list by using an Advanced Find query.
4. You can remove members from a dynamic marketing list by using an Advanced Find query.

Answer: 1, 3, and 4

> The only thing we cannot do with a marketing list, given the options above, is that a marketing list cannot contain both account and contact members; it can only contain one or the other. Other than that, a dynamic marketing list can be copied to a static one, and we can add and remove members of a marketing list by using advanced find.

Q. 8. State true or false: Products can be associated to a campaign and campaign activities.

Answer: False

> Products can only be associated to a campaign.

Q. 9. Which of the following fields are automatically calculated on a campaign? (Choose all that apply.)

1. Total Cost of Campaign Activities.
2. Miscellaneous Costs.
3. Total Cost of Campaign.
4. Expected ROI.
5. Actual ROI.

Answer: 1 and 3

> On the campaign, the only fields that are calculated by the system are the **TotalCostofCampaignActivities** and the **TotalCostoftheCampaign**. When campaign activities are created for a campaign and the cost of the activity is entered by the user, the costs for each activity are rolled up to the campaign. The **TotalCostoftheCampaign** is the **TotalCostofCampaignActivities** plus the value of the **MiscellaneousCosts** for the campaign. Miscellaneous costs are manually entered, and the expected and actual ROI are not fields on a campaign.

Q. 10. Which of the following can be done with a quick campaign?

1. Create an appointment activity.
2. Associate sales literature.
3. Associate products.
4. Create planning activities.
5. Distribute activities of multiple types.

Answer: 1

> Quick campaigns can only distribute one activity type as opposed to multiple campaign activity types. There are also no out of the box reports for quick campaigns, we cannot use templates, no financial information is tracked, no planning activities can be created, and we cannot associated targeted products, price lists or sales literature.

Q. 11. When distributing campaign activities, what are the possible options for assigning an owner to the activity? (Choose all that apply.)

1. You cannot assign the owner of the activity during distribution.
2. The person distributing the activities can own them.
3. Assign to another user or team.
4. Assign to the owner of the campaign.
5. Assign to the owner of the targeted marketing list.

Answer: 2, 3, and 5

> When distributing campaign activities, we can assign an owner during the distribution of the activities. Note that the owner chosen will be assigned to all of the activities distributed— it is all or nothing. Given that the owner can be set to the user distributing the activities, we can choose another user or team, or it can be assigned to the owner of the targeted marketing list.

Q. 12. What are the ways in which a campaign response be created automatically? (Choose all that apply.)

1. Campaign responses cannot be created automatically.
2. Importing using Data Import Wizard.
3. If e-mail tracking is enabled, and an e-mail from a campaign is responded to, the response can be created automatically.
4. By converting an activity to a campaign response.
5. Manually creating a response.

Answer: 2 and 3

> Campaign responses can be imported via the data import tool, which in turn will create the responses automatically. Also, if e-mail tracking is enabled, and an e-mail from a campaign is responded to, a response is automatically created. Although an activity can be converted to a campaign response by using the **Convert** button found on the ribbon, it is still considered manual intervention because a button needs to be clicked.

Q. 13. State true or false: A campaign response can be converted into an account.

Answer: True

> A campaign response can be converted into an account or a contact.

Q. 14. What entities can be created from a campaign response?

1. Lead, Account, Contact.
2. Lead, Account, Contact, Quote, Order, Opportunity.
3. Lead, Quote, Order, Opportunity.
4. Account, Contact, Quote, Order, Opportunity.
5. Quote, Order, Opportunity.

Answer: 2

A campaign response can be converted into a lead, account, contact, quote, order, or opportunity.

Q. 15. What are the options available to a user when exporting data to a spreadsheet?

1. Static Worksheet.
2. Dynamic PivotTable.
3. Dynamic Worksheet.
4. All of the above.
5. None of the above.

Answer: 4

When exporting data using the **Export to Excel** functionality, the spreadsheet can be exported as a static worksheet, a dynamic pivot table, or a dynamic worksheet. If the option for a dynamic pivot table or worksheet is chosen, a database connection is configured in the worksheet. That way, the next time the spreadsheet is opened or refreshed, the latest data will be retrieved and the spreadsheet will be refreshed.

Q. 16. Which of the following types of personal charts can you create? (Choose all that apply.)

1. Funnel charts.
2. Pie charts.
3. Line charts with multiple series.
4. Line charts with single series.
5. All of the above.

Answer: 5

The types of charts that can be created in CRM are column, bar, area, single series line, multiple series line, pie, and funnel charts.

Q. 17. When analyzing data in Dynamics CRM 2011, which of the following can you use? (Choose all that apply.)

1. SSRS reports.
2. SSIS reports.

3. Charts.
4. Auditing.
5. Advanced Find.

Answer: 1, 3, 4, and 5

> SSRS reports, charts, advanced find, and auditing functionality can be used separately or in conjunction with each other to help analyze data within CRM. SSIS or SQL Server Integration Services can be used to help import or integrate data, and there are no reports that are created from SSIS.

Q. 18. What are the required fields needed to setup a goal metric? (Choose all that apply.)

1. Metric Type.
2. Entity Type.
3. Track Stretch Target.
4. Description.

Answer: 1

> When creating a goal metric, the following fields are required:
>
> - **Name**
> - **Metric Type**
> - **Amount Data Type**

Q. 19. What is the first step in defining a goal?

1. Creating a rollup field.
2. Selecting a goal metric, and if no goal metric exists, one needs to be created first.
3. Assigning an owner.
4. Defining a child goal.
5. Defining a goal period.

Answer: 2

> When defining a goal, the following fields are required: **Name**, **GoalOwner**, **GoalMetric**, **GoalManager**, **FiscalPeriod**, **FiscalYear**, **RollupOnlyfromChildGoals** option and **Record Set for Rollup** option. Given the options above, creating a goal metric would be the correct choice. It's also a typical practice to set up all the goal metrics ahead of time, before creating any goals.

Q. 20. Which of the following statements describes the difference between a goal metric and a goal target?

1. Goal target is a way to measure a goal, and a goal metric is a way to measure value over a given period of time.
2. Goal target is a way to measure your expectations, and a goal metric is a way to capture data around ROI.
3. Goal target is a way to capture an expected value or dollars, and goal metric is a way to measure the dollars.
4. Goal target is a way to measure a goal metric, and a goal metric is a way to track actual revenue.
5. Goal target is a way to measure a goal metric, and a goal metric is a way to measure a goal.

Answer: 5

> A goal metric is a way to measure a goal and a goal target is a way to measure a goal metric. For example, a goal metric could be a count of the number of cases solved. The goal would be to achieve a certain number of cases resolved, and the metric can be used to measure that. A goal target is the target you wish you achieve for the goal metric.

Q. 21. What is the primary difference between a custom activity and custom entity? (Choose the best one that applies.)

1. Custom activities can be customized.
2. Custom activities can be added to a queue.
3. Custom activities can be used to track text messages.
4. Custom activities inherit all the properties of the base activities.
5. Custom activities inherit all the properties of a custom entity.

Answer: 4

> Custom activities can obviously be customized, and can be used to track things such as text messages. But the defining feature of custom activities is that they will inherit all the properties of the base activity entity.

Q. 22. Which of the following are required fields when creating a lead?

1. Topic.
2. Topic, Last Name.
3. Topic, Last Name, Company Name.
4. Topic, Last Name, Company Name, Lead Source.
5. None of the above.

Answer: 3

> When creating a lead, the list of required fields is: **Topic**, **Last Name**, **Company Name**, and **Owner**. Again, the owner field is automatically pre-populated with the user creating the record, but it is a required field.

Q. 23. State true or false: An e-mail activity can be converted into a lead.

Answer: True

> An e-mail activity can be converted into an opportunity, case, lead, and can also be promoted to a campaign response.

Q. 24. How can an opportunity be created from a lead? (Choose all that apply.)

1. Qualify the lead and convert it to an account or contact; create the opportunity with the values of the lead, and then attach it to the account.
2. Qualify the lead and convert it to an opportunity.
3. Qualify the lead and convert it to an account, contact and opportunity.
4. Create the opportunity with the values of the lead, and then attach the opportunity to the account or contact.
5. None of the above.

Answer: 2 and 3

> A lead can be qualified, and then converted into an opportunity. Using this process will attach the lead to the originating lead field on the opportunity form.

Q. 25. How can you send a customer or even an internal user a piece of sales literature from within Dynamics CRM? (Choose all that apply.)

1. Create an e-mail message, add the sales literature attachment, and send the e-mail message.
2. Open the sales literature and send it as an e-mail message.
3. Open the attachment tied to the sales literature and send it to the customer as an e-mail message.
4. Create an e-mail message, add the sales literature record, and send the e-mail message to the customer.

Answer: 1 and 2

> One of the benefits of sales literature is that it can be attached to an e-mail message and be sent. To do this, create an e-mail message and simply attach the sales literature to the message and then send it. The other option is from a sales literature record, where a user can click on the **Send An E-mail** button.

Q. 26. What records can a competitor be attached to? (Choose all that apply.)

1. Accounts.
2. Products.
3. Sales Literature.
4. Opportunities.
5. Contacts.

Answer: 2, 3, and 4

> A competitor can be tied to products, sales literature, leads, and opportunities. This is defined as an *N:N* (many-to-many) relationship between the competitor entity and the other entities.

Q. 27. State true or false: An e-mail can be converted into an opportunity.

Answer: True

> An e-mail activity can be converted into an opportunity, case, lead, and can also be promoted to a campaign response.

Q. 28. Your company's default CRM currency is set to U.S. Dollar, but you created an opportunity for a customer that deals in British Pounds. After the opportunity was created, you realized you forgot to change the currency to British Pounds for this customer. What is the easiest way to change the currency?

1. Open the opportunity, and then change the currency.
2. Create a new opportunity that has the correct currency, and then delete the original opportunity.
3. Create a copy of the opportunity, change the currency on the copy, and then delete the original opportunity.
4. Change the default currency for your user account, and then open the opportunity and run the Recalculate Opportunity command.

Answer: 1

> This is a commonly-asked question, and the **Currency** field is like any other lookup on any other entity. Once an opportunity has been created, we can change the **Currency** lookup value to another currency. Changing the value will prompt the user with a warning to check all money fields on the form. Once saved, the currency symbols will be changed to the new currency selected, but the amounts will not be converted. For example, if we entered a value for the **EstimatedRevenue** of an opportunity to be $1,000, and then change the currency to Euro, the opportunity's **EstimatedRevenue** will be changed to € 1,000.

Q. 29. What are the required fields when creating an opportunity? (Choose all that apply.)

1. Topic.
2. Potential Customer.
3. Est. Revenue.
4. Sales Stage.
5. Rating.

Answer: 1 and 2

[When creating an opportunity, the required fields are **Topic**, **Potential Customer**, **Status**, **Currency**, and **Owner**. The **Owner** field is pre-populated with the user creating the record, **Currency** is pre-populated with the system's default currency and the status is automatically set to **Open** when an opportunity is first created.]

Q. 30. Which of the following is required to be set/done when closing an opportunity as won?

1. Close all open activities on the opportunity.
2. Actual Revenue.
3. Estimated close date.
4. Must have at least one opportunity product.

Answer: 2

[When closing an opportunity, a new dialog will appear and the required fields that need to be set are: **Status**, **Status Reason**, **Actual Revenue**, and **Close Date**.]

Q. 31. What are the various statuses of an opportunity?

1. Open, Won, Lost.
2. Won, Lost.
3. Won, Canceled, Lost.
4. Open, Canceled, Closed.
5. Open, Won, Canceled, Lost.

Answer: 1

[An opportunity can have a status of Open, Won, or Lost.]

Q. 32. What is a unit group?

1. A way to group two products together based on a common theme.
2. A single value for a group of measurements of a product.

3. A compilation of the different measurements that a product is available in.
4. A way to track costs of products for price lists.

Answer: 3

> A unit group in CRM is a compilation of different measurements that a product is available in.

Q. 33. What in Dynamics CRM must be created first before you can create a product?

1. Currency.
2. Price list.
3. Discount list.
4. Unit group.

Answer: 4

> When creating a product, the required fields are: **Id**, **Name**, **UnitGroup**, **DefaultUnit**, and **DecimalSupported**. There will always be a **Currency** already set up during installation of Dynamics CRM, and this will default to the system default currency when creating the product, but that is not required. A price and discount lists can be created at any time.

Q. 34. What entities can a product be associated to?

1. Sales Literature.
2. Accounts.
3. Competitors.
4. Contacts.
5. Contract Line.

Answer: 1, 3, and 5

> A product can be associated to leads, sales literature, other products, price lists, contract lines, cases, invoice products, order products, price list items, queue items, and quote products.

Q. 35. How would you set up different prices for products in Dynamics CRM 2011?

1. Create product and then add that product to different price lists.
2. Create product and then add that product to different price list items.
3. Create a product for every price list.
4. Create a product, create a price list, create a price list item and add the product to the price list item.
5. None of the above.

Answer: 4

> Setting up different prices in Dynamics CRM involves the creation of the product first, then the price list, and then the price list item. Associating the product to a price list item that is tied to a price list is how one product can have different prices.

Q. 36. All of an organization's customers want a discounted price as they purchase more units of a product. What is the best way to achieve this?

1. Apply a manual discount to the product when they are purchased.
2. Set up a discount list with an amount or percentage off the list price for ranges of quantities purchased.
3. Set up a discount list with the discounted price for ranges of quantities purchased.
4. Override the price of the product.
5. All of the above.

Answer: 2

> To set up discounts for a product, the use of discount lists can be applied. Discount lists in Dynamics CRM involve volume discounts. This means that for certain quantities of a product ordered, a discount in either a dollar amount or percentage will be applied. Many other organizations use the term quantity breaks, which means that when certain quantities of products are ordered, a certain per unit price is set. This is not the case with Dynamics CRM, as it employs discounts rather than a set price.

Q. 37. When setting the rounding option for a price list item, what is the field dependant on?

1. Quantity Selling Option.
2. Pricing Method.
3. Amount.
4. Rounding Amount.
5. Rounding Policy.

Answer: 5

> When creating a price list item, the **Rounding Option** of a price on the price list is not enabled until the **Pricing Method** is set to a value that includes a percentage, and the **Rounding Policy** is set to a value other than **None**.

Q. 38. What is the best option for creating a quote for a customer that has an existing opportunity and have that opportunity related to the quote?

1. Create the new quote and relate the existing opportunity.
2. Create the new quote and get the products from the existing opportunity.
3. Create the new quote directly from the existing opportunity.
4. Create the new quote and re-associate the products from the opportunity to the quote.

Answer: 3

> A quote can easily be created from an existing opportunity for a customer by simply creating the new quote directly from the opportunity. Doing so allows all the opportunity products to be added as quote products. The options are valid, but it's not the easiest or best option.

Q. 39. What are the various statuses of a quote?

1. In Progress, Open, Won, Revised, Lost or Canceled.
2. Open, Won, Lost.
3. Lost, Won, Canceled.
4. Open, Closed, Canceled.
5. Open, Closed, Revised.

Answer: 1

> A quote can have a status of **In Progress**, **Open**, **Revised**, **Lost**, or **Canceled**.

Q. 40. When an order is created from a quote and the pricing changes, how can the order reflect the updated prices?

1. It can't; the order will need to be canceled or deleted, and then re-created with the new price list.
2. Create a new order with the same products and change the price list.
3. Click on the **Use Current Pricing** button.
4. Change the price list on the order.

Answer: 3

> When an order is created from a quote and the price changes, clicking on the **UseCurrentPricing** button will update the price in the quote to the new price. This can be a potentially troublesome option because often customer quotes are static and a customer might expect the price quoted even if prices go up.

Q. 41. How can an invoice be created? (Choose all that apply)

1. Manually.
2. From a quote.
3. From an order.
4. From another invoice.
5. From an opportunity.

Answer: 1, 3, and 5

> An invoice can be created automatically or manually from an opportunity or generated from a quote or an order.

Q. 42. If you're on an invoice product, how can you get to the invoice?

1. Click on the invoice lookup field.
2. Open a new window, copy the invoice detail URL, and then change the entity name from invoice detail to invoice.

3. Click on the left hand navigation and click on invoices.
4. From an invoice detail record, you cannot get to the invoice record.

Answer: 4

> An invoice product is a unique entity in Dynamics CRM in that most of the security permissions for this entity are inherited from the privileges set for an invoice. Also, even though there is a relationship from invoice to invoice product, the lookup field cannot be placed on the invoice product form. The field is locked down and is not customizable.

Q. 43. What can a user do with the Microsoft Dynamics CRM 2011 Outlook client? (Choose all that apply)

1. Synchronize activity records that the employee owns.
2. Synchronize activity records assigned to a team that the user is a part of.
3. Automatically create contact or lead records from tracked e-mail messages while online.
4. Automatically create contact or lead records from tracked e-mail messages while offline.

Answer: 1, 2, and 3

> The Microsoft Dynamics CRM 2011 Outlook client allows us to perform almost any action that the Dynamics CRM 2011 web client would allow. A unique feature of the Dynamics CRM 2011 Outlook client is that when a user is online, tracked e-mail messages can be used to automatically create a contact or lead record.

Q. 44. Which statement is true about the use of Microsoft Dynamics CRM 2011 Outlook client?

1. Deleting a contact record in Microsoft Dynamics CRM for which you are the owner will delete the contact from Outlook.
2. Deleting a completed task that is tracked in Outlook will delete the task activity record from Microsoft Dynamics CRM.
3. Deleting an e-mail message in Microsoft Dynamics CRM will delete the tracked e-mail message from Outlook.

4. Deleting a tracked e-mail message in Outlook will delete the e-mail message from Microsoft Dynamics CRM.

Answer: 2

> Using the Microsoft Dynamics CRM 2011 Outlook client, deleting a completed task that is tracked (has a connection to task record in Dynamics CRM) will delete the task record from Dynamics CRM. Deleting contacts and/or e-mail messages from either the Outlook client or the web client will not "synch" or delete them in the other system.

Q. 45. How can a case be resolved when it has open activities?

1. Close the open activities, and then close the case.
2. You can close the case even if there are open activities.
3. Close the case, and then close the open activities.
4. Close the case and leave the activities open.

Answer: 1

> Cases cannot be resolved when they have open activities associated to them. Associated means that the activity has its regarding field referencing a case. One of the nuances of a case is that when resolving it all open activities must be closed.

Q. 46. Which of the following statements about cases in Microsoft Dynamics CRM 2011 are true? (Choose all that apply.)

1. Cases can be assigned to teams.
2. A case must be assigned a subject.
3. Custom activity types can be converted into cases.
4. Only out of the box activities can be converted to a case.

Answer: 1 and 3

> New to Microsoft Dynamics CRM 2011, as opposed to previous version of Dynamics CRM, cases, as with many other record types, can be assigned to teams. Like other activities, a custom activity can also be converted into a case. A case does have the option of having a subject, but it's not required.

Q. 47. Which of the following actions can be taken on a resolved case? (Choose all that apply.)

1. Creating notes.
2. Adding activities.
3. Assigning a new owner.
4. Modifying the case fields.

Answer: 1

> Once a case is resolved, it's pretty much read only, so the only action allowed is adding notes. Because all open activities need to be resolved to close a case, adding activities is not allowed. Because the form is read only, assigning a new owner or modifying fields on the form is also not allowed.

Q. 48. How can a case be tied to a specific queue? (Choose all that apply.)

1. Add the case to the queue directly.
2. Assign the case to the queue.
3. From any view, select the case and assign the case to the queue.
4. From any view, select the case and route the case to a queue.

Answer: 1

> A case can be added to a queue directly from the case form. A case can only be assigned to a user or team, and not to a queue. A case can be added to a queue from any view as well, but routing a case to a queue means that the case is already tied to another queue.

Q. 49. What is required when creating a knowledge base article? (Choose all that apply.)

1. Knowledge base article template.
2. Title.
3. Subject.
4. Key Words.
5. Language.

Answer: 1, 2, and 3

> The following fields are required when creating knowledge base article: **Title** and **Subject**. This is a bit of a trick question because in order to create a knowledge base article, a knowledge base article template must be used, so that is also a valid option.

Q. 50. If you deactivate a Knowledge Base article template, what happens to the knowledge base articles created from that template that are in various stages of the publishing process?

1. All articles based on the deactivated template are disabled.
2. Nothing happens to draft articles, but published articles get deactivated.
3. All articles based on the deactivated template are still active.
4. Unapproved and Draft articles using the article template are deactivated.

Answer: 4

> When a knowledge base article template is deactivated, no new knowledge base articles can be created from the template, and any unapproved or draft knowledge base articles using the template are also deactivated.

Q. 51. What are the different options for searches that can be performed on a knowledge base article?

1. Full Text, Keyword, Title, Subject, Article Number.
2. Article Number, Exact Word Search, Use Like Words Search.
3. Exact Word Search, Similar Word Search, Full Text.
4. Full Text, Keyword, Exact Word, Article Number.
5. Full Text, Keyword, Exact Word, Use Like Word.

Answer: 1

> When searching for knowledge base articles, we can use a **Full Text Search**, **Keyword Search**, **Article Number**, and **search by Title or Subject**. This is also a bit of a trick question because the question asks for the search options. There are different "types" of searches, which can include exact word or use like words, but these are not the different search options.

Q. 52. Which of the following actions can you perform with knowledge base articles? (Choose all that apply.)

1. Attach an article to a case.
2. Attach an article to a product.
3. Attach an article to a campaign.
4. E-mail an article to a contact.
5. Attach an article to a marketing list.

Answer: 1

> A knowledge base article can be attached to a case or sales literature, and only a link to the knowledge base article can be e-mailed.

Q. 53. Which of the following is true about deactivating and deleting queues? (Choose all that apply.)

1. When a queue is deactivated, all queue items are removed from the queue.
2. A queue cannot be deleted if it contains queue items.
3. Besides 1 and 2, a queue can be deactivated or deleted anytime.
4. All of the above.
5. None of the above.

Answer: 4

> When a queue is deactivated, all queue items are removed from the queue. A queue cannot be deleted if it contains queue items, and a queue can be deactivated or deleted at any time.

Q. 54. What happens when something is added to a queue?

1. A queue item is created associated to the queue and to the record being associated.
2. The record is directly added to the queue.
3. A queue item is created and associated to the record added and associated to nothing else.

4. The record becomes deactivated until someone chooses to work on the item.
5. The worked on field automatically gets set to the name of the user adding the record to the queue.

Answer: 1

> When something is added to a queue, a queue item is created and the queue item is associated directly to the queue. The record is never directly tied to the queue and the worked on field only gets set when a user chooses the item to work on from the queue.

Q. 55. When users are added to a team, how is the security role on the team applied?

1. The security role on the team supersedes that of the users.
2. The security role of the user supersedes that of the team.
3. The role of the user with the highest privilege is applied to all the users.
4. The privileges are additive between the team and user.

Answer: 4

> Users in Dynamics CRM must have at least one security role defined for them. The security role is a collection of privileges for each entity in the system. When users are added to a team, the user's privilege still applies but the privileges defined for the team will be added as well. For example, if a user has read permission for an account, but does not have write permission and then is added to a team whose security role gives users write privilege for the account, then the user now inherits that privilege.

Q. 56. State true or false: A team can be deleted; a user cannot.

Answer: True

> In Microsoft Dynamics CRM, a user cannot be deleted, but a team can be deleted.

Q. 57. What are the advantages of a team? (Choose all that apply.)

1. It allows users to work collaboratively across an organization.
2. It is one way in which users from different business units can work on a record when individual security roles might not allow that.

3. It lets multiple users create a record at the same time.
4. It allows multiple users to own a record at the same time.

Answer: 1 and 2

> The introduction of teams in Dynamics CRM 2011 has been a tremendous addition because it allows users to work collaboratively across an organization. Let's say we have two users with a security role that allows them to only see accounts in their respective business units. Let's now say those two users need to see some accounts outside each of their business units. We can create a team with the proper privilege and add these two users to the team. This can be accomplished by using Dynamics CRM sharing as well, but this is another option. Teams do not allow multiple users to create a record at the same time. Option 4 is not a correct option in that CRM allows a team to own a record, but this is not the same thing. For example, My Active Accounts view will not show accounts owned by teams that I am a member of so I don't own the record.

Q. 58. What are the required fields when creating a contract template? (Choose all that apply.)

1. Name.
2. Abbreviation.
3. Billing Frequency.
4. Allotment Type.
5. Calendar.

Answer: 1, 2, 3, 4, and 5

> When creating a contract template, the required fields are **TemplateName**, **Abbreviation**, **AllotmentType**, **BillingFrequency**, and **Calendar**.

Q. 59. What are the different contract allotment options?

1. Number of cases, time, and coverage dates.
2. Numbers of cases, time for each case, begin and end dates.
3. Time, Coverage Dates, and length of each case.
4. Number of Active Cases, time, and coverage dates.

Answer: 1

When selecting an allotment type for a contract template, the valid options are **Number of Cases**, **Time for Each Case**, and **CoverageDates**.

Q. 60. What statuses of a contract make it ineligible to delete?

1. Draft, Invoiced.
2. Invoiced, Active.
3. Draft, Active.
4. Canceled, Expired.
5. Draft, Canceled, Expired.

Answer: 2

A contract has the following statuses and explanations:

- **Draft**: The means the contract can still be worked on, but it cannot be associated to a case.
- **Invoiced**: Once a contract is saved, the default status is "Draft." The contextual ribbon now displays a button to invoice the contract. This can only be done if contract lines have been created. Once a contract is in the invoiced state, it cannot be edited or deleted.
- **Active**: The next stage in the contract life cycle is "Active." A contract will automatically be set to active when the contract has started, i.e. the start date of the contract = today's date. This is the only status that allows a contract to be associated to a case. A contract with this status cannot be edited or deleted.
- **OnHold**: Once a contract is activated, it can be placed on hold at any time. Once on hold, the contract cannot be edited or deleted.
- **Canceled**
- **Expired**: Once the end date of the contract has been reached, the contract status automatically gets changed to expired.

Q. 61. If a contract is in the active status, what can you do with the contract?

1. Delete the contract.
2. Edit the contract.

3. Add contract lines.
4. Add it to an opportunity.

Answer: 3

> A contract will automatically be set to active when the contract has started, i.e. the start date of the contract = today's date. This is the only status that allows a contract to be associated to a case. A contract with this status cannot be edited or deleted, but you can add contract lines to the contract.

Q. 62. When a contract is on hold, what can you do?

1. Add contract lines.
2. Edit the contract.
3. Copy contract.
4. Add the contract to a case.

Answer: 3

> When a contract is on hold, the only options available are **Copy Contract**, **Release Hold**, and **Set Calendar**.

Q. 63. What resource allocation should be used if you want to distribute work evenly across all resources?

1. Even.
2. Least Busy.
3. Distributed.
4. Shared.

Answer: 2

> A least busy criteria means the resource with the most availability will be scheduled first, and while randomly resource allocation type will schedule the resources on a random basis.

Q. 64. Where is the configuration for the resources required to perform a service?

1. In the resource selection rules section.
2. In a resource group.
3. On the user record.
4. On the resource record.

Answer: 1

> A selection rule determines the resources required to perform a service. A resource group is a way to group resources according to a set of criteria, which could be skill sets, for example. The user record allows us to define a user's work schedule and there is no such thing as a resource record.

Q. 65. How can the capacity of a facility be set? (Choose all that apply.)

1. Edit the resource selection rule.
2. Edit the equipment's work schedule.
3. Edit the service selection rule.
4. Edit each facility's work schedule.

Answer: 3 and 4

> The capacity of a facility can be set by editing the service selection rule for a service or by editing the user's work schedule. Equipment cannot have a work schedule and editing the service selection rule defines the resources required to perform the specific service.

Q. 66. What fields are required to create a service activity? (Choose all that apply.)

1. Account.
2. Contact.
3. Service.
4. Start Time.
5. Subject.

Answer: 3, 4, and 5

> When creating a service activity, the following fields are required: subject, service, start time, end time and owner. Although the owner field is defaulted to the user creating the record, it's still a required field.

Q. 67. What is the scheduling scenario that defines one customer working with one service person?

1. Individual scenario.
2. Individual contributor scenario.
3. Singular scenario.
4. One person scenario.

Answer: 1

> **Individual Scenario** is the most simple/basic example of service scheduling. In this scenario, Dynamics CRM can schedule one individual to meet with a customer. For example, let's say a client of Race2Win Insurance Company raised an issue with a duplicate bill being sent. Race2Win can offer someone from the billing department to go to the client site, meet with the person that raised the issue and resolve it.

Q. 68. When setting up a user's work schedule, how can it be configured to observe holidays the business observes?

1. Don't schedule the user on holidays.
2. Click on exclude holidays in the user's record.
3. When setting up a user's weekly schedule, click on **Observe**, under the business closures option.
4. When setting up a user's weekly schedule, click on **Acknowledge**, under the business closures option.
5. When setting up a user's weekly schedule, click on **Off**, under the business closures option.

Answer: 3

> When setting up a user's weekly schedule, click on **Observe**, under the business closures option.

Q. 69. Where are customer service preferences configured?

1. On the service activity record.
2. On the account or contact record.

3. On the account, contact, or lead record.
4. On the user's record.

Answer: 2

> Customer service preferences are found in a tab on the account or contact form. When setting up customer service preferences, the preferences are copied to the service activity.

Q. 70. State true or false: When setting up customer service preferences, the preferences are copied to the service activities.

Answer: False

> The customer's preferences are taken into consideration when the Schedule feature is used, but the values are not copied to the service activity.

Q. 71. What does the service scheduling engine do?

1. Gives users the best option for the resource to use to complete the given service.
2. Automatically schedules resources and resolves any conflicts.
3. Uses the selection rule for the service as the primary factor.
4. Starts up, schedules all services, and then goes back to sleep.

Answer: 1

> According to documentation found on MSDN (which is also noted in this book), CRM provides functionality to enable appointment-based service scheduling. You can define services, resources and work schedules, and service locations. A scheduling engine manages appointments and service availability, and can be tuned to optimize scheduling in order to reduce costs and required resources. Thus the service scheduling engine gives the user the best option for a resource to complete the given service.

Q. 72. What are the different ways in which a service activity can be rescheduled? (Choose all that apply.)

1. Open the activity and change the dates.
2. Open the activity and click on schedule.
3. Close the original service activity and create a new one with the new date.
4. Clone the service activity and reset the date of the cloned activity.

Answer: 1 and 2

> A service activity can be rescheduled either by modifying the activity dates or by opening the activity and clicking on **Schedule**.

Q. 73. What are the different status reasons of a service activity?

1. Open, Won, Lost.
2. Completed, Canceled, No Show.
3. Completed, Canceled, Lost.
4. Completed, Canceled, Did Not Show.
5. Completed, Canceled, No Appointment.

Answer: 2

> The different status reasons of a service activity are **Completed**, **Canceled**, or **No Show**.

Q. 74. What are some advantages of the service calendar? (Choose all that apply.)

1. Helps resolve scheduling conflicts.
2. Helps search for service activities.
3. Shows a list of all appointments, including service activities, for a user.
4. Automatically adjusts for daylight savings.

Answer: 1, 2, and 3

> The service calendar helps users to resolve scheduling conflicts, search for service activities—especially using the filtering capabilities of the calendar—and it shows a list of all appointments, including service activities for a user.

Q. 75. What does the service activity volume report display? (Choose all that apply.)

1. Total duration of all tasks.
2. Total number of activities.
3. Total count of service activities.
4. Total duration of all service activities.
5. Total sum of hours worked on service activities.

Answer: 3 and 4

> CRM does not provide out of the box charts for service activities, however like anything in Dynamics CRM, these can be configured very easily. Out of the box, Dynamics provides the service activity volume report.
>
> The service activity volume report is a bar chart that displays the total count of service activities or total duration of all service activities. Another option for this report is to group the data by user, facility/equipment, service, site, customer and status reason.

Bonus question

Q. 1. State true or false: Microsoft Dynamics CRM 2011 is awesome.

Answer: Come on, really?

C
Answers to Self-test Questions

Chapter 2, Activities and Notes

Q. 1.	1, 3, 4, 5
Q. 2.	2, 4
Q. 3.	2, 4
Q. 4.	1, 2, 3, 5
Q. 5.	4
Q. 6.	1, 2, 3
Q. 7.	2, 3, 4
Q. 8.	2
Q. 9.	3
Q. 10.	1, 2, 3

Chapter 3, Managing Marketing Automation Applications – Marketing Lists and Campaigns

Q. 1.	1, 2, 4
Q. 2.	1
Q. 3.	1, 5
Q. 4.	1, 3
Q. 5.	3, 4
Q. 6.	True
Q. 7.	False
Q. 8.	2
Q. 9.	2, 3, 5
Q. 10.	False

Chapter 4, Managing Sales Applications

Q. 1.	2
Q. 2.	1, 2, 4, 5, 6
Q. 3.	3
Q. 4.	1, 3, 4
Q. 5.	False
Q. 6.	3
Q. 7.	4
Q. 8.	1
Q. 9.	3
Q. 10.	1

Chapter 5, Managing the Product Catalog and Order Processing

Q. 1.	5
Q. 2.	2
Q. 3.	4
Q. 4.	1
Q. 5.	3
Q. 6.	1, 2
Q. 7.	True
Q. 8.	False
Q. 9.	1, 3
Q. 10.	True

Chapter 6, Managing CRM 2011 Outlook Client

Q. 1.	2
Q. 2.	1, 2, 3
Q. 3.	2
Q. 4.	1, 2
Q. 5.	4
Q. 6.	True
Q. 7.	5
Q. 8.	True
Q. 9.	False
Q. 10.	False

Chapter 7, Managing Service Management Applications

Q. 1.	1, 4
Q. 2.	1, 2, 4
Q. 3.	1, 3
Q. 4.	1
Q. 5.	1, 2, 3, 4
Q. 6.	1
Q. 7.	2
Q. 8.	1
Q. 9.	4
Q. 10.	2

Chapter 8, Managing Service Scheduling Applications

Q. 1.	4
Q. 2.	3
Q. 3.	1
Q. 4.	1, 2, 4
Q. 5.	5
Q. 6.	1, 2, 3
Q. 7.	2
Q. 8.	1, 3, 4
Q. 9.	1, 3
Q. 10.	1, 3

Index

A

B

C

M

N

O

P

Q

T

U

V

W

[PACKT] enterprise
professional expertise distilled
PUBLISHING

Thank you for buying

Microsoft Dynamics CRM 2011 Applications (MB2-868) Certification Guide

About Packt Publishing

Packt, pronounced 'packed', published its first book "Mastering phpMyAdmin for Effective MySQL Management" in April 2004 and subsequently continued to specialize in publishing highly focused books on specific technologies and solutions.

Our books and publications share the experiences of your fellow IT professionals in adapting and customizing today's systems, applications, and frameworks. Our solution based books give you the knowledge and power to customize the software and technologies you're using to get the job done. Packt books are more specific and less general than the IT books you have seen in the past. Our unique business model allows us to bring you more focused information, giving you more of what you need to know, and less of what you don't.

Packt is a modern, yet unique publishing company, which focuses on producing quality, cutting-edge books for communities of developers, administrators, and newbies alike. For more information, please visit our website: `www.packtpub.com`.

About Packt Enterprise

In 2010, Packt launched two new brands, Packt Enterprise and Packt Open Source, in order to continue its focus on specialization. This book is part of the Packt Enterprise brand, home to books published on enterprise software - software created by major vendors, including (but not limited to) IBM, Microsoft and Oracle, often for use in other corporations. Its titles will offer information relevant to a range of users of this software, including administrators, developers, architects, and end users.

Writing for Packt

We welcome all inquiries from people who are interested in authoring. Book proposals should be sent to `author@packtpub.com`. If your book idea is still at an early stage and you would like to discuss it first before writing a formal book proposal, contact us; one of our commissioning editors will get in touch with you.

We're not just looking for published authors; if you have strong technical skills but no writing experience, our experienced editors can help you develop a writing career, or simply get some additional reward for your expertise.

[PACKT] enterprise
professional expertise distilled
PUBLISHING

Microsoft Dynamics CRM 2011 Application Design

ISBN: 978-1-84968-456-9 Paperback: 236 pages

Develop applications for any situation with our hands-on guide to Microsoft Dynamics CRM 2011

1. Create your first application quickly and with no fuss
2. Develop in days what it has taken others years
3. Provide the solution to your company's problems

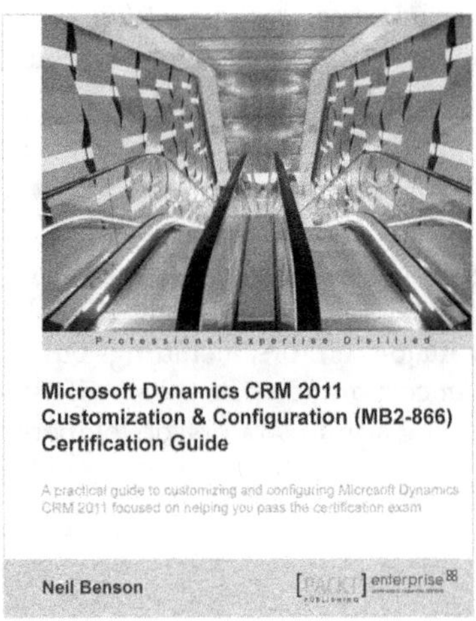

Microsoft Dynamics CRM 2011 Customization & Configuration (MB2-866) Certification Guide

ISBN: 978-1-84968-580-1 Paperback: 306 pages

A practical guide to customizing and configuring Microsoft Dynamics CRM 2011 focused on helping you pass the certification exam

1. Based on the official syllabus for course 80294B to help prepare you for the MB2-866 exam
2. Filled with all the procedures you need to know to pass the exam including screenshots
3. Take the practice exam with 75 sample questions to assess your knowledge before you sit the real exam

Please check **www.packtpub.com** for information on our titles

[PACKT] enterprise
professional expertise distilled
PUBLISHING

Microsoft Dynamics CRM 2011: Dashboards Cookbook

ISBN: 978-1-84968-440-8 Paperback: 266 pages

Over 50 simple but incredibly effective recipes for creating, customizing and interacting with rich dashboards and charts

1. Take advantage of all of the latest Dynamics CRM dashboard features for visualizing your most important data at a glance
2. Understand how iFrames, chart customizations, advanced WebResources and more can improve your dashboards in Dynamics CRM by using this book and eBook

---

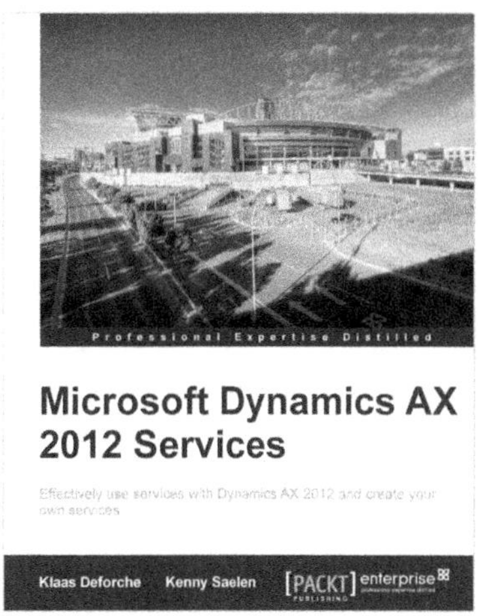

Microsoft Dynamics AX 2012 Services

ISBN: 978-1-84968-754-6 Paperback: 196 pages

Effectively use services with Dynamics AX 2012 and create your own services

1. Learn about the Dynamics AX 2012 service architecture
2. Create your own services using wizards or X++ code
3. Consume existing web services and services you've created yourself

Please check **www.packtpub.com** for information on our titles

www.ingramcontent.com/pod-product-compliance
Lightning Source LLC
LaVergne TN
LVHW080022210926
848481LV00011B/3083
9781849686501